38199357

D1222136

Condemning Students to Debt

COLLEGE LOANS
AND
PUBLIC POLICY

Condemning Students to Debt

COLLEGE LOANS AND PUBLIC POLICY

Richard Fossey
Mark Bateman

EDITORS

Teachers College, Columbia University
New York and London

Published by Teachers College Press, 1234 Amsterdam Avenue, New York, NY 10027

Library of Congress Cataloging-in-Publication Data
Condemning students to debt : college loans and public policy /
   Richard Fossey and Mark Bateman, editors.
      p.   cm.
   Includes bibliographical references (p.   ) and index.
   ISBN 0-8077-3743-7 (cloth : alk. paper)
   1. Student loan funds—United States.   2. Student aid—United States.   3. Federal aid to higher education—United States.   4. Default (Finance)—United States.   I. Fossey, Richard.   II. Bateman, Mark.
   LB2340.2.C66   1998
   378.3'62—dc21   98-9215
ISBN 0-8077-3743-7 (cloth)

Printed on acid-free paper

Manufactured in the United States of America

05   04   03   02   01   00   99   98   8   7   6   5   4   3   2   1

We dedicate this book to our parents:

Jim and Helen Fossey
of Anadarko, Oklahoma

and

Bob and Juanell Bateman
of Beaumont, Texas

and to their faith in American education

Contents

Foreword

It is altogether timely that Richard Fossey and Mark Bateman have collected in one volume an excellent and exhaustive treatment of the many policy issues involved in the explosion of debt for college. Higher education has become, by the close of this century, a virtual necessity for anyone seeking a reasonable shot at the American Dream, and yet its cost to the student and his or her family has skyrocketed at this historical moment. With 4 years of tuition (not to mention room and board and related costs) approaching $15,000 or more in public universities, and $60,000 to $80,000 or more in private universities, the price of higher education has clearly gone beyond the point where a student can realistically hope to "work his way through college." Our country's response has been to turn to loan financing as the answer, but as the essays in this volume show, the problems and difficulties associated with that answer are legion.

How did this curious situation come to pass? Did anyone plan this approach to student finance, or did the system evolve by inadvertence? What are the consequences of relying heavily on debt finance? Were better options overlooked or discarded? And what might be done about the situation in which we currently find ourselves? These are the types of questions that the authors address in the chapters that follow.

Ironically, we know that the federally guaranteed student loan program (GSL), had its birth in 1965 as a counter to a proposed tuition tax credit, and not as a well-conceived program in its own right. The Treasury Department was mightily concerned about the revenue loss that a tax credit for tuition would produce, and thus GSL was born as a loan of convenience for middle class families facing cash-flow problems in meeting college costs. The original program was not intended to be subsidized, and its true purpose was to save the Treasury money. From these simple beginnings arose a program that is now the centerpiece, not only of federal student aid, but of the financing of the entire enterprise of higher education itself.

Since that fateful decision was made over 30 years ago, higher education has undergone dramatic change in scope and scale of activities. The baby-boom generation washed through our colleges and universities, sharply increasing enrollments. In order to accommodate the shift from an elite to a mass form of higher education, existing campuses expanded, new campuses were built, and virtually every town of any size acquired its own community college. An expanding economy and strong support for increased access to higher education resulted in sharply increased state, federal, and private outlays to pay for such growth. In 1972, the federal government enacted historic legislation that enshrined the country's commitment to access by creating Basic Educational Opportunity Grants (BEOG), subsequently renamed Pell Grants. Loans at this time were still a supplemental form of aid, designed in large measure to enable a degree of choice in the institution attended.

During these heady days, economists provided a rationale for investment in higher education through the theory of human capital, in which college degrees were shown to "pay off" through higher lifetime earnings. Other economists studied the factors that contributed to economic growth and highlighted the important role of improved quality of the workforce through education. Traditional arguments regarding the social benefits of an educated citizenry were thus buttressed by hard-nosed evidence that higher education paid-off in investment terms, both to the individual and to society. These findings laid the intellectual base for borrowing to pay for college, because the student could pay off the debt with higher earnings, and still be ahead financially.

However, the 1970s turned out to be a troubled decade. The 1973 oil embargo ushered in a period of slow growth, coupled with high inflation, forcing economists to coin a new term: "stagflation." Furthermore, as the large baby-boom cohorts of college graduates entered the labor market, many could not find jobs that paid the high wages they had come to expect. As college tuitions began to rise at double digit rates toward the end of the decade, fear swept many middle class families that college might be priced beyond their means, prompting Congress to enact the Middle Income Student Assistance Act of 1978 (MISSA). Among other features, this legislation opened GSL to all students, regardless of family income, and produced an explosive growth of borrowing because of the opportunity for arbitrage. Families realized that they could borrow under GSL at subsidized and capped interest rates, while depositing funds in the money market at considerably higher rates. It took the Congress three years to close this loophole, but not before loan volume jumped from $1.7 billion in 1977 to nearly $7.2 billion in 1981. This experience is but one example of the unintended consequences that have marked the history of federal student loans, discussed in considerably more depth in the papers that follow.

Given the sharp boost to borrowing in the late 1970s prompted by MISSA, the history since that time has seen a steady shift in the balance of student aid from grants to loans. In part this shift occurred because in the

Reagan years, grant programs were not strongly supported by the administration, while loans remained the one true entitlement program that were not limited by appropriation levels, like Pell grants and other forms of federal aid.

In addition to the sharp increase in borrowing for undergradute education, many graduate and professional programs rely heavily on student loans as the main source of aid—this is true of most programs in law, medicine, and graduate business. As a consequence, we have reached a stage where a student may emerge from a Bachelor's degree program with debt of $12,000 to $15,000, only to enter a professional school and face further debt of $50,000 to $80,000 or more. These facts alone would warrant the analyses in this volume, for the nation clearly needs to re-examine its policies and purposes in loading this amount of debt upon the shoulders of its younger citizens. Many think we have gone too far in burdening college students with debt finance, while others argue that a debt crisis can be forestalled by improved repayment terms and conditions. These are among the critical issues that the authors help us to examine and which should inform the development of sound public policy. In preparing this excellent volume, the editors have done all students, current and potential, a most valuable service. As Congress engages in its periodic reauthorization of federal higher education programs, one hopes that they will consider the ideas presented here.

David W. Breneman
Curry School of Education
University of Virginia

Acknowledgments

This book is the product of many people's hard work and creativity, and I would like to thank these people now.

First, I wish to thank the writers who provided chapters for this volume. These authors are among the most respected scholars in the field of student loans, and I am grateful to them for joining this project and contributing their insight.

In addition, I would like to thank the many people who contributed their comments and suggestions during various stages of the editing process. In particular, my colleagues at Louisiana State University were supportive during every step of the writing and editing process, and several read manuscripts. I especially wish to thank William "Bud" Davis, Chad Ellett, Terry Geske, and Becky Ropers-Huilman.

Several other people assisted in various ways. Jay Heubert of Harvard University read part of the manuscript and provided helpful comments and criticisms. Dale Plauche of Plaquemine Bank and Trust answered my questions on commercial banking. Sydney Owens of Cambridge, Massachusetts provided important research materials. Edward St. John at Indiana University and Daniel Layzell of Tallahassee, Florida, through their writings, shaped my ideas about student loans and public policy. Faye Zucker provided invaluable editorial advice; and Lori Tate of Teachers College Press shepherded the project through the production process. My thanks to them all.

In addition to the people named above, I would like to acknowledge the people who encouraged me in my transition from the private practice of law to academia. Their support helped make it possible for me to work on a project such as this. In particular, I wish to thank the attorneys and associates of Bankston & McCollum, my former law firm in Anchorage, Alaska. I especially wish to thank Bill Bankston, Chris Gronning, Steve O'Hara, Jim McCollum, Beth Schmidt, and John Sedor. I also wish to thank Jeanne Adair, Joe Donnelly, Cynthia Forrest, Linda Greyser, Jay Heubert, Mini Major, Sydney Owens, Manny Rivera, and Jeff and Naomi Stonberg for their friendship and support during my studies at Harvard.

Finally, I wish to thank my wife, Kim; my children, Austin and Polly; and my stepchildren, Elizabeth and Charlie for their patience and love. They have enriched my life more than I can say.

Introduction

Richard Fossey

A college education is fast becoming indispensable to an individual's economic self-sufficiency. The salary gap between graduates of high school and of college has rapidly expanded in recent years. Without additional education or training, most high school graduates cannot command a wage that will support a family, pay for health care, or permit them to own a home or prepare for retirement.

Unfortunately, as any college student can attest, the cost of higher education is going up. In recent years, college tuition costs have risen faster than both the rate of inflation and median family income.

Governmental funding for higher education has not kept up with these rising costs. Lagging economies in some regions and the increasing costs of other social services have forced state governments to cut back on financial support for public colleges and universities. The federal government has shifted its financial support for higher education away from grants for needy students and toward federally guaranteed student loans.

As governmental support declines, students and their families are paying more and more of the total cost of higher education. And since few families have the discretionary income to pay tuition costs as they come due, they have financed the cost of higher education with federally guaranteed student loans.

This book is an effort to chronicle the burgeoning role of student loans in higher education finance and to identify the policy issues that are raised by this development. In the following chapters, some of the nation's leading authorities in higher education policy identify the important issues that have emerged from the federal student loan program. In 10 chapters they identify five major themes.

Theme 1. Expanding access to postsecondary education is in the national interest. First, as Terry G. Geske and Elchanan Cohn explain in Chapter 2, our national interest requires a policy of broad access to postsecondary education.

Thus, the design and implementation of the federal student loan program, which was created to expand educational opportunities, is of utmost importance to the national welfare.

Geske and Cohn set the context for all the chapters that follow with their discussion of the private and social benefits of postsecondary education in the United States, both monetary and nonmonetary. For individuals, an educational investment is likely to lead to a higher income, better health, and a more satisfying lifestyle. For society as a whole, an educated population contributes to a healthier economy, reduced crime, and greater citizen participation in political and civic functions.

On the other hand, individuals who have no postsecondary education are particularly handicapped in today's information-driven and highly technological society. President Clinton (whom the authors quote) stated the matter well when he said that education "is the fault line, the great Continental Divide, between those who will prosper and those who will not in the new economy."

Thomas Mortenson also takes up this theme. As he observes in Chapter 3, the nation has seen median family income stagnate or decline. At the same time, there have been major shifts in income distribution, with highly educated workers becoming wealthier while poorly educated and low-skill workers have seen declines in their standard of living.

In this economic environment, Mortenson argues, education becomes increasingly important as the means of improving the nation's overall social welfare. A greater proportion of the population must be educated at the postsecondary level, if we hope to narrow the gap between the nation's rich and its poor.

Theme 2. Inconsistency in student loan policy. A second theme of the book, explored by several authors, is the incoherence and inconsistency that characterizes the history of federal student loan policy. As James C. Hearn explains in Chapter 4, the nation's growing reliance on student loans to finance postsecondary education has proceeded without a clear and consistent goal, proper oversight of loan programs, or adequate evaluation. Instead, as Hearn explains, federal loan policy has been "incrementalist" in nature, generally reacting to fiscal and political pressures, rather than developing from a core philosophy about higher education participation and finance. Typically, policy makers have justified various federal loan initiatives based on disparate and sometimes conflicting policy grounds.

Over the years, the student loan program has grown enormously; today about half of the nation's undergraduate students pay at least some of their education costs with borrowed money. Yet policy makers have no clear idea of the short- or long-term impact on students, individual institutions, or higher education as a whole.

Theme 3. Increasing federal regulation of higher education. A third theme, articulated by Jamie P. Merisotis in Chapter 5, concerns the dramatic increase in federal regulation of higher education that has accompanied the federal college loan program. According to Merisotis, approximately 7,000 sections of the Code of Federal Regulations relate to postsecondary student loans. During one 12-month period in the early 1990s, institutions received, on average, a new federal directive every other day.

In addition, the various accrediting bodies, which have traditionally functioned as the bearer of higher education's own quality standards, are coming under federal regulation, which is shaping them into quasi-governmental agencies. These accrediting bodies now enforce not only higher education's own academic norms, but federal standards and mandates as well.

Today, Merisotis explains, federal regulation of postsecondary education has gone far beyond an accounting for federal funds into core areas of higher education policy, including "time-to-degree, job placement, and tuition and fees." Much of the impetus for burgeoning federal regulations has been concern about fraud and abuse among the proprietary schools. But the undeniable result has been a blizzard of federal rules for hundreds of the nation's most respected and well-run colleges and universities and their once autonomous accrediting bodies.

Theme 4. Rising costs are making higher education inaccessible to more and more families. As David Campaigne and Don Hossler outline in Chapter 6, Congress intended for the federal student loan program to provide greater access to postsecondary education for worthy individuals who could not otherwise afford to participate. Unfortunately, as college costs soared and student indebtedness rose, the impact of loans on students' educational decisions has not always been benign. The evidence is growing that for many middle- and lower-income individuals, loans are beginning to make higher education more—not less—difficult to obtain and to have some impact on the kinds of institutions these students attend.

It is now known, Campaigne and Hossler write, that low-income families are more averse to taking out educational loans than are middle- and upper-income families. It is not surprising, then, to see college enrollment lagging among low-income families as the emphasis of federal student aid policy shifts from grants to loans. In addition, their reluctance to incur indebtedness seems to be pushing low-income students away from 4-year colleges and toward less expensive 2-year institutions.

Moreover, even middle-income families cannot absorb the cost of higher education from current income. Since 1980, as Mortenson explains, tuition and fees at public institutions have increased at an inflation-adjusted rate of about 5% per year. Meanwhile, median family income has remained flat.

Mortenson makes clear that the student loan program has not offset the effect of the rising cost of going to college in terms of providing college access to low-income families. In 1970, when inflation-adjusted costs were much lower, a student from a family in the top quartile of income was about six times more likely to have a bachelor's degree by age 24 as was a student from the bottom quartile of family income. Today, in spite of an expanded student loan program, a student in the top quartile is 10 to 13 times more likely to have a college degree by age 24 as is a student from the bottom quartile of family income.

Theme 5. Some student borrowers do not benefit. Finally, a fifth overarching theme is this: Not all students who take out student loans are benefited. Many—low-income students, single parents, and minority individuals, in particular—are defaulting. And many more who do not default are heavily burdened by their student loan commitments. Without any question, a certain portion of students see the quality of the lives decline rather than improve because they borrowed money to finance their education.

Volkwein and Cabrera take up this theme with their discussion of student loan defaults, a problem that grew steadily from the 1970s until the early 1990s. They ask a fundamental question: Can student loan default rates best be explained by examining the types of students who default or the characteristics of the institutions the students attend?

Studies have shown that for-profit trade schools have the highest loan default rate, much higher than have 4-year colleges and universities. This is an indication that the proprietary schools bear a major part of the responsibility for the nation's high student loan default rate. In recent years, the proprietary school sector has come under increasing public and congressional scrutiny as havens for student loan fraud and abuse.

In their chapter, Volkwein and Cabrera suggest that blaming proprietary schools for the student loan default problem may not be appropriate. The characteristics of individual borrowers, they argue, not the organizational characteristics of the institutions they attend, exert the strongest influence on default behavior. Specifically, minority students (African American or American Indian) and students from low-income families have high default rates, as do single parents who do not complete their degrees. Proprietary schools have high default rates, they conclude, because they enroll high numbers of students at high risk for default, not because of the nature of the schools themselves.

Volkwein and Cabrera also point out the tension that many postsecondary institutions are experiencing as they attempt to keep enrollments up and loan default rates down. On the one hand, they are encouraged to expand educational opportunities for minorities, low-income individuals, and those for whom additional education would improve their life circumstances. Additionally, it is in institutions' interest to keep enrollments up, to maintain revenues, even if it means accepting students who are at greater risk of failure. On the other hand, the federal government is increasing the pressure on institutions to improve their graduation rates and lower their loan default rates.

More and more, postsecondary institutions are being forced to steer a difficult course—one that involves improving student selection and admission criteria while maintaining high enrollment levels. Institutions that choose to continue a policy of admitting weaker students, Volkwein and Cabrera conclude, will need to provide strong academic and social support to avoid unacceptable noncompletion and default rates.

In Chapter 8, Michael Coomes also focuses on the vexingly high student loan default rate among the nation's proprietary trade schools. In fact, Coomes's comprehensive description of the nation's for-profit trade schools may be the most complete picture to date on this highly diverse, ever changing, and profit-driven sector of postsecondary education. Coomes concludes that the overall picture of proprietary school participation in the federal student loan program is complicated and unclear, making a general condemnation of the proprietary schools problematic.

Coomes notes, for example, that the overall student loan default rate has gone down significantly since its high in 1991, led by significant improvement in the repayment rate of proprietary school students. Thus, although the bulk of student loan defaults come from the proprietary schools, the problem appears to be diminishing.

Echoing the findings of Volkwein and Cabrera, Coomes points out that the best predictors of loan default are the characteristics of the students themselves, not the type of school attended. Thus, as noted earlier, although propriety schools have the highest loan default rates, that is largely because of the types of the students they enroll—low-income and minority students—not the types of schools these students attend.

Moreover, Coomes notes that the percentage of "problematic" proprietary schools (as defined by the Department of Education) varies greatly from state to state, ranging from 41% in Louisiana to zero in Maine and Guam. This suggests that better state regulation of the for-profit trade schools can play a major role in bringing fraud and abuse under control.

Richard Fossey is another contributor who examines the student loan default problem. In Chapter 9, he focuses on individuals who file for bankruptcy to escape their student loan indebtedness. Without question, federal law is unsympathetic. Unless a debtor can show "undue hardship," educational loans cannot be dissolved in bankruptcy until 7 years after they become due. Moreover, the courts have been remarkably harsh in interpreting the undue hardship rule; some have ruled that only "the certainty of hopelessness" about one's long-term economic future qualifies as undue hardship.

The courts' harsh treatment of student loan defaulters is based on the notion that these people are acting in bad faith. Subsequent to obtaining a valuable education, the popular sentiment seems to be, it is disreputable to use the bankruptcy courts as a means of reneging on a lawful obligation. However, as Fossey argues in Chapter 10, the popular view of loan defaulters as scheming scofflaws is incorrect. On the contrary, many loan defaulters are in serious financial difficulties, often brought on by unemployment, illness, or divorce. Some debtors received no financial benefit from their educational experience, and so did not improve their economic situation enough to service their loans.

Together, Chapters 8, 9, and 10 sketch out a disturbing picture of student loan defaulters that is at odds with the popular stereotype. Defaulters are not, by and large, middle-class individuals trying to evade paying for a valuable education. They are instead, a host of unfortunate debtors for whom an investment in postsecondary education did not pay off.

This book concludes with some reflections on the future of the federal student loan program and some suggestions for improving it. The conclusion contains, among other things, discussion of the American Council on Education's suggestions for improving the program, along with recent federal legislation to provide tax relief to student borrowers and their families.

Without a doubt, technical interventions—statutory, administrative, and regulatory—will make the federal student loan program more economical for its beneficiaries and more efficient. These reforms will not bring the program into harmony with the national interest, however, unless the higher education community and its stakeholders recognize a moral obligation to the millions of individuals who take out federally guaranteed loans to obtain a postsecondary education. At a minimum, these stakeholders—colleges, universities, trade schools, the Department of Education, lenders, and guaranty agencies—must do two things. First, they must do everything possible to contain costs so that the amount of money students need to borrow is kept to a minimum. Second, they must make every effort to ensure that the money that students borrow is invested in worthwhile educational experiences.

Our nation's well-being depends on a higher education system that is accessible and affordable to anyone who can benefit. Student loan policy, in its present form, may not be advancing that goal as well as it might. It is the purpose of this book to help move higher education policy in a new direction.

CHAPTER I

The Dizzying Growth of the Federal Student Loan Program

WHEN WILL VERTIGO SET IN?

Richard Fossey

Measured by its impact on individual lives, the federal student loan program is one of the national government's most successful policy initiatives in the field of higher education. Created by the Higher Education Act of 1965, the program has helped millions of Americans pursue postsecondary education. Indeed, federally guaranteed student loans is a major reason that higher education enrollment has grown from less than 6 million students in 1965 to approximately 15 million today.

Nevertheless, during the life of the student loan program, a storm cloud has hovered over this otherwise glowing policy success—the program's high loan default rate. During the late 1980s, the default rate grew each year until by 1991, an astounding 22% of student loan debtors defaulted within 2 years of beginning repayment. Year after year, the media have publicized the fact that a substantial number of so-called deadbeats took out student loans and failed to pay them back.

Recently, however, the default rate has gone down dramatically. According to the U.S. Department of Education, the default rate was cut in half in just 3 years—to 11% in 1994. According to U.S. education secretary Richard Riley, this drastic decline provides evidence that the Clinton administration's commitment for "reinventing government" by making it more efficient is paying off (Riley, 1997).

Does this mean the default rate is under control? Perhaps. Nevertheless, in spite of the falling default rate, there are disquieting signs that education-related debts are becoming more burdensome for student borrowers. Just as disturbing, the General Accounting Office has repeatedly criticized the Department of Education's management of the student loan program, particularly the way the department collects and processes loan data. In recent years, loan volume has ballooned—more than doubling in just 6 years. To-

7

gether—rising volume, poor program management, and ever more burden-some individual debt loads—could portend a resurgence of student loan de-faults to a magnitude never before seen. Even if default rates stay down, growing debt loads will negatively impact millions of individual borrowers who are burdened with onerous long-term loan payments. Ultimately, the cumulative strain on these individual debtors will surely affect the national economy.

THE BURGEONING FEDERAL STUDENT LOAN PROGRAM: A BRIEF OVERVIEW

When Congress enacted the Higher Education Act in 1965, it intended the legislation to provide a modest benefit to middle-class college students and their families. It was not expected to draw significantly from the federal bud-get, allowing federal money to be channeled to low-income students in need of grants. Over time, however, student loans assumed a larger and larger role in higher education finance, and now constitute one of the largest sources of funds for postsecondary students (Gladieux, 1996). Today, about half of all students graduating from 4-year colleges have college loan obligations; and the vast majority of this debt is guaranteed by the federal government.

Few Americans realize just how large the federal student loan program has grown, especially in the past few years. In 1965, when the program was first introduced, it loaned less than a quarter of a billion dollars for postsec-ondary education. By 1993, that figure had grown to $20 billion. Since then, the program has been growing almost exponentially. In 1997, the federal government guaranteed about $30 billion in student loans (U.S. Department of Education [USDOE], 1997), a 50% increase in just 4 years.

Some would say that the growing federal presence in higher education finance is fortunate. The cost of higher education has risen dramatically dur-ing the past 20 years, straining the capacity of traditional funding sources—state governments and students' families—to pay for it. At the state level, downturns in regional economies have forced some state governments to reduce higher education's share of their total state budgets. In addition, the increasing costs of other social services—health care, law enforcement, and corrections, in particular—have contributed to this trend (Layzell, 1996).

At the same time, students' parents are contributing less to the total cost of college education than they did a generation ago. Bruce Johnstone (1996) identified three factors that help explain this phenomenon. First, more and more postsecondary students are older than the traditional college-attending age group, and financially independent from their parents. It is not surpris-ing to find that these older students have less parental assistance than had their younger counterparts. Second, the nation's higher divorce and separation rate has had an effect on parents' ability and willingness to pay for their children's education costs. Third, many parents seem less willing to save or sacrifice for their children's college education than were parents of past generations.

To these factors, a fourth should be added. A flat economy for middle-class wage earners, coupled with accelerating college costs, has reduced the number of parents who are able to pay their children's college expenses from savings or current income, even if they desire to do so. As several scholars have noted, college costs have outstripped family income and the annual inflation rate for well over a decade.

As the student loan program expanded, a few commentators expressed concern about growing default rates. In the late 1980s, the number of students defaulting on their educational loans increased every year until by 1991, the default rate reached 22%. Among trade school students, the rate was substantially higher—more than 40% in the early 1990s.

Fortunately, the student loan default rate has come down steadily since 1991. In January 1997, the Department of Education estimated a rate in the range of 11% for the cohort of borrowers who were scheduled to begin paying their loans in 1994 (Sanchez, 1997).

This dramatic decline in default rates—a 50% reduction in only 3 years—occurred for two reasons. First, the Department of Education and various lending agencies began an aggressive debt collection campaign. In 1995, the department seized federal income tax refunds from more than 770,000 student loan defaulters (USDOE, 1996b) and 140,000 would-be borrowers were denied new student loans because of previous defaults (USDOE, 1996a). Second, the department targeted institutions with high default rates—mostly proprietary trade schools—and disqualified them from participation in the program. Since the largest number of loan defaulters are former trade-school students, eliminating these schools from the student loan program had a significant impact on default rates.

For many, the Department of Education's rapid progress in reducing default rates provided impressive evidence that the student loan program is under control. As the Clinton administration began its second term in 1997, no federal policy maker or higher-education interest group recommended that the program be cut back or eliminated.

On the contrary, in the late 1990s, most higher education policy discussions began from the premise that the federal student loan program is a permanent fixture of higher education finance. In 1997, Congress approved a modest tax credit for postsecondary expenses and authorized student borrowers to take a tax deduction for some of their student loan interest expenses. However, these actions did not alter the basic structure of the federal student loan program. That same year, a group of 22 higher education associations, led by the American Council on Education, made recommendations for modifying and extending the student loan program. None of the groups' proposals involved dramatic changes to the program, much less its elimination (American Council on Education, 1997b).

Complacency about the student loan program may well be justified. Without question, the program has made it possible for hundreds of thousands of individuals to pursue postsecondary education, which might have otherwise been unobtainable. It has been student loans that have largely filled the void left by the states' diminishing role in funding public colleges and universities. In addition, as Geske and Cohn point out in Chapter 2 of this book, the economic benefits of higher education are substantial. For most students, the return on their investment in higher education justifies the burden of debt they assume when they take out education loans (King, 1996).

WILL DEFAULT RATES START BACK UP?
SOME DISQUIETING SIGNS

Nevertheless, there are some disquieting signs that the student loan program may be creating some serious problems for American higher education and its clients and that these problems may be growing. In fact, we should not be surprised if loan defaults begin rising again.

Accelerating Growth

First of all, the rapidly accelerating growth of the student loan program—from less than $13 billion to $30 billion in annual loans in just 6 years—is itself a cause for concern. In recent years, student loan indebtedness increased almost three times faster than college costs and four times faster than personal incomes (Merisotis & Parker, 1996, p. 18). This seems to be an indication that college students are developing a higher tolerance for education-related debt than had students in the past, a tolerance that may not be in their long-term personal interest.

Currently, student loans constitute the fourth largest sector of consumer debt—after home mortgages, automobile loans, and credit card obligations (Reinebach, 1996). Research and policy analysis have not kept up with this explosion in student loan debt. Consequently, we have no clear picture how a lending program of such enormous size will affect the national economy in the coming years, not to mention the financial planning decisions of millions of student loan debtors. We do know that personal bankruptcy filings are on the increase and that credit card debt is rising. It seems certain that the student loan program, which increases consumer debt by $30 billion a year, will have some measurable impact on the nation's economic health. Just what that effect will be is not clear.

In addition, the loan program's rapid growth puts the declining loan default rate in a new perspective. In Financial Year (FY) 1991, when the cohort default rate had reached 22%, the student loan program guaranteed about $13 billion in student loans. Since then, the rate has declined by half, but student loan volume has more than doubled. Even if the Department of Education succeeds in keeping cohort default rates in the 10% range, the dollar amount going into default each year will be quite large, probably larger than 1991, when the cohort default rate had reached its record high.

Student Loans Are Becoming More Burdensome

Not only has the student loan program grown dramatically, there are also worrisome signs that individual borrowers are finding their student loan obligations more burdensome than in the past. If so, the default rate, which recently went down, may start back up again, as debtors find themselves unable to service their student loan debt.

A primary reason for worry concerns the kind of student loans many individuals now receive. Until 1992, all federally guaranteed student loans were *subsidized;* the government paid accruing interest costs during the time that borrowers were enrolled as students. Today, about one third of student loans are *unsubsidized.* For unsubsidized loans, interest costs accrue to student borrowers as soon as their loan funds are disbursed; and these costs are added to the loan principal that students must repay after their studies come to an end. For example, a freshman who borrows $2,500 a year for college expenses and matriculates in four years has a loan obligation of more than $12,000—the $10,000 she actually received plus four years' accumulated interest. Obviously, a student who takes out an unsubsidized loan will have significantly higher monthly loan payments in the postcollege years than would a student who receives the same dollar amount from a subsidized loan.

Another sign that loans are becoming more burdensome concerns the average amount of debt that students now incur. As David Campaigne and Don Hossler explain in Chapter 6 in this volume, the average student's cumulative indebtedness grew by 153% between 1985 and 1991, from $6,488 to $16,417. Unfortunately, borrowers' income has not kept up with their growing debt burden. The writers note that as a percentage of gross income, cumulative debt rose from 6.23% to 9.52% between 1985 and 1991. During the same period, annual gross income only grew by 5.5%.

As Merisotis and Parker (1996) pointed out, some types of students are more burdened than others by student loan debt. In particular, students with the most financial need—older students, minorities, part-time students, and independent students—have increased their debt burden faster than have traditional-age college students.

> From 1990 to 1993, full-time undergraduates saw their borrowing increase by an average of 8 percent. Part-time students experienced a much higher 17 percent jump during the same period. Traditional college-age students—18- to 24-year-olds—saw their debt levels rise by 4 percent, while 25- to 34-year-olds experienced a 20 percent increase, and 35- to 44-year-olds a 29 percent jump. Debts for White students rose by 9 percent between 1990 and 1993, while climbing 19 percent for non-White students. (p. 19)

In addition to older, minority, and part-time students, another group may be particularly burdened by student loans: the unprepared student. A significant number of postsecondary students will find themselves borrowing tuition money not only for standard college courses but also for remedial courses—designed to repair the effects of a substandard high school education. Students in this predicament are doubly penalized: First, their entry into the job market is delayed by the remedial education process; second, their student loan burden is increased by the cost of remedial education.

A large number of students take remedial courses. According to the National Center for Educational Statistics (Lewis, Farris, & Greene, 1996), 29% of first-time freshmen took at least one remedial course in the fall of 1995. Among minority students, the figure is considerably higher. A study of remedial education in the southern states found that African American and Hispanic students were about twice as likely as were White students to be enrolled in a remedial education course (Ansley, 1991, p. 7).

According to a recent report from the General Accounting Office (GAO), little financial aid goes to students who take remedial courses. In the fall of 1995, only about 13% of the aid granted to underclassmen went to such students (GAO, 1997d, p. 3). But the figure is much higher at 2-year institutions, where almost a quarter of all financial aid is awarded to students taking remedial courses (p. 5).

Increasingly heavy loan burdens and the rising number of unsubsidized loans—what are the consequences for postsecondary students? No one can say for sure. It seems reasonable to anticipate a higher default rate in the coming years, although most former students will continue to make their monthly loan payments even though it will be harder for them to do so. Perhaps the more important questions are these: What purchases will these debtors forego as a result of their heavier loan burdens? How will their career decisions be affected? What will be the impact on debtors' plans to have and raise children?

Storm warnings from the U.S. General Accounting Office. Finally, we have a third reason to worry about the student loan program. According to the U.S. General Accounting Office (GAO), there are serious problems with the program's management and design. In a 1997 report, the GAO described fundamental flaws in the student loan program and concluded that "the financial interests of the U.S. taxpayers are not well served" (1997c, p. 52).

For several years, the GAO has referred to the student loan program as a "high risk" area. Again and again, it has called attention to fraud and abuses in the program, particularly in the proprietary school sector. The GAO has also turned up evidence of mismanagement: for example, loans being given to ineligible students and students being given additional loans even though they had defaulted on earlier obligations (GAO, 1995b).

Perhaps the most alarming problem that the GAO identified is the Department of Education's lack of accurate data about how the student loan program is operating. The GAO pointed out this problem in 1992, in 1995, and again in 1996 (1992, 1995a, 1996). In the 1996 report, it concluded that "unreliable student loan data" (p. 7) prevented the Department of Education from reasonably estimating program costs. In particular, the GAO determined that the department did not have procedures in place to ensure that billing reports from guaranty agencies and lenders—the institutions that actually administer the loan program—were reliable.

In a February 1997 report, the GAO (1997c) said again that student loan data were unreliable. "As a result," it concluded, "the Department cannot obtain complete, accurate and reliable FFELP [Federal Family Education Loan Program] data necessary to report on its financial position" (p. 14). In other words, due to faulty information, the Department of Education may not have an accurate picture of its student loan liabilities. Although the GAO identified about $13 billion in loan guarantee liabilities in a 1997 report (1997c, p. 49), the actual figure could be larger.

In addition to calling for better data control, the GAO identified two fundamental flaws in the student loan program, flaws that continue in spite of corrective legislation that Congress has passed from time to time over the years. First, as the program is now structured, the federal government bears nearly all the risk of loan losses, giving the guaranty agencies and lenders little incentive to keep defaults to a minimum. Second, the program has increased its lending to students who run a high risk of default—low-income students and students who attend proprietary schools or other nontraditional postsecondary institutions.

According to the GAO (1997c), these two flaws have increased the student loan program's costs and contributed to high default rates.

> Some proprietary school operators have enriched themselves at the expense of economically disadvantaged students, while providing little or no education in return. Faced with large debts and no new marketable skills, these students have often defaulted on their loans. Lenders and guaranty agencies who have little financial risk have also contributed to the default problem. Had sufficient risk-sharing arrangements been in place, lenders and guaranty agencies would have had an incentive to monitor the kind of education their borrowers were receiving and their repayment practices. (p. 25)

One cannot read the GAO reports on the student loan program without a sense of foreboding. Taken together, these reports constitute a series of warnings about a massive government program's flaws. With each passing year, the program grows larger, and it becomes increasingly dangerous to ignore these warnings.

In fairness, Congress and the Department of Education have taken steps to make the student loan program more efficient and to reduce fraud and abuse. The declining default rate is evidence of that. Nevertheless, the fundamental problems that the GAO identified—inadequate information from lenders and guaranty agencies, mismanagement, and insufficient safeguards against imprudent lending—have not been remedied.

THE HIGHER EDUCATION COMMUNITY'S LACK OF CONCERN

As we have seen, the higher education community, policy makers, and legislators have several reasons to be concerned about the federal student loan program. Its rapid growth, the growing burden on individual debtors, and the GAO's warnings about program flaws all point to the need for a comprehensive review of a program that exerts an enormous influence on higher education institutions and their students.

Surprisingly, college and university leaders have expressed little concern about this mammoth and unruly program, even in broad discussions about higher education's many problems. For example, in *Crisis in the Academy,* Christopher Lucas (1996) reviewed several critical issues facing higher education at the close of the 20th century: disagreements about curriculum content, lack of consensus on mission, and the need for better accountability by the professoriat; but the college student's growing debt burden went unremarked. Likewise, Clark Kerr (1997), the eminent higher education scholar and former president of the University of California, wrote an insightful article about "the increasingly indeterminate future" of higher education in the United States, without making any mention of the federal student loan program.

Kerr (1997) and Lucas (1996) are not alone in giving the student loan program short shrift when reviewing higher education's major challenges. Little research exists on the topic. Such research that does exist has been concentrated in two areas: (a) the effect that loans have on borrowers while they are students; for example, their impact on college access, college choice, and student persistence; and (b) factors associated with loan defaults, including the characteristics of loan defaulters and institutions with high default rates. Very little research exists on the effect that student loans have on individuals during the loan repayment period. Nor is it clear how the student loan program has affected fiscal policy at the institutional level (Burd, 1997).

So far, the higher education community has expressed little concern about the student loan program. Colleges and universities have certainly benefited from the program's growth; student loans are a major reason that institutions have been able to raise tuition in recent years at twice the rate of inflation. Although students are becoming increasingly burdened by their college loans, most still pay them back. In fact, default rates have come down in recent years, reversing an earlier trend.

But the past may be no indication of the future. Student loan volume is growing. Students now borrow at the rate of about $90 billion every 3 years. We may reach some "tipping point" when the dynamics of the program change fundamentally for students, institutions, and the national economy.

THE NEED FOR BETTER INFORMATION, MONITORING DEVICES, AND RESEARCH

Surely it is time, if not for worry, at least for greater vigilance. At a minimum, we need to do three things to make sure that the benefits of the student loan program are not overwhelmed by negative consequences.

First, we need to get better information about how the student loan program operates, and we need to do this quickly. As the GAO has repeatedly warned, the Department of Education has no clear idea what its student loan liabilities are. Currently, student loan data are contained in at least 11 nonintegrated data systems, a situation that makes it difficult for the department to get accurate and timely information about students and institutions, and that has left the program vulnerable to fraud, waste, and mismanagement (GAO, 1997b). What is needed, according to the GAO, is an integrated information technology or "systems architecture" for managing the department's financial aid programs (p. 3). Until this is done, it will be impossible to monitor the student loan program adequately.

Second, we need to pay close attention to some key indicators of loan repayment behavior. Historically, students who attended 4-year institutions have had the lowest default rate, only about 6% (GAO, 1997e). If the default rate for this category of students—those least likely to default—begins creeping up, that will be a warning that individual debt loads are becoming more burdensome. We also need to watch the repayment patterns of borrowers who build good repayment records in the first few years after their loans become due. Most borrowers who default do so almost immediately, within a year or 2 after their payment obligations begin. If a significant number of borrowers begin defaulting on loans after 3 or 4 years of regular loan payments, that too will be a signal that loan obligations are becoming more burdensome for individual borrowers.

Third, we need more research on the effect that student loans have on borrowers during the repayment stage. We know that many individuals pass up satisfying careers in order to take better-paying jobs that will enable them to meet their loan obligations (Kilps, 1997). However, we have no idea how many people have been affected in this way by their student loans. We know that defaulters are banned for life from further participation in the student loan program and that thousands of would-be borrowers are denied new educational loans every year for this reason. We have no notion of how many people in this predicament are individuals who took out a student loan to pay for a worthless proprietary school program and were then unable to pay their debt.

CONCLUSION

In closing this chapter, it is appropriate to recall an article written by Wellford Wilms, Richard Moore, and Roger Bolus (1987), analyzing student loan default rates as they were going up during the mid-19980s. Just as "a chronic cough often foreshadows a serious illness," the authors wrote, "escalating default rates testify to an underlying malady in the [student loan] program itself" (pp. 51–52).

Ten years later, we have seen loan default rates cut in half, but the "chronic cough" has not gone away. Other signs, just as portentous, indicate that the nation's mammoth student loan program still has serious ills. Student loan volume is mushrooming; individuals are assuming heavier debt loads, and the program continues to evade sound management.

Everyone in the higher education community should be worried about these developments. So far, it has mostly been trade school students who have been seriously injured by student loans. Thousands borrowed money that exceeded the value of their training programs. Many went into default and are foreclosed from further participation in the student loan program.

The day may come, however, when not just trade school enrollees, but large numbers of college graduates, will be negatively affected by their loan obligations. At present, few college and university students borrow so much money that their student loans significantly diminish the economic value of their educational experience. But annual loan volume doubled in just 6 years, and the average student's debt burden continues to rise. If we persist on our present course, loan obligations may some day devalue the benefits of higher education to a far greater extent than most of us can now imagine.

REFERENCES

American Council on Education (1997a, February 6). Clinton's higher education initiatives. Washington, DC. Author.

American Council on Education (1997b, March 19). Recommendations for Reauthorization of the Higher Education Act. Washington, DC: Author.

Ansley, A. A. (1991). They came to college? *A remedial/developmental profile of first-time freshmen in SREB states.* Atlanta, GA: Southern Regional Education Board.

Burd, S. (1997, May 30). Do federal loans encourage tuition increases? *Chronicle of Higher Education,* p. A18.

Gladieux, L. E. (1996). Federal student aid policy: A history and an assessment. In *Proceedings of the National Conference on the Best Ways for the Federal Government to Help Students and Families Finance Postsecondary Education* [Online: <http://www.ed.gov/offices/OPE/ppi/FinPostSecEd/>]

Johnstone, B. (1996). The United States. In D. W. Breneman, L. L. Leslie & R. E. Anderson (eds.), *ASHE reader on finance in higher education.* Needham Heights, MA: Simon and Schuster.

Kerr, C. (1997). Speculations about the increasingly indeterminate future of higher education in the United States. *Review of Higher Education, 20,* 345–356.

Kilps, J. (1997, July/August). Gambling on an education: The opportunities and limitations of student loans. *Sojourner,* pp. 32–35.

King, J. (1996). Student aid: Who benefits now? *Educational Record, 77,* 21–27.

Kramer, M. (1996). Stresses in the student financial aid system. In D. W. Breneman, L. L. Leslie, & R. E. Anderson (eds.) *ASHE reader on finance in higher education.* Needham Heights, MA: Simon and Schuster.

Layzell, Daniel. (1996). The financing of colleges and universities: Changing roles and emerging issues. Unpublished paper.

Lewis, L., Farris, E., & Greene, B. (1996). *Remedial education at higher education institutions in fall 1995, NCES-584.* Washington, DC: National Center for Educational Statistics, U.S. Department of Education.

Lucas, C. J. (1996). *Crisis in the academy: Rethinking higher education in America.* New York: St. Martin's Press.

Merisotis, J. P., & Parker, T. D. (1996). College debt and the New England family. *Connection, 11,* 18–19.

Reinebach, A. (1996, July 1). Catching the wave: Student loans emerge as the next big asset class in the sizzling ABS sector. *Investment Dealers' Digest,* p. 12.

Riley, R. (1997, January 9). Press briefing by Secretary of Education. Washington, DC: Author.

Sanchez, R. (1997, January 10). Economy, crackdown, pay off in college loan default rate. *The Washington Post,* p. A2.

United States Department of Education (1996a, March 22). ED crackdown on high-default schools shows results: Trade school rates drop sharply. [Press release]. U.S. Department of Education Home Page: <http://www.ed.gov./index.html>.

United States Department of Education (1996b, January 22). National student loan default rate hits all-time low. Washington, DC: Author.

United States Department of Education (1997, January 9). Press Briefing by Education Richard Riley and Assistant Education Secretary David Longanecker. U.S. Department of Education Home Page:<http://www.ed.gov./index.html>.

United States General Accounting Office (1992). High risk series: Guaranteed student loans (GAO/HR-93-2). Washington, DC: Author.

United States General Accounting Office (1995a). High risk series: Student financial aid (GAO/HR-95-10). Washington, DC: Author.

United States General Accounting Office (1995b). Student financial aid: Data not fully utilized to identify inappropriately awarded loans and grants (GAO/HEHS-95-199). Washington, DC: Author.

United States General Accounting Office (1996). Financial Audit: Federal Family Education Loan Program's Financial Statements for Fiscal years 1994 and 1993 (GAO/AIMD-96-22). Washington, DC: Author.

United States General Accounting Office (1997a). Debt collection: Improved reporting needed on billions of dollars of delinquent debt and agency collection performance (GAO/AIMD-97-48). Washington, DC: Author.

United States General Accounting Office (1997b). Department of Education: Multiple, nonintegrated systems hamper management of student financial programs (GAO/T-HEHS/AIMD-97-132). Washington, DC: Author.

United States General Accounting Office (1997c). High risk series: Student financial aid. (GAO/HR-97-11). Washington, DC: Author.

United States General Accounting Office (1997d). Student Financial Aid: Federal aid awarded to students taking remedial courses (GAO/HEHS-97-142). Washington, DC: Author.

United States General Accounting Office (1997e). Student loans: Default rates at historically Black colleges and universities (GAO/HEHS-97-33). Washington, DC: Author.

Wilms, W. W., Moore, R. W., & Bolus, R. E. (1987). Whose fault is default? A study of the impact of student characteristics and institutional practices on guaranteed student loan default rates in California. *Educational Evaluation and Policy Analysis, 9,* 41–54.

CHAPTER 2

Why Is a High School Diploma No Longer Enough?

THE ECONOMIC AND SOCIAL BENEFITS OF HIGHER EDUCATION

Terry G. Geske and Elchanan Cohn

President Clinton, when seeking support for his administration's educational policies, often declared that "education is the fault line, the great Continental Divide between those who will prosper and those who will not in the new economy" (Nichols, 1996, p. 3A). Although education has always been a basic determinant of the quality of human life, there is considerable evidence that it is now playing an even more important role in shaping the economic opportunities and successes of countries and individuals. The new demands of the labor market, with its increased emphasis on high technology and global competition, include a more highly skilled, adaptable work force.

This chapter begins with a brief overview of the role of government in higher education, including a review of those arguments typically used to justify governmental involvement. Next, the various types of benefits that accrue to society and individuals from higher education are described and classified. Following an examination of a variety of social or external benefits associated with higher education, a general survey is provided of selected research studies containing estimations of the economic benefits of higher education. This survey focuses on those monetary and nonmonetary benefits that substantially contribute to the quality of our lives.

In this survey, we first examine the magnitude of the monetary returns (i.e., increased lifetime earnings) that can be expected from a college education. We then present examples of nonmonetary benefits (i.e., increased productivity in activities outside the labor market) that also flow from this education. These nonmonetary benefits can significantly affect the quality of human life by impacting health, family life, consumption behavior, and asset management. The survey is not exhaustive, and considerable selectivity has been exercised. Moreover, the emphasis throughout this chapter is placed on the overall conclusions of the research surveyed. The difficult research design questions, methodological problems, and measurement issues involved in this type of research are not addressed.

THE ROLE OF GOVERNMENT IN HIGHER EDUCATION

Perhaps the most common argument in favor of government's role in higher education is the alleged existence of "external" benefits. These are benefits that are created by higher education, but which are not captured by the student or his or her family. An educated individual, for example, may be more civic-minded, and his or her increased productivity could result in the greater productivity of coworkers, employees, and employers (see Wolfe, 1995). Since they cannot be captured by the person paying for the education, these benefits may escape the benefit–cost calculus when it comes to a decision on whether (or where or in which program and field of study) to enroll in an institute of higher education (IHE). A likely result is that the private demand for higher education will be less than the social demand. With the process left to the private market, underenrollment would result (relative to the ideal level of enrollment, which would be driven by the social demand that also includes the external benefits). The foregoing provides a rationale for government intervention, in the form of subsidies to individuals, institutions, or both, operation or control of IHEs, or both.

Economic Growth and Income Distribution

Several studies demonstrate the important role of education in promoting economic growth (for a survey, see Cohn & Geske, 1990; see also Carnoy, 1995). In Denison's (1985) analysis, for example, improvements in education were responsible for 20% of the growth rate of real national income between 1929 and 1948 (and 49% from 1973 to 1982). The role of education is even more pronounced in the rise in the growth rate of real national income *per person employed*. To the extent that economic growth is a national priority, government support of higher education is likely to increase investment in education and to spur economic growth.

Perhaps a more compelling argument in favor of government support of higher education is that unsubsidized, private higher education would be open almost exclusively to high-income families, denying higher education to the lower-income masses. There are two arguments here. First, if financial markets make it difficult—frequently impossible—for low-income families to borrow for higher education without government interference, then even if *all* of the benefits of higher education can be captured by the students and their families, still a large number of students would not enroll, simply because they lack the necessary funds. Ignoring egalitarian arguments, such a situation is *inefficient*, because some human resources are not being developed to their full potential. This situation would call for government action, most notably some form of a government-guaranteed (perhaps subsidized) student loan program.

In addition, government subsidies to education could help redress an unequal distribution of income, provided that society believes that the current distribution of income is undesirable. Supplying grants, loans, and other forms of subsidies to economically disadvantaged members of society is one form of income equalization. To the extent that this redistribution is consistent with the amelioration of the inefficiency described above, governments might be able to improve equity and efficiency simultaneously, which seems to be preferable to other policies (e.g., welfare) that tend to improve equity only at the expense of efficiency.

Other Reasons for a Government Role

Another argument in favor of a government role in education is that decisions concerning an investment in higher education involve risk and uncertainty. Since a student may be uncertain about his or her ability to complete college successfully, and since the magnitude of the returns from schooling are not likely to be known for certain, students might be reluctant to pursue particular college careers, which can be costly both to the individual and to society. Government programs that reduce such risk and uncertainty might be helpful. Examples of such programs include the Educational Opportunity Bank (based on income-contingent loans) and the Education Credit Trust (see Cohn & Geske, 1990, pp. 364–367).

Finally, the federal government has been involved in higher education in order to pursue various federal objectives—from the desire to reward GIs who fought wars for the United States, to an attempt to close the technological gap with the former USSR that was so dramatically exposed when that country launched its first Sputnik satellite. The present role of the federal government is focused on helping able but relatively poor students (through grants and loans) and on special projects that are considered to be in the national interest, such as research grants, library support, and the "information superhighway."

TYPES OF EDUCATIONAL BENEFITS

Several scholars, most recently Solmon & Fagnano (1995), have provided taxonomies of educational benefits. These taxonomies include the benefits that the economy obtains from educational research, the cultivation and discovery of (potential) talent, the increased ability of educated individuals to adapt to new job opportunities and rapidly changing technology, and the provision of human resources for sustained economic growth. In addition, schooling provides for better citizenship, the ability to appreciate and recognize a wider range of cultural and other services, and the chance to give the next generation better education and, therefore, a better future.

Various Classification Schemes

For analytical purposes, educational benefits can be conveniently partitioned into a number of different categories, including direct and indirect returns, monetary and nonmonetary benefits, consumption and investment benefits, and private and social benefits. With regard to the consumption and investment categories, a product (or service) is placed in the consumption category if it yields satisfaction (or utility) in a single period only. On the other hand, a good is placed in the investment category if it is expected to yield satisfaction in future periods only. There are, of course, goods for which it is difficult to draw a sharp distinction between the consumption and investment aspects—that is, goods that yield satisfaction now and are also expected to yield satisfaction in the future. Education is a product that is best characterized by the "in between" classification.

Private benefits are those that accrue to the individual who is being educated. Social benefits include private benefits as well as benefits that accrue to other members of society. There are basically two types of benefits that belong in the social but not the private domain. These include (1) tax payments associated with the educational benefit (that is, income taxes paid out of one's lifetime income stream) and (2) external benefits, which, as noted earlier, are benefits that are due to the educational investment but that the individual cannot capture. Although the measurement of private benefits has improved over the years, that of social benefits or externalities (with the exception of tax payments) remains problematic. Because the external benefits of education are very difficult to estimate and value, only limited empirical research has addressed these benefits, which might further justify public investment in higher education.

Intergenerational Effects

At the same time, there are educational benefits that may not accrue until a generation later. Studies show that persons are more likely to complete a given level of education if their parents are (or were) more highly educated. The intergenerational effect is the increment in a person's education that can be ascribed to the incremental education of the parent. Thus, some of the higher expected earnings of the children could be traced back to their origin in the increased educational investment by their parents. Therefore, if our investigation of the benefits of education is confined to the parents only, some (perhaps serious) underestimation of benefits would result. Spiegelman (1968) concluded that the sum of social and private intergenerational benefits amounted to more than half of the direct benefits estimated for the Title I program of the Elementary and Secondary Education Act in California.

SOCIAL OR EXTERNAL BENEFITS

The social benefits of education include, in addition to private benefits, those benefits that may be attributable to education but that are so diffused among the population that individuals are unable to appropriate them. A brief listing of major external benefits has been provided by McMahon (1987), who points out that these benefits are

> (1) necessary to effective democracy and democratic institutions, (2) important to efficient markets and adaptation to technical change, (3) lower crime rates and reduced penal system expense, (4) lower welfare, medicaid, unemployment compensation, and public health costs, (5) reduced imperfections in capital markets, (6) public service in community and state agencies, and (7) complementarities in production. (pp. 134–135)

Although it may be impossible to measure and quantify most of these external benefits, some work has been done, for example, with regard to the benefits of increased political participation and the costs associated with criminal behavior. For example, Withey (1971) discusses results of "a study of 87 cities around San Francisco" (p. 83). Although the most highly educated persons in these cities were not represented on city councils, college education is highly related to the probability of being represented on a council: "In the population of these cities, 57 percent have more than a high school diploma, but 95 percent of councilmen are educated above that level" (p. 83).

There is some evidence that more educated persons are less prone to commit crime. Spiegelman (1968) presents some insights regarding juvenile crime, and Ehrlich (1975) presents additional data on the relationship between education and crime. Webb (1977) provides some information on the educational background of inmates in correctional institutions versus that of the general population. She calculates the cost of crime attributable to inadequate education as ranging between $7 billion and $14 billion in 1970. Finally, Phillips, Votey, and Maxwell (1972) show that labor market status is a sufficient factor to explain rising youth crime rates. Since education is associated with higher labor force participation rates, it can be argued that increased education could help in reducing the crime rate.

Other Nonmarket Benefits

Feldman and Newcomb (1969) offer a comprehensive analysis of the impact of college on student behavior and beliefs. Their summary of various studies suggests that "students going through college increase their interest in aesthetic and cultural values, decrease their adherence to traditional religion and other traditional values, [and] become more realistic and less moralistic in their ethical judgments. They also take an increasingly liberal rather than conservative position on political and socioeconomic issues and become more open minded as measured by scales on authoritarianism, dogmatism, ethnocentrism, and prejudice" (Gurin 1971, pp. 27–28). Strumpel (1971) utilized a variety of studies to describe the effect of higher education on economic behavior. He shows that persons with more education are much less likely to be unemployed or to be on strike and to lose work time due to illness, unemployment, or strike. An individual with a higher education is less likely to have many different jobs or occupations, or to change jobs often within the same occupation. They are much more likely to receive a vacation, especially those of 3 weeks or more, and are much more likely to assign a high rank to their chance for promotion. College graduates are far more likely than others to find their jobs enjoyable and to believe that automation is a good thing.

Mathios (1989) provides evidence that nonmonetary benefits are especially important for individuals with more education. Using the NAS-NRC Twin Offspring sample, Mathios measured nonmonetary benefits on the basis of response to a group of questions regarding nonfinancial job attributes. Earnings equations were estimated for low- and high-education groups, alternatively excluding and including several "compensation factors." He concludes that "the inclusion of the occupational factor variables explains an additional 9 percent of the earnings variation in the [high education] group . . . but only an additional 2 percent of the earnings variation in the [low education] group" (p. 464).

Moreover, the results show that people are willing to substitute certain nonmonetary benefits for a pay increase. For example, individuals who indicate that leisure time is the most important occupational factor are estimated to earn (in 1980) $2,800 less that those for whom leisure time is not important. Similar findings (in qualitative terms) are reported for 15 out of 18 factors studied. The author concludes that issues such as sex discrimination in employment must include consideration of nonmonetary benefits, because "estimated earnings differences may overstate the magnitude of discrimination if nonmonetary rewards are a more important part of total compensation for female workers" (p. 457). Similarly, rates of return to college education may be understated, or differences in rates of return by race and sex that rely exclusively on earnings might mask differences in nonmonetary benefits.

Option Values

Weisbrod (1962) points out that there is a financial option open to students. This option refers to the fact that the completion of one level of schooling (e.g., level *a*) enables one to pursue additional levels of schooling (*a* + *1, a* + *2*, etc.). The returns that one might expect to receive for a higher educational investment (say, *a* + *1*) might induce him or her to invest in a lower educational level (e.g., *a*), even if the expected return on the latter (*a*) would not be sufficient to justify the necessary expenditure. When option values are explicitly considered, the profitabilities of various early educational investments are strongly affected by the probability of completion of higher educational levels, so that one's decision regarding an educational investment is critically affected by the option value.

Nonfinancial options permit a person to exercise a number of choices over the life cycle involving job options, working condition options, leisure-time options, and the like. A college professor, for example, enjoys certain nonfinancial advantages because of his or her position, including a substantial degree of freedom and flexibility in work or the satisfactions associated with teaching and research. Other nonfinancial options of this sort include the "hedging option" (i.e., the flexibility of educated individuals in adapting to new job opportunities, which provide a hedge against unemployment) and the "nonmarket option" (i.e., the fact that with education an individual can perform a variety of activities that could not be done without it).

MONETARY RETURNS

During the past 40 years, numerous studies have been written on the private and social rates of returns to investment in higher education in the United

States.[1] These researchers applied benefit-cost techniques to measure the effects of education on lifetime income, using different methods involving the shape of age-earning profiles, earning differentials, and the present value of lifetime income differentials. In general, the findings of the selected studies reviewed here are based on the internal rate of return (IRR) technique.

Returns to College Education

Historically, estimates of the private rates of return to 4 years of college education have typically ranged from 10 to 15%. (For a summary, see Cohn & Geske, 1990.) Estimates of the social rates of return have been somewhat less, yielding approximately 11 to 13%. In recent years, the disparity between private and social rates has been diminishing, and they are now roughly equivalent (Leslie & Brinkman, 1988). Although the IRR to college appears to have remained fairly stable over the years, there was an apparent reduction in the IRR during the early 1970s. Freeman's (1980) findings indicated a relatively sharp decline in the returns to college education during the 5-year period from 1968 to 1973, when the private IRR dropped from 11% in 1968 to 7.5% in 1973.

More recently, Murphy and Welch (1989) examined the historical record of the monetary returns to higher education. The work by these economists documents that the returns to college education have increased in recent years. They found that the ratio of the average wages of persons completing 16 years of schooling to the average wages of those completing only 12 years was 1.33 during the period of 1975 to 1980, compared to 1.54 during 1981 to 1986. These ratios of 1.33 and 1.54 approximated private rates of return of 8.3 and 13.5%, respectively. Similar results were obtained for population subgroups (men, women, Blacks, and Whites) and also for groups with different labor market experience. Similarly, Cohn and Hughes (1994), who provide updated estimates of the IRRs to college education for 1965–1985, also reported a considerable increase in the returns during the early 1980s. Murphy and Welch concluded that much of the decline in the college wage premium during the early and mid 1970s could be attributed to an oversupply of college graduates during this period.

If the estimates of the returns to education in the United States during the 1970s suggested that Americans were "overinvesting" in education, the more recent estimates during the 1980s revealed a marked change in the payoff to education. Becker (1992) reported that this fairly dramatic upturn in the returns to college education apparently peaked in 1986, but then remained relatively stable at least through 1990. Becker pointed out that the average college graduate, after several years of work experience, "now earns some 50 to 70 percent more than a high school graduate. College graduates, on average, receive $500,000 to $1,000,000 more than high school graduates over their lifetimes" (p. 100). Why the rapid rise in the earnings ratio between college and high school graduates? Becker suggested that one possible explanation may be that a college education has not become worth more, but that a high school diploma has become worth less, because of changing job prospects during the 1980s for high school graduates in the United States.

In a comprehensive study, McMahon and Wagner (1982) examined the considerable variation in monetary returns across major fields (and their related occupations), and across types of public and private institutions (i.e., research universities, comprehensive 4-year colleges, and liberal arts colleges). Students who intended to become engineers, for example, expected a private rate of return (25.5%) twice as large as those who intended to become schoolteachers (12.3%). In addition, expected private rates of return for students planning to earn only a bachelor's degree were low at private liberal arts colleges (8.7%) when compared to rates of return at public and private 4-year comprehensive colleges (21.0% and 18.5%, respectively). Similarly, after examining private returns to specific college majors, Berger (1992) found that individuals who received a bachelor's degree in engineering or in the natural sciences, and sometimes in business, received an earnings premium.

Returns to Graduate Education

The economic returns to graduate programs are generally much lower than for bachelor's degree programs. Although the returns to graduate education are characterized by considerable variation, the private payoff, for the most part, has ranged from 2 to 10%, though several studies have reported very low, even negative, returns to graduate education (Cohn & Geske, 1990, pp. 110–114). At the same time, there are some exceptions, such as the IRR for a 3-year PhD program calculated by Ashenfelter and Mooney (1968)—10.5%; the higher IRRs for PhD economists employed in business estimated by Siegfried (1971)—as high as 23.6%; and the average IRRs calculated by Weiss (1971)—over 12%.

Returns to Different Groups

For the most part, the results discussed previously have been "average returns," combining the returns to education for numerous disparate race–sex–ability groups. Considerable evidence, however, suggests that the returns to education differ significantly among various groups in society. The economic returns to African Americans and females, for example, have increased in relative terms, as efforts toward integration, affirmative action, and other programs on behalf of minorities have become more effective (Cooper & Cohn, 1997; Jud & Walker, 1982; Link, Ratledge, & Lewis, 1976; Welch, 1973).

Hoffman (1984) examined Black-White differences in returns to higher education for the 1970s and found that the earnings differential between the college educated and the high school educated decreased for young White males, but increased for Blacks. Hoffman's findings suggested that the Black-White earnings gap had narrowed to the point that predicted earnings (based on 1977 data) were equal for both black and white college graduates. Becker (1992) also pointed out that the increased earnings for college graduates throughout the 1980s appear to have benefited minorities more than their White counterparts. These studies suggest that education is a much more important determinant of earnings for Blacks than for Whites.

Some evidence is available that suggests that differential returns to education by sex may be due to various attributes of the male-female groups under consideration, such as labor market experience, commitment to full-time participation in the labor force, continuity in employment, or types of skills and professions for which individuals are qualified. Daymont and Andrisani (1984) argued that a substantial portion of the gender differential in hourly earnings among recent college graduates can be attributed to differences between men and women in preference for occupations and in preparation (college major) for these occupations. Similarly, Ferber and McMahon (1979) suggested that increased education and a shift to "male" occupations may result in higher rates of return for women.

The overall level of returns to investment in higher education indicates that, in general, such an investment is profitable both for the individual and for society. It must be recognized, however, that college education is not universally profitable, with rates of return varying considerably by major fields and types of institution. If certain college and university programs yield very low and even negative returns, why do individuals continue to enroll in such programs? One response to this question is that college education (and education in general) bestows not only labor market benefits but also various types of non-labor-market benefits, including private nonmonetary benefits.

NONMONETARY BENEFITS

A major problem in estimating the full or true returns to education has to do with our inability to quantify and to value the nonmonetary benefits associated with education. In general, there are three basic categories of non-monetary benefits of education.[2] The benefits falling into the first category related to the pure consumption effects of schooling (e.g., the enjoyment of learning and discovery) and those falling into the second category related to the effects of schooling on the nonwage dimensions of labor market remuneration (e.g., fringe benefits, working conditions, and employment stability) have already been mentioned. The third category includes the effects of schooling on productivity in activities outside the labor market (e.g., in household production and in capital markets). The survey of studies presented in this section focuses on the third category, and more specifically on the beneficial effects of education on health, family life, consumption behavior, and asset management.

Education and Health

Extensive research has documented the positive correlation between increased schooling and good health. Grossman (1976) found that schooling positively affects health, and since past health is controlled for in his model, he argues that the evidence supports a causal relationship that runs from schooling to current health. Grossman's findings indicate that a one-year increase in schooling is associated with a 3.5% increase in health capital when only age is held constant. This increase in health capital declined to 1.2% when all relevant variables are held constant (e.g., age, background characteristics, ability levels, wage rates, job satisfaction).

Given an assumed demand function for health, Grossman (1976) suggested, "schooling raises productivity in the production of health by 2.4 percent at a minimum" (p. 179). Grossman compared this nonmarket productivity effect of schooling on health to the market productivity effect of 5.5% in the hourly wage rate for his sample. "Although the nonmarket productivity effect of schooling may appear to be small in an absolute sense, it is approximately 40 percent [2.4 ÷ 5.5] as large as the market productivity effect" (p. 179).

Other researchers have also documented the relationship between schooling and health. Edwards and Grossman (1981) found that parental schooling levels (after controlling for differences in earnings) are positively correlated with the health status of their children. Lefocowitz (1973) argued that there is a causal relationship between levels of education and individual health status and that the observed correlation between income and medical deprivation appears to be a consequence of education's relationship with both variables. Orcutt, Franklin, Mendelsohn, and Smith (1977) observed that increased schooling (and higher relative income) are correlated with lower mortality rates for given age brackets. Finally, Sander (1995) pointed out the positive effect of schooling on health behavior by documenting that schooling reduces the odds that people smoke. He found that "men and women with more schooling are less likely to smoke and more likely to quit smoking" (p. 23). This finding was particularly true for college graduates.

Education and Family Life

Considerable empirical work has focused on the effects of education on family life, including marriage, family planning, and the rearing of children. With regard to marriage, Michael (1982) argued that education facilitates a more productive sorting of men and women in the marriage market. In turn, this marital sorting may lead to subsequent benefits such as more stable marriages and positive assortative mating by intelligence, which increases the probability of parenting "bright" children.

In terms of family planning, Michael (1975b) argued that education directly affects family size and fertility behavior through the efficiency with which parents process information about contraceptive products and techniques. Michael's analyses disclosed that more-educated couples tend to adopt contraceptive practices more readily and at an earlier stage in marriage than do less-educated couples. In addition, more-educated couples are better informed about and more receptive to new contraceptive techniques, and thus engage in more effective fertility control than do less-educated couples.

In addition, education affects the quality and quantity of time that parents devote to their children. Hill and Stafford (1980) found that more-educated women spend substantially more time with preschool children than do less-educated women—between two and one-half and three and one-half times as much per child. Moreover, Leibowitz (1975) found that although more-educated women generally spend more time in the labor market than do other women, they are also less likely to work when they have preschool or school-aged children in the home. In addition, although aggregate time devoted to home production is about the same for the different education levels, women with more education spend less time in home maintenance activities and considerably more time in child care activities.

Leibowitz (1974; see also Rosenzweig & Wolpin, 1994) argued that there is evidence that this home production, primarily through parental time inputs, increases preschool and childhood stocks of human capital. She found that a mother's education is significantly related to her child's IQ, and that preschool home investments strengthened this relationship beyond the genetic endowment factor. Murnane (1981) also documented a significant relationship between a mother's education and her children's cognitive skills.

Similarly, he concluded that this relationship reflects, at least in part, the positive influence of home environment, including the quality of child care.

Consumption Behavior and Asset Management

Michael (1975a) compared the effect of education on consumer behavior in the home or nonmarket sector with the effect of education on earnings in the labor market. He used a household production model to examine how education affects consumer expenditure patterns. He argued that if more-educated persons are more productive in nonmarket activities, families with more education should produce a higher level of output (commodities) for a given quantity of inputs (time and money). Accordingly, Michael reasoned that more-educated households will have more real wealth (in terms of commodities) and that these households will, in effect, behave as if they have more real income (the equivalent of greater money income).

Michael labeled this effect of schooling on real income through nonmarket productivity the "consumption income effect." To verify and estimate this consumption income effect, Michael structured an empirical test to determine if differences in education levels influence consumer behavior in the same manner that they influence money income. Michael concluded that education produces a positive effect on the efficiency of consumption, and he estimated that the effect of schooling is approximately 60% as great in nonmarket activities as in the labor market. In addition to Michael's work, other studies have provided substantial evidence that individuals with more education seek out, and are better informed, about consumer goods markets.

Solmon (1975) analyzed the relationship between education and savings behavior. He hypothesized that more-educated individuals will save a higher proportion of income, and that they will also tend to exercise different savings alternatives. Overall, his various analyses supported the basic proposition that more-educated individuals have a higher propensity to save and are more efficient at managing their savings portfolios. Solmon also examined the relationships between schooling and individuals' attitudes with respect to portfolio management, savings objectives, and risk preference. He concluded that "at least with respect to inflation, the more educated are more sophisticated (or efficient) investors" (pp. 279–280). He inferred from these findings that the more highly educated are more likely to accept risk, to be more informed and rational in investment decision making, and to plan ahead with a longer time horizon.

Initial attempts to quantify and value these nonmonetary benefits suggest that estimates of the returns to schooling may be considerably understated. After surveying and describing various nonmarket effects of schooling such as those just discussed, Haveman and Wolfe (1984) attempted to place an appropriate value on them. They speculated that benefit-cost studies that have focused exclusively on increased earnings may have captured only about 50% of the total value of an additional year of schooling. Whether the value of a college education is underestimated by more or less than 50% is not clear; what is clear is that attention must be paid to benefits of this type. Indeed, in many instances, investment in higher education is justified almost exclusively in terms of expected nonmarket benefits, rather than increased income for graduates.

CONCLUSION

This brief survey suggests that both governments and individuals gain substantial economic benefits from investments in higher education. Although there will always be disagreement over the magnitude and extent of the social or external benefits associated with higher education, these types of benefits will always be an important consideration for governments. Most informed observers would agree that a highly educated population assures a well-informed, more active citizenry, which strengthens our democratic processes at all governmental levels. Yet, despite a number of solid economic arguments that justify a strong governmental role in higher education, the commitment to higher education at both the federal and state levels has declined in recent years.

During the early 1990s, federal outlays for higher education, on an annual basis, averaged about $12 billion, which represented slightly less than 1% of total federal outlays. At the state level, however, where education is a major responsibility, the bulk of a state's budget is typically devoted to education. In recent years, however, state governments have been paying less, and families and students have been paying more, of the total cost of higher education. For governments, the consequences of reducing their investments in higher education may not be felt immediately, or even within the next several years. But the consequences of these cutbacks will become manifest in the future as reduced social benefits become increased social costs in other public budget components (e.g., increased health, welfare, unemployment, and penal costs). Given the growing importance of education and the changing labor market, families know that they simply cannot afford to bypass an investment in higher education. For parents, the consequences of foregoing investments in higher education will be realized immediately as their children fail to capture those important private monetary and nonmonetary benefits that higher education yields and that can immeasurably enhance the quality of their lives.

NOTES

1. This section and the next draw heavily from Geske (1995). For a review of similar studies that have estimated the rates of return to investment in higher education in about 50 other countries, see Cohn and Geske (1990) and Psacharopoulos (1994).

2. For a more extensive discussion of nonmonetary benefits, see Cohn and Geske (1992).

REFERENCES

Ashenfelter, O., & Mooney, J. D. (1968, February). Graduate education, ability and earnings. *Review of Economics and Statistics, 50,* 78–86.

Becker, W. E. (1992). Why go to college? The value of an investment in higher education. In W. E. Becker & D. R. Lewis (Eds.), *The economics of American higher education* (pp. 91–120). Boston: Kluwer.

Berger, M. C. (1992). Private returns to specific college majors. In W. E. Becker & D. R. Lewis (Eds.), *The economics of American higher education* (pp. 141–195). Boston: Kluwer.

Carnoy, M. (ed.) (1995). *International encyclopedia of economics of education* (2nd ed.). Oxford: Elsevier.

Cohn, E., & Geske, T. G. (1990). *The economics of education* (3rd ed.). Oxford: Pergamon.

Cohn, E., & Geske, T. G. (1992). Private nonmonetary returns to investment in higher education. In W. E. Becker & D. R. Lewis (Eds.), *The economics of American higher education* (pp. 173–195). Boston: Kluwer.

Cohn, E., & Hughes, Jr., W. W. (1994). A benefit-cost analysis of investment in college education in the United States: 1969–1985. *Economics of Education Review, 13* (2), in press.

Cooper, S. T., & Cohn, E. (1997, Summer). Internal rates of return to college education in the United States by sex and race. *Journal of Education Finance, 23,* 101–133.

Daymont, T. N., & Andrisani, P. J. (1984, Summer). Job preferences, college major, and the gender gap in earnings. *Journal of Human Resources, 19,* 408–428.

Denison, E. F. (1985). *Trends in American economic growth, 1929–1982.* Washington, DC: Brookings.

Edwards, L. N., & Grossman, M. (1981). Children's health and the family. In R. M. Scheffler (Ed.), *Advances in health economics and health services research* (Vol. 2). Greenwich, CT: JAI Press.

Ehrlich, I. (1975). On the relation between education and crime. In F. T. Juster (Ed.), *Education, income and human behavior* (pp. 318–338). New York: McGraw-Hill.

Feldman, K. A., & Newcomb, T. M. (1969). *The impact of college on students.* San Francisco: Jossey-Bass.

Ferber, M. A., & McMahon, W. W. (1979, Summer). Women's expected earnings and their investment in higher education. *Journal of Human Resources, 14,* 405–420.

Freeman, R. B. (1980, Winter). The facts about the declining economic value of college. *Journal of Human Resources, 15,* 124–142.

Geske, T. G. (1995). The value of investments in higher education: Capturing the full returns. *Zeitschrift für Internationale Erziehungs- und Sozialwissenschaftliche Forschung* (Journal for International Education and Social Science Research, Germany), *12* (1), 121–139.

Grossman, M. (1976). The correlation between health and schooling. In N. E. Terleckyj (Ed.), *Household production and consumption* (pp. 147–211). New York: Columbia University Press.

Gurin, G. (1971). The impact of the college experience. In S. B. Withey (Ed.), *A degree and what else? Correlates and consequences of a college education* (pp. 25–54). New York: McGraw-Hill.

Haveman, R. H., & Wolfe, B. L. (1984). Schooling and economic well-being: The role of nonmarket effects. *Journal of Human Resources, 19* (3), 377–407.

Hill, C. R., & Stafford, F. P. (1980). Parental care of children: Time diary estimates of quantity, predictability, and variety. *Journal of Human Resources, 15* (2), 219–239.

Hoffman, S. D. (1984). Black-White differences in returns to higher education: Evidence from the 1970s. *Economics of Education Review, 3* (1), 31–21.

Jud, G. D., & Walker, J. W. (1982, Fall). Racial differences in the returns to schooling and experience among prime-age males: 1967–1975. *Journal of Human Resources, 17,* 623–632.

Lefocowitz, M. J. (1973, March). Poverty and health: A reexamination. *Inquiry,* 3–13.

Leibowitz, A. (1974, May). Education and home production. *American Economic Review, 64,* 243–250.

Leibowitz, A. (1975). Education and the allocation of women's time. In F. T. Juster (Ed.), *Education, income and human behavior* (pp. 171–198). New York: McGraw-Hill.

Leslie, L. L., & Brinkman, P. T. (1988). *The economic value of higher education.* New York: Macmillan.

Link, C., Ratledge, E., & Lewis, K. (1976, March). Black-White differences in returns to schooling: Some new evidence. *American Economic Review, 66,* 221–223.

Mathios, A. D. (1989). Education, variation in earnings, and nonmonetary compensation. *Journal of Human Resources, 24* (3), 456–468.

McMahon, W. W. (1987). Externalities in education. In G. Psacharopoulos (Ed.), *Economics of education: Research and studies* (pp. 133–137). Oxford: Pergamon.

McMahon, W. W. & Wagner, A. P. (1982). The monetary returns to education as partial social efficiency criteria. In W. W. McMahon and T. G. Geske (Eds.), *Financing education: Overcoming inefficiency and inequity* (pp. 150–187). Urbana: University of Illinois Press.

Michael, R. T. (1975a). Education and consumption. In F. T. Juster (Ed.), *Education, income and human behavior* (pp. 235–252). New York: McGraw-Hill.

Michael, R. T. (1975b). Education and fertility. In F. T. Juster (Ed.), *Education, income and human behavior* (pp. 339–364). New York: McGraw-Hill.

Michael, R. T. (1982). Measuring non-monetary benefits of education: A survey. In W. W. McMahon and T. G. Geske (Eds.), *Financing education: Overcoming inefficiency and inequity* (pp. 119–149). Urbana: University of Illinois Press.

Murnane, R. J. (1981). New evidence on the relationship between mother's education and children's cognitive skills. *Economics of Education Review, 1* (2), 245–252.

Murphy, K., & Welch, F. (1989). Wage premiums for college graduates: Recent growth and possible explanations. *Educational Researcher, 18* (4), 17–26.

Nichols, B. (1996). Clinton makes future his centerpiece. *USA Today,* 14, June 5, 1996, p. 3A.

Orcutt, G. H., Franklin, S. D., Mendelsohn, R., & Smith, J. D. (1977, February). Does your probability of death depend on your environment? A microanalytic study. *American Economic Review, 67,* 260–264.

Phillips, J., Votey, Jr., H. L., & Maxwell, D. (1972, May-June). Crime, youth, and the labor market. *Journal of Political Economy, 80* (pt. 1), 491–504.

Psacharopoulos, G. (1994). Returns to investment in education: A global update. *World Development, 22* (9), 1325–1343.

Rosenzweig, M. R., & Wolpin, K. I. (1994). Are there increasing returns to the intergenerational production of human capital? *The Journal of Human Resources, 29* (2), 670–693.

Sander, W. (1995). Schooling and smoking. *Economics of Education Review, 14* (1), 23–33.

Siegfried, J. J. (1971, April). Rate of return to the Ph.D. in economics. *Industrial and Labor Relations Review, 24,* 420–431.

Solmon, L. C. (1975). The relation between schooling and savings behavior: An example of the indirect effects of education. In F. T. Juster (Ed.), *Education, income and human behavior* (pp. 253–294). New York: McGraw-Hill.

Solmon, L. C. & Fagnano, C. L. (1995). Benefits of education. In M. Carnoy (Ed.), *International encyclopedia of economics of education,* 2nd ed. (pp. 114–124). Oxford: Elsevier.

Spiegelman, R. G. (1968). A benefit/cost model to evaluate educational programs. *Socio-Economic Planning Sciences,* Volume I, 443–460.

Strumpel, B. (1971). Higher education and economic behavior. In S. B. Withey (Ed.), *A degree and what else? Correlates and consequences of a college education* (pp. 55–79). New York: McGraw-Hill.

Webb, L. D. (1977). Savings to society by investing in adult education. In *Economic and social perspectives on adult illiteracy: A conference report* (pp. 52–73). Tallahassee, FL: Florida Department of Education.

Weisbrod, B. A. (1962, October). Education and investment in human capital. *Journal of Political Economy, 70,* (Supplement), 106–123.

Weiss, Y. (1971, December). Investment in graduate education. *American Economic Review, 67,* 833–852.

Welch, F. (1973, December). Black-White differences in returns to schooling. *American Economic Review, 67,* 893–907.

Withey, S. B. (1971). Some effects on life-style. In S. B. Withy (Ed.), *A degree and what else? Correlates and consequences of a college education* (pp. 81–93). New York: McGraw-Hill.

Wolfe, B. L. (1995). External benefits of education. In M. Carnoy (Ed.), *International encyclopedia of economics of education,* 2nd ed. (pp. 159–163). Oxford: Elsevier.

CHAPTER 3

How Will We Do More with Less?

THE PUBLIC POLICY DILEMMA OF FINANCING POSTSECONDARY EDUCATIONAL OPPORTUNITY

Thomas G. Mortenson

Since 1979, public policy regarding postsecondary education opportunities for students and economic changes that are occurring in the labor market have gone in opposite directions:

- Individual and social welfare are increasingly determined by the educational attainment of workers in the labor force, at the same time that
- Federal and especially state investment in postsecondary education opportunity has been sharply reduced.

To the extent that public policy effectively addresses the economic changes occurring in the labor force, social welfare objectives of public policy can be enhanced. On the other hand, if public policy continues to oppose or ignore these fundamental economic changes, something well short of optimal or maximized social welfare will result.

In this analysis, the conflict between economic change and political priorities is outlined, the known consequences are described, and some recommendations are offered. In the first part of this analysis, I describe the major economic forces, which began about 1973, that are shaping the American economy and individual and social welfare. These changes call for far greater human capital investment than has ever been made in the past. In the second part of the analysis, I outline the sharply reduced social investment in postsecondary education, particularly since about 1979, at the federal level and in 49 of the 50 states. In the third part, I examine the postsecondary enrollment consequences of this reduced social investment. Finally, I describe the evolution and current disarray of public policy and a partial solution to this growing disparity between fundamental economic, demographic, and social change on the one hand and the response of government policy makers on the other.

THE CHALLENGE OF ECONOMIC CHANGE

The changes driving the American economy since the early 1970s are unlike those experienced during the decades following the end of World War II. In the United States—victorious, relatively undamaged by the war, isolated from the rebuilding challenges faced by Europe and in Asia, able to dominate most of the world and exploit its opportunities—the economy in general and the private welfare of families in particular improved rapidly, substantially, and almost continuously in the 1950s and 1960s. In 1994 dollars, median family income increased from $26,060 in 1956 to $41,766 by 1973.[1] Moreover, the benefits of this growth were widely shared among American families. Of this era it could truly be said that the rising tide lifted all boats. There were good jobs and prosperity for all, as long as we ignored certain islands of poverty among us defined by geography, age, race, and ethnicity, and other unpleasant features of American society.

But the growth of postwar American prosperity peaked about 1973, and, on average, we have been stuck there ever since. For more than 20 years, the welfare of Americans as measured by median family income has been stagnant. Measured in 1994 dollars, in 1973 median family income for Americans was $41,766, whereas in 1994 it was $40,159. For many Americans, working harder now does not improve private welfare—at best it allows a worker to keep up with the cost of living or it slows the descent. A growing share of many family budgets is devoted to such basic survival needs as shelter, food, and medical care. That leaves a declining share available for the discretionary purchases that enrich the quality of our lives.

What has occurred since 1973 is a great deal of income redistribution. Change continues to occur, but mainly in ways that benefit a relatively narrow group within the American population. A few groups of Americans are better off today than they were in 1973, whereas many others are worse off. For example, among the socially dependent, the elderly are better off—as measured by poverty rates—whereas children are worse off.

The welfare of individuals and their families is generally measured by income, and income is increasingly determined by educational attainment. Since 1973, those groups that have managed to maintain or improve their standards of living are those with substantial amounts of postsecondary education. Others who thought they could begin their adult lives with a high school education or less have found their incomes and the standards of living those incomes support in virtual economic free fall.

With educational attainment so clearly the dividing line between those who are succeeding and those who are failing in this post-1973 economy, the explanation is clear: Education is human capital in an economy that has rapidly evolved, especially since about 1973, into one in which workers are increasingly dependent on ever greater levels of education and training to be productive in economically valuable in rewardable ways. Those who possess this capital have access to the best-paying jobs in the labor force, attained through their education, training, and certification. Those who do not have such capital are increasingly competing for jobs in a worldwide labor pool filled with workers willing to work for far lower wages than American laborers had been able to earn prior to 1973. Whereas a person used to be able to earn a decent living by being honest and hard-working, now he or she must also be postsecondary educated or trained and certified to have access to the best paying jobs in the labor force—and married to an equally well-educated and hard-working spouse.

These economic shifts since 1973 show no sign of abating, and in fact may be accelerating. The American economy is unlikely to return anytime soon to a time when high-wage/low-skills jobs abound in the labor force. Labor unions are unlikely to bully corporations through labor actions into higher wages—the corporations are increasingly driven to lower labor costs in industries that compete worldwide. The American military no longer offers training and career alternatives to immature, troubled, or uncommitted youth. Since the early 1980s, the military services have acted increasingly like selective-admission colleges and universities. Those without valuable education and training will have access mostly to jobs paying at or near the minimum wage, without medical insurance or retirement or other benefits available to the best-educated workers in the labor force. Moreover, changing economic and technological conditions will require more or less continuous lifetime education and training for workers to just keep pace with the changes propelling the economy.

As if economic and technological change were not enough, several demographic changes are occurring that call for public policy attention. One is the arrival at college age of the echo of the post–World War II baby boom. For the next 18 years, the numbers of high school graduates will increase yearly, putting increased pressure on postsecondary capacity and quality. Moreover, this growth will be disproportionately among minority groups and children from low-income and first-generation families that traditional higher education has not served well in the past. And the growing need for continuous education and training throughout working lives will bring many more older Americans back to campuses to update skills, prepare for new roles, and nurture mature minds.

The public policy challenge is to respond to this need to substantially—

not marginally—broaden opportunities for postsecondary education and training. Broadening means including a far larger proportion of the population than has ever been served before, from a more diverse set of socioeconomic backgrounds than traditional higher education has been comfortable serving in the past. Broadening also means lengthening the exposure of adults to education and training opportunities, and taking those opportunities to places where adults live and work and cannot leave. How well these needs are addressed will determine to a significant degree our individual and social welfare for the foreseeable future.

HUMAN CAPITAL INVESTMENT THROUGH POSTSECONDARY EDUCATION

In the United States, education after high school is financed by a mix of social investment (government appropriations) and private investment (tuition paid by students and their families). According to data from the National Income and Product Accounts (NIPA) for 1993, students and their parents provided about 46% of the funds used to educate students, states provided another 45%, and the federal government provided the remaining 9%.[2]

Over the past 40 years, these proportions have shifted. These decades can be divided into two broad eras. The first lasted from 1952 to 1979. During this period, social investment in the higher education of students expanded, from 49% of the total in 1952 to a peak of 65% in 1979. Concomitantly, the proportion of the total paid by students and their families declined from 51 to 35%. The social investment mix also shifted during this era from entirely states between 1952 and 1958, to growing contributions from both states and the federal government through 1974, followed by declining state contributions offset by further growth in federal contributions through 1979. This growth in federal investment in postsecondary education opportunity was particularly important because, unlike most state investment, the federal investment was focused almost exclusively on financially needy students from low-income family backgrounds.

The second era spans 1979 through the present. During this period, social investment in postsecondary education opportunity has declined. By most measures, the reductions have been about 30%. For example, state tax funds appropriated for higher education per $1,000 of state personal income have declined from a peak of $11.22 in Fiscal Year (FY) 1979 to $7.88 by FY 1996, or a decline of 29.8%. States have diverted budget shares previously committed to higher education to new state budget priorities, especially corrections and Medicaid. At the federal level, costs of student financial aid have been shifted from federal taxpayers to financially needy students by shifting from nonrepayable grant assistance to repayable education loans, then by seeking to shift the costs of these loans to borrowers through higher interest rates, the addition of various loan fees and increased loan collection efforts. The recent congressional discussions about eliminating the federal interest subsidy between leaving school and entering repayment, and capitalizing the in-school interest subsidy were unsuccessful extensions of the effort to shift the cost of the federal education loan program from federal taxpayers to student borrowers.

This is the era of cost-shifting from taxpayers to students and their families. Colleges and universities needing resources to provide the basic dimensions of educational opportunity—capacity, quality, and affordability— have increased tuitions and other student charges to offset losses in state appropriations and the deterioration in federal student financial aid funding. The decline in social investment has been precipitated by many factors, including, but not limited to, social unwillingness to increase taxes to pay for government services, growing interest obligations on accumulated government indebtedness, growing social program costs for those without postsecondary education or training (particularly corrections for males and medicaid for females), an awareness of the very large private returns to individuals who graduate from college and enter the labor market, and an occasional negative press for higher education when basic organizational management problems become public knowledge and are reported in the media.

The cost-shifting to students shows up clearly in inflation-adjusted tuition and fee increases charged to students. Since 1980, public institution tuition and fees have increased at an annual rate of the Consumer Price Index (CPI) plus 4 to 5%. This has occurred while real median family incomes have remained flat.[3]

The cost-shifting from taxpayers to students between 1979 and 1993 can be measured with the National Income and Product Account data. In 1993, students and their parents were paying $14.2 billion more for their higher education than they were in 1979. State taxpayers were paying $9.8 billion less, and federal taxpayers were paying $4.5 billion less, than they were in 1979.

IMPLICATIONS FOR EDUCATIONAL OPPORTUNITY

The cost shift from taxpayers to students has influenced the enrollment decision making by students and their families. Research on these questions began in the early 1950s by econometricians, who have calculated quantitative estimates of the effects of price changes on changes in student enrollment decisions regarding access, choice, and persistence in postsecondary education.

The basic economic principle is straightforward: All other things held constant, if the price that students are charged increases, then fewer will enroll, and if the price decreases, then more will enroll. When the prices of higher education increase, as they have since 1979, fewer students will be able to afford to attend college, fewer will be able to make choices between institutions that are not constrained by affordability considerations, and fewer will be able to persist in their studies as long as they had planned without encountering price obstacles such as cumulative educational debt and the numbers of hours worked. Moreover, these price effects are concentrated more at the lower end of the family income scale than they are at the top.

A more complete statement of the private investment decision is that a student will enroll in college if the net present value of the college investment is greater than the value of the alternatives available to him/her. The net present value of higher education to the student is the present value of benefits less costs. Benefits include the consumptive value of higher education while enrolled (lifestyle), and the investment returns following college graduation (increased earnings). Costs include the direct costs of college attendance (tuition, fees, books, and supplies), indirect costs of living while attending college (food, housing, transportation, personal and medical care), opportunity costs (foregone income), financing costs (interest, principle, and fees associated with borrowing), risk and other costs less nonrepayable student financial aid (scholarships, grants, waivers). All future values are discounted to present value.

Econometricians calculate quantitative estimates of the effects of price or net price (price less gift aid) on student enrollment decisions that define educational opportunity: access, choice, and persistence to degree attainment. These estimates, customarily defined as "Student Price Response Coefficients" or SPRCs, are of the percentage change in enrollment per $100 of price change. As the price of higher education charged to students increases (all other conditions held constant), fewer will enroll by a predictable amount. As the net price decreases (through offsetting student financial aid), more students will enroll. These effects have measurable and predictable effects on choice and persistence decisions of students as well.[4]

Empirically, the enrollment consequences of the cost shift from taxpayers to students since 1979 can be seen in the redistribution of higher educational enrollment and attainment (through age 24) in enrollment data reported by the Census Bureau and data from other sources during this same period. Here we have calculated high school graduation rates, college participation rates, and 4-year college completion rates for unmarried 18- to 24-years-olds by family income quartiles for the years between 1970 and 1994.

The product of these three rates measures the proportion of the population for each income quartile and year that attained a bachelor's degree by age 24.[5]

• In 1994, 8% of those from the bottom quartile of the family income distribution, below about a $22,000 yearly income, earned a bachelor's degree by age 24. This compares to 14% of those from the second quartile of family income ($22,000 to $38,000), 28% of those from the third quartile ($38,000 to $68,000), and 80% of those from the top quartile (about $68,000).

• In 1970, a student born into a family from the top quartile of family income was about six times more likely to have a bachelor's degree by age 24 than was a student born into the bottom quartile. By 1979, at the end of the expansion of social investment in higher educational opportunity, the top quartile student was four times more likely to have a bachelor's degree by age 24 than was the student from the bottom quartile. Now, in the mid 1990s, the student from the top quartile is ten times more likely to have a bachelor's degree by age 24 than is the student from the bottom quartile of family income.

Another interpretation of this redistribution of higher educational opportunity is that what was until fairly recently thought of as the means for bridging the gap in the distribution of private income, wealth, and opportunity has, since 1979, become the means for preserving and deepening the gulf that separates the rich and the poor in America.

PROGRAM CREATION AND LATER DISARRAY

In 1965, public policy, particularly but not exclusively at the federal level, charted a course designed to broaden opportunities for postsecondary education and training as a part of a comprehensive federal social program to reduce the social and economic malignancy of poverty in the United States. The plan was the War on Poverty. The three planks of the platform on which this war was waged were (1) to increase the human capital of the poor by making social investments in their education and health that would make them more valuable to potential employers, (2) to remove irrelevant barriers to their full participation in the labor force through civil rights legislation, and (3) to stimulate the economy to create jobs for these newly capitalized workers when they were ready to enter the labor market.

The specific federal policy regarding higher education was the Higher Education Act of 1965, which created, for the first time, federal need-based student financial aid in the form of Education Opportunity Grants. This federal initiative was paralleled by the creation of state need-based grant programs beginning in the mid-1950s that continue to the present.

The federal course was pursued through about 1979 in the design of effectively targeted and funded programs. This effort made significant progress towards reducing inequality of opportunity for postsecondary education and training as long as the focus and commitment were clear.

But beginning with the 1978 Middle Income Student Assistance Act, the federal effort began to lose focus, and shortly thereafter, funding support began to erode as well. Federal policy design began to shift from the authorization to the appropriations processes of Congress during the recessions of the early 1980s, and thus was inaugurated the federal cost shift from taxpayers to students through the shift from grant assistance to loan assistance. Being less expensive for the federal government but more costly for students, the educational loans were substituted for the federal Pell Grant program. Moreover, fees were added to loans, interests rates were increased, special allowances to lenders reduced, and collection efforts strengthened. All of these efforts shifted the costs of federal student financial aid from taxpayers to aid recipients, particularly those with low income.

But a new social and economic need to broaden opportunities for postsecondary education and training has emerged since the federal student financial aid programs were created in the mid-1960s. Since about 1973, changes in the labor market for workers with different levels of education have produced surpluses of workers without postsecondary education, and relative shortages of workers with postsecondary education, particularly at the highest levels of education. This demand-supply imbalance has produced redistributions in income and concomitant living standards over the past 20 years. Those with a high school education or less are now often competing with workers overseas willing to work for a fraction of what American workers expect and need. The new challenge in this international economy is to increase levels of education and training in the American workforce to make workers more productive and thus justifying higher wages, which produce greater private and social welfare.

This challenge arises in the environment of sharply curtailed social investment in opportunity for postsecondary education and training. We are back to where we began: How can we do much more with much less? At least a partial answer must be found first in doing more with what we have. That is: How can we broaden opportunities for postsecondary education and training with the current, curtailed level of social investment? Any answer must clearly involve substantial reallocation of the existing social resources provided to educate students.

Currently, many students in higher education receive far greater social resources than they "need" to participate in higher education, whereas others receive far less than they need. In this case, need is determined by the same student financial aid formulas used to determine how much (if any) federal, state, and institutional student financial aid an applicant will receive to help him or her finance their college attendance costs:

> College attendance costs
> Less   Expected family contribution
> Equals   Financial need

College attendance costs in this formula include tuition, fees, books, supplies, food, housing, transportation, and personal and medical care. The expected family contribution is calculated by a federal formula that considers student and parental income and assets, family size, number enrolled in college, and other factors. The remaining financial need is then met through a package of scholarships, grants, waivers, and various forms of student self-help such as educational loans and work-study earnings.

The student who receives more social resources than he or she needs has an expected family contribution that is greater than college attendance costs and is enrolled in a public institution where state appropriations reduce tuition charges to well below the costs of education. For example, national average undergraduate tuition and fees at state flagship universities in 1994–95 was about $3,032. If this represents about a third of the cost of educating a student (in FY 1993 it was 32.3%), then the total cost per student is about $9,000 per year. The difference between what the student pays ($3,032) and what a year of university education costs ($9,000) is state taxpayer support of about $6,000 per student per year of education.

For students from families with high incomes, the expected family contribution from need analysis may be greater than the college attendance costs plus the state taxpayer subsidy. For other students, the expected family contribution may fall well short of college attendance costs. These students qualify for need-based student financial aid. It is this great unevenness in the distribution of financial need that requires the reallocation of existing social investments in higher education opportunity, particularly from states, to more effectively meet the demonstrated financial needs of students. Some students currently receive large state subsidies that they would not qualify for were such subsidies need tested. Other students would qualify for larger state subsidies than they currently receive.

The public policy challenge is to broaden postsecondary educational opportunity on a declining base of social investment. Any solution to this dilemma requires attention to at least the following issues.

1. Inefficiencies in current social investment in higher education. Clearly, states can no longer afford to discount tuition below the cost of education for those who cannot demonstrate financial need for such assistance, if the trade-off is denial of educational opportunity for others for financial reasons. Subsidizing the higher education of those who do not need such assistance, at the expense of educational opportunities for others who do, cannot be justified as social policy.

2. Social recognition that higher education costs real money and is an increasingly necessary—not peripheral—social investment. Opportunity costs money: Capacity costs money, quality costs money, and affordability costs money. The potential for producing these dimensions of higher educational opportunity on a declining resources base are highly limited. The social benefits produced by higher education warrant increased (but targeted) social investment.

3. Higher education must be recast from consumption to investment, with the long-term benefits of higher education made clear to future and potential college students. The labor market data are unequivocal: Higher education pays handsome returns to individuals who make the commitment and sacrifices to earn it. Moreover, the labor market promises brutal treatment for people who think that they can attain decent living standards without it. The same lesson applies to society.

NOTES

1. These data are collected in the *Current Population Survey* and published annually in several series of *Current Population Reports,* including the P-20 series on educational attainment, and the P-60 series on income.

2. The historical NIPA data have been published in *National Income and Product Accounts of the United States, Volumes 1 and 2, 1929–1988.* These data have been updated through 1993 in the Survey of Current Business.

3. The family income data have been published in the P-60 series of *Current Population Reports.*

4. The basic reference text for these kinds of analyses is *The Economic Value of Higher Education* by Leslie and Brinkman, 1988, published by the American Council on Education and MacMillan Publishing Company, New York.

5. Most of the data used in this analysis is collected in the *Current Population Survey* and reported by the Census Bureau in the P-20 series of *Current Population Reports* in the school enrollment series. An estimation technique used to derive college completion rates by age 24 using data from the 1980 *High School and Beyond* data file is explained in "Educational Attainment by Family Income, 1970 to 1994" in the November 1995 issue of *Postsecondary Education Opportunity* (Volume 41).

CHAPTER 4

The Growing Loan Orientation in Federal Financial Aid Policy

A HISTORICAL PERSPECTIVE

James C. Hearn

In the past two decades, the federal government has dramatically changed the ways in which it aids the financing of postsecondary students' attendance. From a roughly equal emphasis on student loans and grants, the government has moved toward an approach dominated by loans. Increasingly, federally supported student aid is loan aid, not grant or work-study aid. Largely as a result of this emerging federal emphasis, loans have grown to well over half of all the student financial aid awarded in this country.

The increased use of loans as the primary instruments of federal student aid policy has created new financial challenges in students' and graduates' lives. The effects of students' rising debt levels, in particular, have been much discussed in the popular press, in the chambers of Congress, and among those closely involved in student aid issues. Often, the language used has been that of crisis. For example, a senator closely associated with the rise of federal student aid grants has worried publicly that rising debt levels might be creating "a new class of indentured servants" (Senator Claiborne Pell, cited in Kosterlitz, 1989, p. 921). In a similar vein, College Board president Donald Stewart said recently that we are facing "a deeply mortgaged future. It may be individuals who pay off the educational debts, but we as a society are co-signing the mortgage—and paying a high social cost as well" (College Board, 1995a, p. 11).

The actual short- and long-term implications of the recent loan explosion have been little studied empirically before now, and the severity of the problem is unclear (Baum, 1996). What *is* clear, however, is that the financial aspects of attending college have changed remarkably since the mid-1970s. To aid understanding of that transition, in this chapter I trace the history of student loans in federal financial aid policy. The emergence of the current federal emphasis on loans is best understood by looking back further than the past two decades and by examining more than the federal loan programs alone. Investigating the programs' development since their inception and in broad political, economic, and social context illuminates why particular paths were taken and how the legacy of taking those paths shapes contemporary policies.

The chapter is organized in three parts. The initial section provides a brief overview of the history of federal loans and other forms of federal student financial aid, focusing particularly on trends in dollar outlays and student participants. The following section profiles in more detail the often colorful policy history of the federal loan programs.[1] In the concluding section, I discuss the federal loan programs' evolving role in the financing of higher education.

AN OVERVIEW OF FEDERAL INVOLVEMENT IN STUDENT LOANS

Prior to the passage of the Higher Education Act of 1965, the federal government supplied only one form of aid generally available to all college students: National Defense Student Loans. Originated in 1958, these loans were later renamed National Direct Student Loans, then renamed again, as Perkins Loans. Other federal aid prior to 1965 was specially directed to particular groups, such as that offered through the Servicemen's Readjustment Act of 1944 (the "GI Bill"). As noted in Table 4.1, all federal student aid totaled a little over one billion dollars in 1963–64 (in 1994 dollars).

Activist national education initiatives in the 1960s expanded the total of direct federal student aid outlays. By providing matching and cost-support funds, the federal government also spurred dramatic growth in other forms of aid in that period. By 1970–71, the total of these two kinds of federally *supported* student aid was $12.5 billion in 1994 dollars.[2] A decade later, the total was nearly twice that amount. Thus, total federally supported aid grew over 20-fold between 1963–64 and 1980–81. After relative stability in the 1980s, the number began to grow dramatically again, reaching an estimated total of over $34 billion dollars in 1994–95.

Most of the growth in federal student aid has been in programs providing aid generally available to the American public, rather than in aid targeted for special groups such as veterans. As Table 4.1 reveals, the generally available aid programs were over 32 times larger in 1980–81 than in 1963–64. That growth slowed in the mid-1980s but surged again in the later years of the decade. Then, between 1990–91 and 1994–95, generally available aid awards rose a remarkable 48%. At middecade, the programs were 59 times larger than in 1963–64.

TABLE 4.1. Total Aid Awards for Postsecondary Students in the United States (Selected Years, in Millions of U.S. Constant Dollars).

	1963 –1964	1970 –1971	1975 –1976	1980 –1981	1985 –1986	1990 –1991	Est. 1994 –1995
Federally Supported Aid:							
Generally Available Federal Aid:							
Pell Grants (formerly Basic Grants)	0	0	2505	4088	4866	5436	5570
Supplementary Educational Opportunity Grants (SEOG)	0	499	538	630	559	501	546
State Student Incentive Grants (SSIG)	0	0	53	124	103	65	72
College Work Study (CWS)	0	849	789	1131	895	806	749
Loan Programs:							
Perkins Loans	547	898	1231	1188	959	964	958
Income-Contingent Loans	0	0	0	0	0	0	0
Family Education Loans (Non-Direct):							
Subsidized Stafford Loans	0	3791	3389	10,623	11,360	11,075	13,906
Unsubsidized Stafford Loans	0	0	0	0	0	0	7039
Supplemental Loans for Students (SLS)	0	0	0	0	367	1894	32
Parent Loans (PLUS)	0	0	0	0	330	1059	1637
Direct Student Loans (Ford Program):							
Subsidized Stafford Loans	0	0	0	0	0	0	1073
Unsubsidized Stafford Loans	0	0	0	0	0	0	471
Parent Loans (PLUS)	0	0	0	0	0	0	168
Total Generally Available Federal Aid	547	6038	8505	17,784	19,439	21,806	32,221
Specially Directed Federal Aid	565	6508	14,654	6820	2245	1672	2388
Total Federally Supported Aid	1112	12,546	23,159	24,604	21,684	23,479	34,610
State Grant Aid	269	882	1311	1372	1788	2059	2628
Institutional and Other Grant Aid	1297	3125	3126	2782	4040	6379	8929
Total Federal, State, and Institutional Aid	2679	16553	25,857	28,758	27,511	31,917	46,167

Note: These data are adapted from data supplied by the Gillespie and Carlson (1983) and the College Board (1995). See text for details on the data.

The bulk of this recent growth came in the federally supported loan programs, and those programs now compose the great majority of the generally available federal aid. For reinforcement of that point, consider the other generally available federal programs, for grants and work-study support respectively. Federal grant programs include the massive Pell Grants program and the smaller Supplemental Educational Opportunity Grants (SEOG) and State Student Incentive Grants (SSIG) programs. After adjusting for inflation, federal grant aid has grown little for the past decade, totaling $6.2 billion in 1994–95. The other federal nonloan program, the College Work Study (CWS) program, has actually shrunk since the 1970s, and totaled only $749 million in 1994–95. The combined 1994–95 total of under $7 billion dollars in the Pell, SEOG, SSIG, and CWS programs contrasts dramatically with the over $25 billion committed under the loan programs in that year.

As suggested in the table, the federal government has initiated many loan programs over the years. A brief introduction to those programs will be provided here, with more details to come later in the chapter. Perkins loans, as noted earlier, began in 1958. These are administered by campus aid officials, and funds are supplied directly by the federal government. Income-contingent loans, which allowed students to repay at a set percentage of income, were a separate program for a period in the 1990s, but this program has been discontinued and income-contingent repayment is now provided as an option within other federal loan programs. The Federal Family Education Loan Program (FFELP) includes all the programs based in funds supplied by private lenders, mainly banks and state-licensed or -controlled financing organizations. What is now the subsidized Stafford Loan program under the FFELP was once known as the Guaranteed Student Loan (GSL) program. The unsubsidized Stafford Loan program under FFELP is a newer effort to provide loan funds for students not qualifying for federal subsidies on interest while they are in school. A growing share of federal student loans (one third in 1994–95) is now unsubsidized. The Supplemental Loans for Students program was the predecessor of the unsubsidized Stafford Loan program, and has now been phased out of existence. The final FFELP program is the Parent Loans program, known as the PLUS program, which provides unsubsidized loans to the parents of students who do not qualify for sufficient subsidized loan aid to meet educational costs. Recently, three non-FFELP versions of the Stafford and PLUS programs have been funded on a trial basis: Under the new Ford Direct Student Loan Program (FDSLP), funds for loans are provided by the federal government to college aid offices, which in turn directly allocate the loans to students.

These varied loan programs will be discussed in more detail later in this chapter. For now, it is instructive to examine them as a block. Figure 4.1 traces generally available federally loan support as a percentage of aid awards, using the data of Table 4.1. The solid line, for federally supported loans as a percentage of all generally available federal aid, suggests that the federal government's percentage in loans drifted down from a total orientation to NDSL loans in the year immediately preceding the Higher Education Act of 1965 to just under half in 1976–77. Then, the percentage began a quick climb upward to a range between 65 and 70%, where it stayed until 1992–93. In 1993–94, it rose to 76%. In 1994–95, it rose to 78%. The broad-dashed line, for loans as a percentage of all federal aid, tells a similar story. The distance between this line and the solid line above it narrows because of the decline in specially targeted federal aid. Virtually all targeted aid has been in the form of grants, so the gradual disappearance of those forms of aid spelled substantial declines for grant aid as a percentage of all federal aid.

There has also been notable growth in federally supported loans as a percentage of all federal, state, and institutional aid combined, denoted in the figure by the short-dashed line. Over the years since 1980–81, state grant aid has doubled, and institutional and other grant aid has tripled (see Table 4.1). Still, most of the absolute growth in aid totals has come from the growth of the dollar volume of federal loans. The figure reveals that student financial aid in the United States is increasingly composed of federally supported loan aid. That aid moved from around 20% of all aid in 1963–64 to a low of 17% in 1975–76, then rose to a high of 55% in 1994–95. The fact that federally supported loans are now over half of all aid is especially startling in light of the relatively small role that loans played in overall aid outlays as recently as 20 years ago.

Two elements in the loan data merit further attention: the growth in programs other than the Perkins program, and the increasing use of programs other than the traditional subsidized, nondirect guaranteed student loan program. The increasing dominance of the FFELP and the FDSLP over the Perkins program is clear from the raw data of Table 4.1: Between 1975–76 and 1994–95, the dollar investment in loan programs other than Perkins grew from $3.4 billion to over $24 billion. In the same years, the number of loans other than Perkins loans increased from 922,000 to 7 million (Gillespie & Carlson, 1983; College Board, 1995b). Meanwhile, funding for Perkins loans has grown relatively little in real terms over the years since their inception, and they are not central elements in the recent "loan explosion."

Regarding the second important element in the historical data, policy makers and students have recently made increasing use of programs other than traditional guaranteed student loans. It is instructive to trace the history of the average nondirect subsidized Stafford loan from its inception under the original GSL program to the present. In constant-dollar terms, loans of

FIGURE 4.1. Generally Available Federal Loans as a Percentage of Aid Awards, 1963–1994.

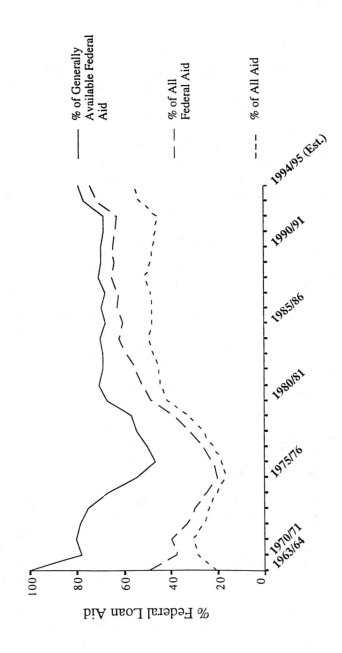

this kind have actually decreased in size since 1970–71, according to data from the College Board (1995a). Thus, the rising spending for subsidized Stafford Loans has gone largely into additional loans for additional students, not into more generous loans to individual students. The increase in the number of students served by the subsidized Stafford program seems to be related more to increasing college costs and to the increasing number of financially independent (and, therefore, usually more needy) college students rather than to major expansion of program eligibility standards. Indeed, financial eligibility requirements for federal aid programs tightened in real terms over the 1980s, and award sizes stagnated. In response, more students and their families have qualified for modest Stafford loans and also have made more extensive use of other sources of aid, including the growing array of alternative federal loan programs.

Two good cases regarding the latter point are the PLUS program and the unsubsidized Stafford program. Both nondirect and direct PLUS loans averaged over $5,000 in 1994–95, and together those programs served an estimated 351,000 students that year. Similarly, both nondirect and direct unsubsidized Stafford loans averaged over $3,500 that year and together provided an estimated 2.1 million students with loans. In both cases, individual loan amounts were substantially larger than those in the longstanding, nondirect, subsidized Stafford loan program. Together, the number of students served by these alternative programs was far from insignificant. While 4.3 million students received the traditional, nondirect, subsidized Stafford loans in 1994–95, 2.7 million received a nondirect, unsubsidized Stafford loan, a direct, subsidized Stafford loan, a direct, unsubsidized Stafford loan, a nondirect PLUS loan, a direct PLUS loan, or a combination of these (College Board, 1995b).

In sum, federal student aid policy progressed from the relatively small NDSL program of the early 1960s to a substantially greater effort with a roughly equal focus on grants and loans in the 1970s, then in the years since has moved to an even more substantial effort with a renewed emphasis on loans. Although the original NDSL (Perkins) program has grown only modestly over the years since the 1960s, other student loan programs have grown dramatically in dollar terms, in variety, and in coverage of the student population. Behind this striking growth is a colorful political history.

THE POLICY HISTORY OF FEDERAL STUDENT LOANS

Federally supported loans for facilitating postsecondary attendance are a relatively new aspect of the finance of higher education in the United States (Kramer, 1991). Some limited, highly targeted federal loans were made in

World War II and, shortly after the war, the Truman Commission, a presidentially appointed panel, argued vigorously for federal student loans (Presidents Commission, 1947; Woodhall, 1988). Nevertheless, federal financial aid up to the late 1950s consisted almost entirely of specially directed grant aid. At that time, however, federal leaders troubled by the nation's military, technological, and scientific status relative to the Soviet Union came to view investment in education as a productive countermeasure. Overcoming longstanding reservations regarding federal activities in education (see Morse, 1977), they implemented the National Defense Education Act of 1958. The National Defense Student Loan (NDSL) program was a prominent feature of the act. Thus, federal loan programs emerged largely out of noneducational concerns, a typical pattern in federal higher education policy making (see Brademas, 1983; Moynihan, 1975; Schuster 1982).

The NDSL program was the first federal loan program, and indeed the first federal aid program, not targeted toward particular categories of college students. Former NDSL director John Morse (1977) has noted that "it was the national panic (not too strong a word) over Russia's success in launching the first satellite that gave federal aid proponents the opening they needed" to overcome federal leaders' historic reluctance to become involved in higher education (p. 3).

NDSL funds were to be awarded to campuses, which in turn would provide loans to full-time students on the basis of need, as determined by institutions. Preference was to be given to students in the sciences, teaching, mathematics, and modern foreign languages. Forgiveness of loan debts was to be granted to students in certain careers, such as teaching. The loans were to be repaid over long terms at a low interest rate (3%). The government contributed $9 to a school's loan fund for every dollar provided by the institution. All repayments were to be reinvested by institutions in further student loans. In 1958–59, 27,600 students received these new loans, which totaled $9.5 million.

In its first few years, the NDSL program's preferences for students in certain fields were removed. Interestingly, the government consistently underestimated the interest from both students and institutions in participation in these loans, and the roster of institutional and student participants grew substantially. The total NDSL funds requested by institutional applicants regularly exceeded appropriations by a factor of 20 or more in the early years of the program, and the government found itself in the novel and awkward position of judging the relative worthiness of different institutions (Morse, 1977).

The NDSL program was the first federal effort to require testing of students' financial need, and the first to involve a contract between the federal government and institutions (Moore, 1983). For our purposes, however, the historically most notable aspect of the NDSL program is its pioneering of the notion of generally available federally supported loans for college students. Before the late 1950s, loans for college students were largely privately or institutionally originated and based on the income and financial positions of the student's parents (Bosworth, Carron, & Rhyne, 1987; Gillespie & Carlson, 1983). Some states (prominently including New York and Massachusetts) and some across-state associations initiated guaranty funds in the 1950s to support commercial lending to students, but interest on these loans was generally not publicly subsidized (see Barger & Barger, 1981). Although some of these efforts served as models for the development of later federal loan programs (Marmaduke, 1983), there was no significant federal support for commercial, institutional, or state lending to students before the NDSL program.

The development of the NDSL program can be viewed as the initiation of the modern era of federal student aid. The consequences of this program and the federal efforts that followed it were profound for those involved in student-aid work at the campus level. Before the late 1950s, student aid administration was not developed as a professional field and student aid offices were far less complex and systematized than today. Analysis of a student's aid eligibility was rather primitive by current standards, often involving simple income cutoffs. The initiation of the NDSL program brought growing demand for institutions to measure accurately their students' actual financial needs. Seeing that their need analysis efforts could benefit from collective wisdom as well as from economies of scale in formula development and processing expenses, institutions increasingly turned to the College Scholarship Service (CSS), a service organization begun by the College Board in 1954. Integrating generalized need analysis routines with the unique need and award standards of each institution, the CSS was a harbinger of aggressive modernizing efforts in student aid in the 1960s and beyond.

Despite the stirrings brought on by the NDSL program, however, the student aid arena remained quite small at the federal level for several years. This was all to change remarkably in 1964–65. A new Social Security benefit for recipients with dependents in college and a new aid program for students in health-related fields were initiated at that time, but these developments were soon overshadowed by the passage of the watershed U.S. Higher Education Act of 1965.

Emergence of Assertive Federal Policy in Student Aid—1965 to 1972

The bywords of higher education in 1965 were *prosperity* and *growth*. Nationally, unemployment and inflation were low, and productivity was rising. In addition, the many children born in the years after World War II were enrolling in college at high rates. Postsecondary enrollments grew steadily, along with the nation's supply of institutions, especially in the community college sector, where new institutions were emerging at the rate of one every week and a half. Dramatic demographic changes in student bodies were in the future, however: Students of this era were more likely than today's students to be full-time, residential, male, and White (Breneman, 1991). Out of this context arose the U.S. Higher Education Act of 1965.

The act was a product of a wide-ranging educational initiative on the part of Congress and President Lyndon Johnson. All told, the 89th Congress passed more than two dozen acts aimed directly at American schools and colleges. Most of those were closely connected to the Democrats' War on Poverty and Great Society efforts, as well as to the Civil Rights Act of 1964. President Johnson and congressional leaders saw action in education as an effective, politically feasible policy mechanism for achieving their broader goals of eliminating poverty and discrimination in the nation. In the president's view, "The answer for all our national problems, the answer for all the problems of the world, comes down . . . to one single word—education" (cited in Gladieux & Wolanin, 1976, p. 17).

Higher education was to reap especially significant rewards from the president's linkage of educational improvement to emerging national priorities. The Higher Education Act encompassed two approaches to federal support: aid to states and institutions and aid to needy students (Gladieux & Wolanin, 1976; Leslie, 1977; Fenske, 1983). College student aid was covered mainly under Title IV of the act. For student aid, the passage of Title IV represented both a philosophical and a fiscal shift. Philosophically, it expanded the purposes of federal student aid in the equity-oriented direction suggested years earlier by the Truman Commission. Fiscally, the act laid the groundwork for massive growth in the dollars and recipients of federal aid to levels unimagined even in the 1950s.

Under Title IV, the existing NDSL program was renewed, the College Work Study (CWS) program established a year earlier was finalized, and the Guaranteed Student Loan (GSL) and the Educational Opportunity Grants (EOG) programs were inaugurated. The CWS and EOG programs, like the earlier NDSL program, were to be delivered through campus offices (as "campus-based" aid, in the federal terminology). The GSL program was also to be administered out of campus aid offices, although private funds were to be loaned. Thus, the student aid elements of the 1965 act were to be delivered largely through existing institutional aid offices.

The new Guaranteed Student Loan program was a particular interest of President Johnson. Johnson had made his way through college with the help of loans from family friends, a bank, a local newspaper publisher, and his college (Caro, 1983; Hansen, 1987). As a consequence, he strongly supported expanding students' opportunities to borrow. As a senator from Texas in the 1950s, Johnson had introduced loan legislation, which failed to pass (Morse, 1977). The GSL program offered more than simple philosophical appeal for Johnson, however: It was designed in good part as a tactical diversion to head off legislation establishing tax credits for higher education attendance (Morse; 1977; Kramer & Van Dusen, 1986). Thus, the GSL program was not aimed primarily at socioeconomically disadvantaged students. Instead, it was initiated as a small, supplementary program operating at low federal cost and serving those not quite needy enough to qualify for the other new, more need-based aid programs (Kramer & Van Dusen, 1986; Hauptman, 1987). Specifically, the program's main intent was to address middle-income families' liquidity problems by facilitating access to funds from private lenders.

Although it was originally conceived as providing no subsidies at all, the GSL program as legislated provided interest subsidies for students while in school as well as funds to assure that states and private nonprofit agencies would work with the federal government to guarantee student loans made by commercial lenders. The initial federal interest rate subsidy was set at 6% a year while the student was in school and 3% during the repayment period, which began 9 months after graduation. The borrower was to pay the other 3%. Only those with family incomes under $15,000 could receive the subsidy, although unsubsidized GSL's were available to others. Students were given 10 years to repay loans over $2,000, and less time to repay smaller loans.

Banks, savings and loan associations, credit unions, and other financial institutions were invited to participate in the program. The guarantees on loans were to be assured through a federally supported guaranty fund in each state, equal to 10% of the face value of the loans, to protect lenders against loss through default, death, or disability of the borrower. The federal government provided states with deposits to be used to build their own guaranty funds, although most states opted to participate instead in the broader Federally Insured Student Loan (FISL) program.

These initial terms met with some concern from lenders, states, institutions, and students. Money was to be tied up in student loans for many years without payback (causing liquidity problems for lenders), the interest rates set by the government were not sufficiently high for lenders, institutions were frustrated by reporting and regulatory control mechanisms, and states were unenthusiastic about beginning their own guaranty agencies under existing guidelines (Morse, 1977; Breneman, 1991).

Having rejected such alternatives as the development of a national student loan bank (see Panel on Educational Innovation, 1967), the federal government moved to refine the GSL program into a more accepted loan policy vehicle. In 1968, it raised the statutory interest rate from to 7% and introduced "reinsurance," which merged existing state guaranty funds with federal insurance support. Nonprofit and state agencies were to provide guarantees, funded by a small administrative allowance, retention of a percentage of collections on defaulted loans, and an insurance premium paid by borrowers. The federal government assured states that it would cover 80% of a state's total losses from student default, death, or disability. This alleviated some of the pressures on state guaranty funds while creating incentives for states to monitor more closely lenders' efforts to collect loan payments.

In 1969, the federal government introduced the "special allowance," which paid all eligible lenders a supplementary amount above the statutory interest rate. The allowance, which was revised every 3 months by a committee of government officials, fluctuated between 1 and 2.5% over the next few years (Moore, 1983). Loan volume grew somewhat as a result, and by 1970, over one million borrowers received just over one billion dollars under the GSL program (Gillespie & Carlson, 1983).

The coming of the early 1970s marked the end of the initial "policy emergence" phase of federal student aid under the Higher Education Act of 1965. Through the combination of new or expanded student aid programs, federal support for spending for generally available student aid grew approximately tenfold between 1963–64 and 1972–73, in constant-dollar terms. Although new grant and work-study programs were a prominent feature of that growth, generally available federal loan programs grew at nearly the same rate.

Years of Policy Refinement and Expansion—1972 to 1978

The academic year 1972–73 marked the beginning of a second phase in the Title IV aid programs history, a phase of policy refinement and expansion. As the 1972 debates on reauthorizing the Higher Education Act approached, policy makers generally agreed that a new, expanded program of aid for college attendance was desirable, but conflict emerged among institutions, policy analysts, interest groups, and politicians over several issues (Gladieux & Wolanin, 1976; Brademas, 1987). After lengthy, detailed, and exhaustive deliberations, rough consensus was reached over the directions of expansion in the aid programs: toward channeling aid to students rather than to institutions, toward greater emphasis on facilitating student choice among institutions and persistence to the desired degree, toward an expanded pool of eligible applicants for aid, and toward a distinct, foundational role for the federal government in efforts to build equality of opportunity through student aid (Gladieux & Wolanin, 1976).

The newly created Basic Educational Opportunity Grants (BEOG) program was central to each of these directions, in that it allowed needy students to take their aid eligibility to the institutions of their choice, rather than relying on the grant funds available at one institution. Informed choices by students among competing institutions were therefore favored, under the assumption that grant portability would make institutions more sensitive to market forces favoring efficiency and quality. The BEOG program was the federal government's first major, direct, need-based grants program. It was to provide a foundation for students' aid packages, onto which other forms of federal, state, and institutional aid would be added. The 1972 reauthorization also brought expansion of the SEOG program, as well as CWS and NDSL (the latter of which was renamed the National Direct Student Loan program). Also that year, Congress initiated the State Student Incentive Grant (SSIG) program, which provided grant aid jointly with states.

In the context of all these new and expanded commitments, policy makers did not expect major growth in the loan programs (Mumper, 1996). That was to prove an accurate forecast: Federally supported loan volumes remained relatively stable throughout the early and mid-1970s, and loans diminished as a factor in federal aid, accounting during this period for only about one half of all generally available federal student aid, one fourth of all federal student aid, and about one fifth of all student aid (see Figure 4.1).

The primary implication of the 1972 amendments for the loan programs involved their relative priority. Loans were thenceforth to be viewed as supplemental aid for facilitating students' choice and persistence, rather than as a core "access" element in aid packages. Whether someone attended college or not was to be addressed mainly through the BEOG program, with loans and other aid programs providing supplemental support for one's attending a preferred school and attaining one's degree.

A second implication of the 1972 reauthorization for the loan programs was especially portentous. The eligible pool of institutions for federal student aid programs was expanded to include proprietary and vocational institutions. This expansion marked a transformation of the target of federal aid policy from "higher education" into "postsecondary education" (Schuster, 1982). Although the significance of this change was little noted at the time, the newly included proprietary and vocational institutions would come to dominate later reports of fraud and high default rates in loan programs.

Analyses of the 1972 reauthorization sometimes paint the results in glowing terms, but, in truth, the debate was a "debacle" of disunity and frustrated hopes for the interest groups representing higher education institutions (Hansen, 1977, p. 242). Most important, those groups favored maintaining campus officials as the dominant forces in student aid, and therefore strongly opposed the development of the portable, "voucher" concept in the basic grants program. After 1972, however, elements of consensus began to arise among interest groups. A "student aid partnership" emerged, consisting of postsecondary institutions and their associations, state government officials involved in aid policy, federal aid officials in the U.S. Department of Health, Education, and Welfare, and private organizations processing aid applications under contract (Fenske, 1983). In the mid-1970s, the partnership began to voice rather uniform views in keeping with a consensually supported focus on equal opportunity (Hansen, 1977). Policy disputes were rare in those years, and the partnership mainly worked together toward incremental operational and bureaucratic improvements in the programs (Hansen, 1977; Fenske, 1983). Federally supported aid grew 60% in real terms between 1972–73 and 1977–78, largely in the grants programs.

The period may be viewed, therefore, as a time of refinement and expansion of loan policy. A major example of refinement is the creation in 1972 of the Student Loan Marketing Association (Sallie Mae). A government-sponsored private corporation that was begun to provide liquidity and facilitate the secondary market in the GSL program, Sallie Mae sought to encourage banks' continuing participation in the program by buying loans and allowing pledges of existing student loans as collateral for new loans.

Other 1972 refinements included the introduction of need analysis to the GSL program, to replace the simple income cutoffs used in earlier years. Later in this period, to combat the influences of inflation on GSL program participation, the income level for student eligibility was raised to $25,000. In addition, the government raised overhead payments to state agencies, allowed states to keep up to 30% of their recoveries on defaulted loans to cover administrative costs, and offered 100% federal reinsurance to those states with low default rates. Also, the "special allowance" for lenders was pegged to an adjustable gross yield of 3.5% above the 90-day treasury bill rate.

Partly as a result of these reforms, the number of state loan agencies and participating financial organizations grew in the mid-1970s. Thus, although some other refinements of the time were restrictive on students and institutions, the general tone of the GSL changes in this period was expansive and the program grew notably after years of relative stability.

In the NDSL program, concern over mounting program costs led to the withdrawal of loan forgiveness for students entering military service or teaching careers. This period also brought regular rises in the administrative allowance for reimbursing institutions' NDSL costs. Overall, NDSL funding was rather stable in the mid-1970s.

Despite the seemingly calm surface surrounding the aid programs, however, this was a period of increasing demographic, economic, and political tensions in higher education (Stampen, 1987). In the late 1970s, those tensions erupted. Congress became concerned over the financial needs of middle-class parents of college-bound students, relative to lower and upper-class students (Brademas, 1987), and controversy arose over how to address the perceived problem. Congress debated between expanding the Title IV aid programs to cover more middle-income students and introducing a new program of federal tuition tax credits for college attendance. On this question, the professional and political allies of the aid partnership found themselves uncomfortably split. Longtime direct student aid proponents such as Senators Moynihan and Kennedy joined a coalition of liberal and conservative senators favoring tax credits. President Jimmy Carter and his allies countered that tax credits were wasteful in that they would go to many families who did not need aid to finance attendance, they were hard to control budgetarily, and they came too late in the academic year to influence attendance in the direction of expanded equality of opportunity.

In the end, the congressional proponents of the traditional student aid approach triumphed. The Middle Income Student Assistance Act (MISAA) was passed as the Higher Education Amendments of 1978. As a response to the perceived "middle-income squeeze," MISAA loosened the definition of need to include more middle-income families in the basic grants program and removed the $25,000 income ceiling on eligibility for GSLs. After passage of the act, any student could receive the GSL interest subsidy during enrollment, as well as the program's attractive 7% repayment rate. MISAA thus defined any student facing college expenses as needy enough to warrant federal support (Brademas, 1987).

The Policy Destabilization of 1978 to 1980–81

The passage of the expansive MISAA legislation initiated a period of destabilization of the federal aid policy agenda. Between 1977–78 and 1980–81, total federally supported aid grew a stunning 59% in constant dollars. Growth in the loan programs was especially strong. The removal of the family income ceiling on GSL eligibility in the context of dramatically rising interest rates in the general economy created substantial incentives for middle and upper-income families with discretionary resources to participate in the program.

In 1979, the government acted to assure more aggressive loan marketing to those very families. Responding to complaints by banks and other lenders that general interest rates had risen enough to make unattractive the full GSL interest rate for lenders (i.e., the statutory loan rate plus the special allowance rate), the government implemented a more liberal, variable special allowance. Soon the full interest rate rose as high as 19.5%.

Presented with an opportunity for inflation-proof, government-guaranteed returns, financial institutions quickly intensified their marketing of GSLs to the public. As families increasingly noticed this easily accessible, non-need-based, program, the number of student borrowers in the GSL program grew to 2.9 million in 1980 (College Board, 1993), and yearly program disbursements began regularly exceeding budgeted appropriations by large margins. Underestimates of demand became characteristic of the years immediately following MISAA.

The period was further troubled by growing controversy over the ultimate directions of the loan programs. Although MISAA was traditional in its use of aid awards rather than tax credits, it was a striking departure from the aid coalition's consensus favoring need-based, grants-oriented aid for the disadvantaged students. An "era of good feeling" in federal aid policy had come to an end, replaced by uncontrolled growth and philosophical uncertainty, especially regarding the appropriate clientele for the GSL program. Most participants and analysts attribute the removal of income caps on GSL eligibility to the combination of middle-class pressure for relief from college costs and heavy lobbying efforts by financing-industry officials (e.g., see McPherson, 1989). Stampen (1987) suggests that resistance to the costs of government oversight was also a factor:

> Senator Jacob Javits of New York argued, to a room charged with certainty about the excess of government regulation, that the ceiling on Guaranteed Student Loans should be eliminated so that middle- and upper-income students could become eligible. He reasoned that it was costing the government more to enforce the regulations excluding them than to remove the ceiling. The government's fiscal note, which turned out to be wildly inaccurate, estimated a cost of $9 million. Senator Javits concluded by saying he was not worried that a Rockefeller or two might receive a loan because they would repay many times through higher taxes after graduation. (p. 10)

MISAA's magnanimous terms stimulated a shift to loans in the overall balance of program allocations under Title IV, after several years of increasing emphasis on grants (see Table 4.1 and Figure 4.1). Viewed in retrospect, the middle years of the 1970s may be seen as a grants-oriented anomaly in the history of federal aid policies. The ratio of loans to other generally available federally supported aid in 1980–81 was similar to that of the mid-1960s and to that of the rest of the 1980s (see Figure 4.1). What is more, the ratio actually grew in the 1990s, leaving the grants orientation of the mid-1970s an ever more distant memory.

Of course, the loans emphasis in the late 1970s involved much more money than was present in the 1960s. It also involved much more controversy. The arrival of painful financial pressures on the government at that time led some critics to worry that Congress and the president had promised aid for all needy students while not reserving the funds necessary to achieve those goals (Gladieux, 1980). Although federal officials sought to step up their formal control and oversight of student aid award processes, many analysts argued that the government was not attending closely enough to program efficiency (e.g., appropriate ways to control fraud, abuse, and waste) and fairness (e.g., the acceptability of the use of the GSL program for investment purposes by upper-income families). Some observers decried the blurring of the original purposes of the Title IV programs as aided populations expanded. What is more, the interests of public and private institutions, of higher-cost and lower-cost institutions, of selective and open-admissions institutions, and of proprietary and traditional institutions began to diverge significantly (Gladieux, 1983; Mumper, 1996; Schuster, 1982).

With controversy and fiscal restraint as a backdrop, the 1980 reauthorization of the Higher Education Act focused on redesigning the student aid programs and managing their growth. Congress created the new Parental Loans for Student program (PLUS). This program of loans for parents of dependent undergraduates was similar to the GSL program, but was open to all regardless of need, provided no interest rate subsidy, allowed larger loans, and featured higher interest rates.

That reauthorization also addressed problems with the MISAA legislation and the difficulties posed by continuing high rates of inflation and interest. Official interest rates on NDSL and GSL loans were raised, but the special allowance for GSL lenders was restricted and the growing GSL-based profits of state lending agencies were curtailed through limiting those agencies' use of tax-exempt bonds to finance student loans.

Although Congress proclaimed as a priority the control of waste, it also imposed ceilings on spending by the Department of Education and thereby reduced the department's audit and program-review capabilities. By the time Ronald Reagan entered office in early 1981, some of the major dislocations of MISAA had been addressed, and the turbulent third phase in the federal aid programs' political history was drawing to an end. The following years would bring a return to some predictability in student aid, but would not bring a return to consensus.

The Policy Drift of 1981 to the Present

The lengthy and ongoing fourth phase in the life of the Higher Education Act may be termed a period of policy drift. The overall size of the federal aid commitment has increased, and loans have continued to grow both in absolute terms and relative to grants. Yet the period has brought no real consensus to the arena regarding growth, loan emphasis, or other policy features.

In the early 1980s, Congress blocked implementation of some aspects of the 1980–81 reauthorization and provided some support for conservatives' efforts to cut federal student aid. College benefits to Social Security survivors were removed and the terms of the new PLUS loan program were toughened. Congress also enacted several measures to slow GSL program growth: Student borrowing was limited by actual need, students with family incomes over $30,000 became subject to need analysis tests for loan eligibility for the first time since 1978, and banks were allowed to charge students a loan origination fee. Loan growth slowed much less than Congress initially expected and hoped, however, and the first year of the Reagan administration was the high-water mark for supporters of retrenching federal student aid.

In the following years, the political rhetoric concerning the aid programs became more heated than ever. In the early 1980s, political conflict over student aid was based not in the details of aid programs themselves, but in the proper funding levels of those programs relative to other social and educational programs. The central parties to the conflict were not so much opposing members of Congress as distinct branches of government. There was an ongoing, almost ritualized battle of wills between the Reagan administration, which favored substantial cutbacks, and the Congress, which tended to oppose such retrenchment. The conflict continued over the years of the Reagan presidency.

Although the relative proportion of total student aid paid by states and institutions, as opposed to the federal government, increased in the 1980s after a long downward trend (see Table 4.1), the overall size of that shift was not nearly so dramatic as one might have expected on the basis of the Reagan administration's rhetoric. It was in this period that Education Secretary William Bennett uttered perhaps the single most famous (or infamous) quotation ever in this arena, arguing for changes in student aid that would require aid-enriched students to pursue "a divestiture of certain sorts: stereo divestiture, automobile divestiture, three-weeks-at-the-beach divestiture" (Fiske, 1985, p. A1).

In the end, the opposing forces reached something of a balance, or an inescapable impasse (Hartle, 1991). The generally available aid programs grew slightly in constant-dollar terms (College Board, 1995b) and by the end of the decade most postsecondary students were receiving at least one kind of federal aid (McPherson & Schapiro, 1991).

Despite the ongoing hostilities between Congress and the Reagan administration, they did share a concern over college students' expanding debt levels, and in this concern they were joined by the popular media (e.g., Fiske, 1986; "The Student Loan Scandal," 1987) and policy analysts (e.g., Hansen, 1987). As participation in loan programs continued to grow in the 1980s, Lawrence Gladieux (1983) of the College Board noted wryly that in an age of Visa, MasterCard, massive consumer credit, and "creative financing," it is perhaps not surprising that loans have been the primary focus of efforts and plans to fill the gap for students and parents. . . . Increasingly, postsecondary education has come to be looked on as another consumer item to be "financed"—stretched out and paid for from the student's and/or parent's future earnings. (pp. 422–423)

Analysts, policy makers, and media observers also shared a concern over a related problem of the period, the increased incidence of loan defaults in both the GSL and the NDSL programs. Default expenses grew sevenfold in the 1980s in constant-dollar terms (U.S. Department of Education [USDOE], 1992). Although analysts noted that students tend to be young and have few assets, the popular media and congressional critics frequently compared their default rates unfavorably with rates for standard consumer and home loans.

Unfortunately, in both the NDSL and GSL programs, the incentives and resources for preventing loan defaults were limited in this period. In the NDSL program, institutions were constrained by costs from becoming debt collectors. In the GSL program, lenders were entirely insured against default losses by the provisions of the program, and USDOE oversight was limited by budget constraints and program structure. In addition, critics argued that as participation by educational institutions and students in the proprietary sector increased dramatically in the 1980s, accrediting bodies in that sector may have failed to effectively police their member institutions' aid practices. Finally, there was a willingness of some lenders to lend to students regardless of their institution's default rates and stability, a willingness of guaranty agencies to guarantee such loans, and a willingness of secondary loan markets to provide ongoing financing (Dean, 1994). In the mid-1980s, Congress imposed more stringent "due diligence" requirements on institutions to reduce defaults, limit multiple disbursement of loans to first-year students, and limit interest billings.

In the 1986 reauthorization of the Higher Education Act, NDSLs were renamed Perkins Loans, borrowers were given the option of consolidating their student loans from various federal programs into a single loan under a single, weighted interest rate, and the Supplemental Loans to Students (SLS) program for independent students was initiated. The SLS program was analogous to the PLUS program for dependent students: it provided a way for students to finance the great majority of their college costs through unsubsidized loans.

Although Congress in this reauthorization also toughened need analysis for loan eligibility, placed a limitation on student borrowing to the assessed amount of need, and allowed lenders to charge borrowers a new premium for insurance, GSL program growth continued, no doubt greatly aided by Congress's raising of the allowable loan size and by declines in loan servicing costs, which attracted more and more financial institutions into the program (USDOE, 1992).

Two of the most notable continuing problems of the 1980s in the federal loan programs were problematic loan administration and the ever increasing complexity of the programs. Widely publicized cases of noncompliance in loan servicing lessened public and congressional confidence in the integrity of the loan programs and the quality of their management (Dean, 1994). At the same time, frequent articles catalogued complaints about complexity from policy analysts, aid officers, and students (e.g., see Flint, 1991; "17 Changes in 4 Years," 1990; Wilson, 1988). One of these articles even lampooned in full-page cartoon form the detailed, lengthy process of loan generation and disbursement (Wilson, 1987, p. 25). Kramer and Van Dusen (1986), portrayed the guaranteed student loan program as a Rube Goldberg contraption: "a long series of devices accomplishing by extravagant means something terribly simple, like opening a tin can or putting out the cat" (p. 18). Ironically, the Education Department found that its efforts to meet public demands for greater fiscal integrity in the programs often meant earning the ire of aid officers and others frustrated by program complexity. Sometimes, the department made such sudden regulatory changes that institutions found themselves formally out of compliance without having known of the original, newly instituted regulations (Dean, 1994).

Tuition, fees, and other expenses of college-going rose at unprecedented rates in the 1980s, and the loan programs picked up the majority of the federal contribution to meeting those expenses. Between 1980 and 1990, the number of student borrowers in the GSL program grew from 2.9 million to 3.7 million (College Board, 1993, 1995b). As a result of this rapid, largely unplanned growth in the student loan programs, growth in grant programs was restricted. An increasing share of a limited pool of federal dollars was going to support the expanding volume of the federal loan programs. The federal government's expenses in supporting lenders and guaranteeing loans more than doubled between 1980 and 1985, then grew another 12% between 1985 and 1990 (USDOE, 1992).

Mumper (1996) has termed the late 1980s and early 1990s a period of "continuing deterioration" in the loan programs (p. 100). The U.S. General Accounting Office issued a scathing report in 1992, and congressional attention to loan problems also rose noticeably as the new decade began. Senator Sam Nunn brought his Permanent Senate Subcommittee on Investigations into the loan arena, focusing on abuses among proprietary schools and among private participants in the student loan industry. That committee (Nunn, 1990) found "overwhelming evidence that federal student loan programs and, particularly, those involving trade and proprietary schools, are riddled with fraud, waste, abuse, and pervasive patterns of mismanagement. . . . [W]e did not hear of even a single part of the guaranteed student loan program that is working efficiently and effectively (p. 1)." Senator Nunn concluded that "nothing less than a comprehensive, sustained, and intensive reform effort is needed" (cited in Mumper, 1996, p. 100). Senator Edward Kennedy, noting that "student loan programs may be just one step ahead of disaster" (cited in Mumper, p. 100), endorsed reform as well, and Congress in the early years of the decade enacted legislation aimed at cutting off institutions with especially high student loan defaults.

As the 1992 reauthorization of the Higher Education Act arrived, a number of problems in the loan programs demanded federal attention. Program costs continued to rise, management questions continued to plague program leaders, lower-income students continued to receive more loans and less grant aid than many thought advisable, debt obligations among all kinds of students continued to grow, and rapidly rising college costs convinced many to argue for expanded loan eligibility for middle-income students.

The 1992 presidential campaign figured prominently in debates on these problems. Bill Clinton proposed a national service program to replace existing student loan programs (Clinton, 1992). Clinton linked national service initiatives with student loan reform by stressing that loan programs make repaying the loan a priority, which in turn encourages students to take high-paying jobs offering few returns to society, rather than low-paying jobs that benefit society (Mumper, 1996). After winning a campaign in which this and other student aid issues were frequently discussed, Clinton as president began to pursue formal adoption of his ideas.

His proposals have met with mixed success. Congress passed a scaled-back version of the national service idea, with each award limited to $4,750 a year and the number of participants limited to no more than 100,000 people. Another goal of the administration, alternative GSL repayment periods for students, was implemented. The small federal Income Contingent Loans program was replaced by the offering of income-contingent repayment as an option in other federal loan programs. Congress in 1992–93 also expanded eligibility for the GSL and NDSL programs, raised the limit on yearly undergraduate borrowing, placed eligibility analysis for all Title IV programs under the rather liberal "Federal Methodology," and reduced Pell eligibility for single independent students and dependent students with earnings. Each of these moves increased the demand for loans further (Zook, 1994). Finally, Guaranteed Student Loans were renamed Stafford Loans, and those loans and the PLUS and SLS loans were folded into the Federal Family Education Loan Program (FFELP).

These last changes were closely connected to the most dramatic policy option considered in the reauthorization of the Clinton years: instituting a "direct lending" program to replace the traditional guaranteed student loan approach. Under this new program proposed by Clinton, institutions would lend federal funds directly to students, without the use of private funds or the involvement of private financial institutions. Direct student loans were broached as an approach to lowering institutions' administrative costs by eliminating the need to deal with multiple private lenders and guaranty agencies participating in the Stafford Loan program. In concert with this change, it was argued, the complexity of the loan programs would be reduced and management in federal student loans improved. Coloring the direct lending debate were proponents' concerns over indications that the student-loan business was making many people in the financing industry extraordinarily wealthy (see Regional Financial Associates & Jenkins, 1991; Zook, 1993). On the negative side, many institutions expressed concerns over new administrative burdens potentially associated with the direct lending efforts. Their opposition was reinforced by analyses by Sallie Mae and the Congressional Research Service (Dean, 1994).

In the end, Congress, in August 1993, adopted a compromise, trial version of the direct lending program, under which direct lending could be instituted voluntarily at institutions while the traditional nondirect guaranteed loan program would also continue. Volunteer institutions could disburse subsidized Stafford loans, unsubsidized Stafford loans, and PLUS loans directly to students. Both sides expressed confidence that time would tell that theirs was the superior alternative (Zuckman, 1993).

Under the terms of the compromise, the volume of direct loans could grow as a proportion of all lending to as much as 60% of all federal loans by 1998. Private capital is replaced as a source of loan funds by federal treasury funds, secured by the issuance of treasury bonds or the use of tax receipts. Institutions perform the administrative functions formerly performed by private and state lenders. Loan servicing is performed by federally supported contractors. Schools are required to process adjustments in loan amounts, notify servicing contractors of changes in student status, and maintain records of funds receipt and disbursement. The Ford Direct Student Loan Program was adopted as an option by many institutions around the country and began disbursing funds in 1994–95. Intriguingly, Congress left many of the specifics of the program open for interpretation and refinement.

Between the early and mid-1990s, the landscape of student loans changed notably. Contrary to the expectations of many and the hopes of some, growth in the loan programs accelerated rather than slowed. Between 1990–91 and 1994–95, the number of student borrowers in the Stafford program grew from 3.7 million to 6.2 million (College Board, 1995b). Stafford loans came to be provided in traditional and direct form and in subsidized and unsubsidized form. Those with need received the subsidized loan for which the government paid interest during the years in school. Those without measurable need received the new unsubsidized Stafford loan, for which the interest rate was higher, and the student paid the interest accrued during attendance. Unsubsidized Stafford loans grew dramatically after their inception, mainly because of the discontinuation of the unsubsidized SLS program, which served similar purposes and was phased out in 1994–95 (College Board, 1995b).

Interestingly, the 1990s have brought noteworthy decreases in the loan participation rates of students and institutions in the proprietary sector. Stafford loans and other federal loans are now far less tilted to the for-profit sector than they were in the 1980s. Specifically, students in the proprietary sector received only ten% of the subsidized Stafford loans in 1993, down from a high of 35% in the mid-1980s (College Board, 1995b). At the institutional level, most of the more than 500 institutions that dropped out of the federal loan programs between 1992 and 1995 were from the proprietary sector (Zook, 1995). It is in that sector that many of the worst abuses of federal aid programs have occurred, and in that sector that default rates have tended to be highest (Hansen, 1987; Mortenson, 1990). These declines in loans in the for-profit sector suggest indirectly that recent actions to address high default rates in the federal loan programs have been successful on at least some grounds.

CONCLUSION: FEDERAL LOAN EXPANSION IN BROADER CONTEXT

It is impossible to examine the dramatic increase in federal loan support without considering other developments taking place at roughly the same time. While federal loan efforts have been evolving since their great expansion in the late 1970s, total enrollments have risen (rather than falling, as anticipated by many analysts), the demographic characteristics of students have become more diverse, and delayed entry and part-time enrollment have increased (Hearn, 1992). At the institutional level, student aid has increasingly been viewed as an integral element in a wide variety of concerns, including admissions, fund raising, student services, and public relations (Brademas, 1983). At the same time, because of its close connections to concerns regarding cost patterns, tuition levels, grant support, program duplication, and educational quality, student aid has become a more prominent vehicle for states' initiatives in postsecondary education. Each of these trends is tightly related to the changes in federal loans.

It is especially important to examine simultaneously financing trends at the federal, state, and institutional levels. As Table 4.1 suggests, the federal retreat from grants and movement into loans since the 1970s has been met by some expansion in grant aid for students at the state and institutional levels. States' abilities to respond effectively to changes in federal aid have been hampered, however, by their own economic and political difficulties. Most notably, state efforts have been constrained by uncertainty over the financial feasibility of both the traditional "low-tuition-low-aid" approach to student support and the alternative "high-tuition-high-aid" approach to financing public institutions (Fischer, 1990; Hearn, Griswold, & Marine, 1996). That uncertainty over appropriate tuition and aid levels has also troubled private institutions. Under pressure, some states and some private institutions have been forced to adopt what is in essence the worst of both approaches, a "high tuition-low aid" approach (Griswold & Marine, 1996). That is, tuitions have been allowed to rise without parallel increases in student aid. A somewhat less regrettable state and institutional response, but still troubling and quite central to the concerns in this chapter, are efforts to use loans rather than grants as the dominant form of student aid in high-tuition-high aid approaches (see St. John, Andrieu, Oescher, & Starkey, 1994).

Clearly, the dramatic rises in public and private institutions' tuition levels since 1980 are closely linked to the parallel expansion of student loans. As colleges' costs for salaries and other items have risen, the burden of meeting those costs has increasingly been placed on students and their families. In some ways, these new demands on them have been immediately felt. For example, need analysis and eligibility analysis formulas for determining students' aid levels have been tightened, bringing more stringent expectations for parental contributions to college expenses, student savings, and summer work earnings, as well as tougher requirements for students wishing to be certified as financially independent of their parents. But much of the increased financial burden on students and their families has been deferred in impact, via demands that students finance more of their college attendance through loans. Postsecondary institutions, financial institutions, and governments are increasingly providing aid to be repaid later, after students are presumably more established in their adult careers. In essence, unable to slow the growth in college costs, unable or unwilling to devote further governmental resources to meet those costs, and unwilling to demand more short-term contributions from students and their families, policy makers have placed much more of the burden of financing attendance on students' future lives. As the imagery and language of "downsizing" and "cost control" have come in the past decade to dominate policy arenas at the local, state, and national levels, many postsecondary leaders are reluctantly accepting students' high debt levels as ongoing facts of life.

It can be argued that appreciably higher student loan levels represent almost as significant a historical development in federal aid policy as the GI Bill or the original Higher Education Act of 1965. Yet, in contrast to those earlier events, the loan explosion has taken place incrementally over a period of years. Some years are more significant than others, of course, but there is no single watershed year in federal loan policy. Mark Twain's old parable of the hot-water frog seems apropos: Dropped in boiling water, a frog will promptly jump out, but dropped in cool water which is being slowly heated to boiling, a frog might well end up being boiled to death. Of course, the consequences of loan expansion are not nearly so dire for students or policy makers. Still, as Twain warns us, intense scrutiny of one's emerging environment is always warranted.

ACKNOWLEDGMENTS

This chapter benefited substantially from the helpful comments of two veteran analysts of federal student loan policy: John Lee, President of JBL Associates of Bethesda, Maryland and Keith Jepsen, Director of Financial Aid at New York University. My research assistant James Eck also deserves thanks, as do Sharon Wilford and Sammy Parker, who assisted me in earlier work on the political history of federal student aid efforts.

NOTES

1. Reference to the work of a number of authors is essential to understanding the policy history of federal student loans. Primary sources for the present work were Gladieux and Wolanin (1976), Morse (1977), Moore (1983), Gillespie and Carlson (1983), Gladieux (1983), Fenske (1983), Hartle (1991), Dean (1994), St. John (1994), College Board (1995b), and Mumper (1996). A political history of all the federal aid programs (including grants and work study as well as loans) is presented in Hearn (1993). Each of these sources may be consulted for further details and perspective on the historical analysis presented here.

2. Several points should be made about the data of Table 4.1 (for details, see College Board, 1995b). First, federally supported aid totals include some funds supplied by institutional, private, and state sources. Importantly, totals for Family Education Loans are for the amounts for the loans themselves, not for the amount supplied by the federal government for subsidies and repayments on those loans. The actual funds supplied by the federal government are substantially smaller than the totals for these loans themselves. Second, the amounts in the table include aid for undergraduate, graduate, and professional students. Third, total loan amounts are underestimated because private loans by individuals, corporations, and schools are

not included in figures, and are essentially incalculable (College Board, 1995b). Finally, reported loan values in Table 4.1 are for loan commitments, not the final loan amount, but the two totals are virtually identical.

REFERENCES

Barger, H., & Barger, G. (1981). *College on credit: A history of United student aid funds, 1960–1980.* Indianapolis, IN: Hackett.

Baum, S. (1996, Winter). Is the student loan burden really too heavy? *Educational Record, 77*(1), 30–36.

Bosworth, B., Carron, A., & Rhyne, E. (1987). *The economics of federal credit programs.* Washington, DC: Brookings Institution.

Brademas, J. (1983). Foreword. In R. H. Fenske, R. P. Huff, & Associates (Eds.), *Handbook of student financial aid* (pp. ix–xiii). San Francisco: Jossey-Bass.

Brademas, J. (1987). *The politics of education: Conflict and consensus on capitol hill.* Norman, OK: University of Oklahoma Press.

Breneman, D. W. (1991). Guaranteed student loans: Great success or dismal failure? In D. W. Breneman, L. L. Leslie, & R. E. Anderson (Eds.), *ASHE reader on finance in higher education* (pp. 377–387). Needham Heights, MA: Ginn Press.

Caro, R. A. (1983). *The years of Lyndon Johnson: The path to power.* New York: Vintage Books.

Clinton, W. (1992). *Putting people first.* New York: Times Books.

College Board. (1993). *Trends in student aid: 1983 to 1993.* Washington, DC: Author.

College Board. (1995a, December). College costs and student loans up. *College Board News, 24*(2), 1, 11.

College Board. (1995b). *Trends in student aid: 1985 to 1995.* Washington, DC: Author.

Dean, J. (1994). Enactment of the federal Direct Student Loan Program as a reflection of the education policy making process. In J. Jennings (Ed.), *National issues in education: Community service and student loans* (pp. 157–178). Bloomington, IN: Phi Delta Kappa International.

Fenske, R. H. (1983). Student aid past and present. In R. H. Fenske, R. P. Huff, & Associates (Eds.), *Handbook of student financial aid* (pp. 5–26). San Francisco: Jossey-Bass.

Fischer, F. J. (1990). State financing of higher education: A new look at an old problem. *Change, 22*(1), 42–56.

Fiske, E. (1985, February 12). New secretary sees many "ripped off" in higher education. *The New York Times,* pp. A1, B24.

Fiske, E. (1986, August 3). Student debt reshaping. *The New York Times,* pp. 34–38, 40–41.

Flint, T. A. (1991). Historical notes on regulation in the federal student assistance programs. *Journal of Student Financial Aid, 21*(1), 33–47.

Gillespie, D. A., & Carlson, N. (1983). *Trends in student aid: 1963 to 1983.* Washington, DC: College Board.

Gladieux, L. E. (1980, October). What has Congress wrought? *Change, 26–27.*

Gladieux, L. E. (1983). Future directions of student aid. In R. H. Fenske, R. P. Huff, & Associates (Eds.), *Handbook of student financial aid* (pp. 399–433). San Francisco: Jossey-Bass.

Gladieux, L. E., & Wolanin, T. R. (1976). *Congress and the colleges: The national politics of higher education.* Lexington, MA: Lexington (Heath).

Griswold, C. P., & Marine, G. M. (1996). Political influences on state policy: Higher-tuition, higher-aid, and the real world. *Review of Higher Education, 19* (4), 361–389.

Hansen, J. S. (1977). *The politics of federal scholarships: A case study of the development of general grant assistance for undergraduates.* Unpublished doctoral dissertation, The Woodrow Wilson School, Princeton University.

Hansen, J. S. (1987). *Student loans: Are they overburdening a generation?* New York: College Board.

Hartle, T. W. (1991). The evolution and prospects of financing alternatives for higher education. In A. M. Hauptman & R. H. Koff (Eds.), *New ways of paying for college* (pp. 33–50). New York: ACE-Macmillan.

Hauptman, A. M. (1987). The national student loan bank: Adapting an old idea for future needs. In L. E. Gladieux (Ed.), *Radical reform or incremental change?: Student loan policy alternatives for the federal government* (pp. 75–89). Washington, DC: College Board.

Hearn, J. C. (1992). Emerging variations in postsecondary attendance patterns: An investigation of part-time, delayed, and non-degree enrollment. *Research in Higher Education, 33,* 657–687.

Hearn, J. C. (1993). The paradox of growth in federal aid for college students: 1965–1990. In J. C. Smart (Ed.), *Higher education: Handbook of theory and research (Vol. 9).* (pp. 94–153). New York: Agathon.

Hearn, J. C., Griswold, C. P., & Marine, G. M. (1996). Region, resources, and reason: A contextual analysis of state tuition and student-aid policies. *Research in Higher Education, 37* (3), 241–278.

Kosterlitz, J. (1989, April 15). Losers by default. *National Journal, 47,* 924–925.

Kramer, M. (1991). Stresses in the student financial aid system. In A. M. Hauptman & R. H. Koff (Eds.), *New ways of paying for college* (pp. 21–32). New York: ACE-Macmillan.

Kramer, M., & Van Dusen, W. D. (1986, May/June). Living on credit. *Change, 18* (3), 10–19.

Leslie, L. L. (1977). *Higher education opportunity: A decade of progress.* (ERIC/AAHE Higher Education Research Report No. 3). Washington, DC: American Association for Higher Education.

Marmaduke, A. S. (1983). State student aid programs. In R. H. Fenske, R. P. Huff, & Associates (Eds.), *Handbook of student financial aid* (pp. 55–76). San Francisco: Jossey-Bass.

McPherson, M. S. (1989). Appearance and reality in the Guaranteed Student Loan

Program. In L. E. Gladieux (Ed.), *Radical reform or incremental change?: Student loan policy alternatives for the federal government.* Washington, DC: College Board.

McPherson, M. S., & Schapiro, M. O. (1991). *Keeping college affordable: Government and educational opportunity.* Washington, DC: Brookings Institution.

Moore, J. W. (1983). Student aid past and present. In R. H. Fenske, R. P. Huff, & Associates (Eds.), *Handbook of student financial aid* (pp. 5–26). San Francisco: Jossey-Bass.

Morse, J. (1977). How we got here from there: A personal reminiscence of the early days. In L. Rice (Ed.), *Student loans: Problems and policy alternatives* (pp. 3–15). New York: College Board.

Mortenson, T. G. (1990). *The impact of increased loan utilization among low family income students.* Iowa City, IA: American College Testing Program.

Moynihan, D. P. (1975). The politics of higher education. *Daedalus, 104,* 128–147.

Mumper, M. (1996). *Removing college price barriers: What government has done and why it hasn't worked.* Albany, NY: SUNY Press.

Nunn, S. (1990, October 10). Opening statement to the Permanent Subcommittee on Investigations (Hearings on Abuses in Federal Student Aid Programs). Washington, DC: United States Senate.

Panel on Educational Innovation. (1967). *Educational Opportunity Bank—A report of the Panel on Educational Innovation to the U.S. Commissioner of Education, the Director of the National Science Foundation, and the Special Assistant to the President for Science and Technology.* Washington, DC: GPO.

President's Commission on Higher Education. (1947). *Higher education for American democracy.* Washington, DC: GPO.

Regional Financial Associates, & Jenkins, S. (1991). *Lender profitability in the student loan program.* Report prepared for the U.S. Department of Education. West Chester, PA: Regional Financial Associates.

St. John, E. P. (1994). *Prices, productivity and investment: Assessing financial strategies in higher education.* (ASHE-ERIC Higher Education Report No. 3). Washington, DC: School of Education and Human Development, George Washington University.

St. John, E. P., Andrieu, S. C., Oescher, J., & Starkey, J. B. (1994). The influence of student aid on within-year persistence by traditional college-age students in four-year colleges. *Research in Higher Education, 35*(4), 455–80.

Schuster, J. H. (1982, May). Out of the frying pan: The politics of education in a new era. *Phi Delta Kappan 63*(9), 583–591.

Seventeen changes in four years: Johns Hopkins grapples with new loan rules. (1990, December 5). *Chronicle of Higher Education, 37*(14), p. A24.

Stampen, J. O. (1987). Historical perspective on federal and state financial aid. In California Postsecondary Education Commission (Ed.), *Conversations about financial aid.* Sacramento, CA: Author.

Student Loan Scandal, The. (1987, October 8). *The New York Times,* p. 26Y.

U.S. Department of Education. (1992). *Guaranteed Student Loans Program data book, FY91.* Washington, DC: Author.

U.S. General Accounting Office. (1992). *Transition series: Education issues* (Report No. GAO/OCG-93-18TR). Washington, DC: U.S. General Accounting Office.

Wilson, R. (1987, April 15). Critics blast Guaranteed Student Loan Program, charging it is too complex and is poorly policed. *Chronicle of Higher Education, 33* (31), pp. 1, 24–26.

Wilson, R. (1988, March 16). Student-aid analysts blast loan program, urge big overhaul. *Chronicle of Higher Education, 34* (27), pp. 1, 24.

Woodhall, M. (1988). Designing a student loan program for a developing country: The relevance of international experience. *Economics of Education Review, 7*(1), 153–161.

Zook, J. (1993, June 9). For Sallie Mae's top executives, 1992 was a very good year. *Chronicle of Higher Education, 37,* p. A23.

Zook, J. (1994, April 27). Record-setting debt: Changes in federal law have brought huge increases in student borrowing. *Chronicle of Higher Education, 39,* p. A21.

Zook, J. (1995, July 21). Congressional panel warned of growing Pell Grant fraud. *Chronicle of Higher Education, 41*(45), p. A26.

Zuckman, J. (1993, August 14). Both sides hope to be No. 1 in dual loan system test. *Congressional Quarterly Weekly Report, 51,* pp. 2230–2231.

CHAPTER 5

Federal Student Aid Regulations
NEXT STEPS

Jamie P. Merisotis

INTRODUCTION

Federal regulation of colleges and universities has been a major topic of policy discussions within the higher education community in the 1990s. Prompted by major changes in the institutional eligibility requirements for the Title IV student aid programs during the 1992 reauthorization of the Higher Education Act, this discussion is likely to take on new intensity as the new millennium approaches.

The context for federal regulation has its genesis primarily in the student aid programs authorized under Title IV of the Higher Education Act of 1965. Beginning with the initial passage of the act, the appropriate level of federal oversight needed to ensure program integrity and protect the taxpayer investment in these programs has been of concern (Trivett, 1976). Such concerns have incrementally escalated over the past 2 decades and have surfaced with increasing regularity as major items for policy discussion during the reauthorizations of the Higher Education Act, which generally occur every 5 years.

Three issues have elevated the importance of federal regulation as a matter of public discourse. One is that the federal investment in student aid has grown dramatically. Aid awarded through federal Title IV programs increased from $2.6 billion in 1974–75, to $13.4 billion in 1984–85, to $32.7 billion in 1994–95. Even after adjusting for inflation, this represents a real increase of more than 400% over the past 2 decades (College Board, 1995).

Second, a large portion of the increase in funds awarded to postsecondary students has been for those attending for-profit proprietary institutions. Beginning in the early 1980s, the dollar amounts and proportions of total student aid monies awarded to proprietary students has steadily increased. This in turn resulted in greater scrutiny on the number of institutions certi-

76

fied by the U.S. Department of Education to participate in federal aid programs (Lee & Merisotis, 1990).

Third, macrolevel public policy concerns have centered on the increasing regulation of colleges and universities by the federal government. A 1994 study found that Title 34 of the Code of Federal Regulations—which is primarily concerned with student assistance programs—contained over 7,000 different sections, many of which were duplicative or conflictive of other sections. In addition, between August 30, 1992 and September 1, 1993, the U.S. Department of Education sent 171 "Dear Colleague" letters to campuses, with a new federal directive contained in each one. This volume translated into a new regulation roughly once every other day. These letters were in addition to routine requests for comments on proposed regulations from the Federal Register, the primary means by which the department solicits input from college and university officials on new regulations (Merisotis, 1994).

The future of federal regulations pertaining to student assistance programs is uncertain. However, an analysis of the problems with the current regulatory construct could help to illuminate the challenges confronting the existing system and help to frame an agenda for policy reform in the coming years.

HISTORY OF THE OVERSIGHT TRIAD

The federal regulatory system created under the Higher Education Act consisted of a "triad" of oversight mechanisms designed to protect consumers and ensure the appropriate management of federal resources. This "three-legged stool" of oversight included (1) licensing by the state in which the institution operates, (2) accreditation by an agency recognized by the secretary of education, and (3) federal eligibility and certification. Each of these components contained specific procedures and requirements.

Under the triad, state licensure was the first step in the process. The law made no specific demands on states except that they license schools; as a result, licensure requirements varied widely, depending on the unique history of institutional oversight in a single state (Gold, 1990). However, as the only entity in the triad with the authority to approve institutions before they opened—and close them down for violating law or regulations—states wielded significant power in the triad process.

Once licensed, institutions also had to demonstrate that they were accredited by an agency recognized by the secretary of education. From a federal policy perspective, this placed the majority of the responsibility on the accrediting agencies themselves, who usually had to petition the secretary for recognition (and renewal) every 5 years. The secretary's decision was heavily influenced by the Advisory Committee on Accreditation and Institutional Eligibility, whose members were appointed by the secretary.

The final step in the triad was the completion of a two-part process known as eligibility and certification. Institutions were required to complete a two-part application and forward it to the Division of Eligibility and Certification in the Department of Education. Part one, the eligibility section, essentially affirmed that the institution was appropriately licensed and accredited. Part two, the certification section, required schools to certify that they had the administrative and fiscal capability to manage federal student aid funds. This was demonstrated by the submission of audited financial statements, staffing data, satisfactory academic progress standards, default rates, student withdrawal rates, and other information.

The original triad process remained virtually unchanged for more than 20 years. It was not until the 1992 reauthorization that significant changes to the federal regulatory system were enacted.

The Currently Authorized System

The system of federal oversight created during the 1992 reauthorization consists of three parts: federal eligibility and certification requirements, accreditation standards, and the State Postsecondary Review Entity (SPRE) program. Each of these parts are contained in a new section under Title IV, known as Part H, the Program Integrity Triad.

Federal Eligibility and Certification Requirements

Under the new regulatory system, all institutions have substantial reporting and compliance responsibilities, including

- a new financial audit required every year;
- annual compliance audits;
- a comprehensive review every 4 years to establish or to maintain federal aid eligibility;
- new standards of financial responsibility (monitored through the annual financial statements);
- new special requirements for institutions with vocational programs;
- new reporting requirements and restrictions for additional locations or branch campuses;
- new requirements for program length; and
- new standards for satisfactory academic progress.

Accreditation Standards

Before 1992, the federal government did not regulate higher education accreditation, although institutional accreditation by a federally recognized entity has been required for Title IV eligibility since the early 1970s. The 1992 amendments explicitly regulate accreditation for the first time through a minimum list of standards that must be in place for federal recognition. The law also provides for a detailed review and recognition process for would-be Title IV "gatekeepers." It requires that accrediting agencies meet standards set by the secretary concerning their purpose, reputation, and methods of review, and sets 12 standards for an accrediting agency's review of an institution.

The impact of changes in accreditation standards are likely to be minimal for most regionally accredited institutions in the short term. However, under the new law all accreditors are required to conduct unannounced "inspections" at least once in the accreditation cycle for all institutions that offer nondegree vocational programs. In addition, accreditors are required to conduct more prereviews of new campuses or off-campus locations.

State Postsecondary Review Entity Program

The most significant—and politically volatile—change in the federal eligibility process was the creation of the State Postsecondary Review Entity (SPRE) program. Specifically, Part H

- calls for the establishment of a SPRE in each state
- provides federal funds to each state for performing SPRE functions set forth by the secretary and authorizes the appropriation of $75 million for fiscal year 1993, and such sums as may be necessary for each of the four succeeding fiscal years
- specifies criteria, or "triggers," necessary to prompt the state review of an institution of higher education (IHE); the triggers are as follows:

1. a cohort default rate equal to or greater than 25%;
2. a cohort default rate equal to or greater than 20%, and either more than two thirds of undergraduates receiving Title IV aid or two thirds or more of education and general expenditures from Title IV funds;
3. two thirds or more expenditures from Title IV funds;
4. a limitation, suspension, or termination action against the institution during the past 5 years;
5. an audit finding during the two most recent audits resulting in repayment of more than 5% of Title IV funds;

6. a citation for failure to submit audits in a timely fashion;
7. a year-to-year fluctuation of more than 25% in Title IV received by students funds not accounted for by changes in the programs;
8. failure to meet standards of financial responsibility;
9. a change of ownership resulting in a change of control;
10. for private institutions only, being in Title IV programs less than 5 years; and
11. a pattern of student complaints related to the management or conduct of Title IV programs, or relating to misleading or inappropriate advertising of the institution

• sets forth review standards concerning institutional maintenance of student records, financial and administrative capacity, curriculum, tuition, admissions requirements, successful job placement and state license exam performance (at proprietary schools), address of student grievances, publicity, refund policy, graduation rates, and withdrawal rates
• states that IHEs may have their eligibility for Title IV programs terminated based on state reviews.

The political history of the SPRE program has been a volatile one. The Washington-based higher education associations targeted the program in the 1992 reauthorization as their number one priority for elimination. Having failed in that effort, the associations continued coordinated efforts to eliminate SPRE, leveling a range of criticisms on the program, including infringement on academic freedom, overregulation, duplication with accreditation, and a host of other complaints. Though efforts in the U.S. House of Representatives to permanently repeal the SPRE language ultimately failed, the program was effectively derailed in the 1995 budget when the $20 million in funding for the program was eliminated (Zook & Cordes, 1995).

IDENTIFIED PROBLEMS

Political considerations notwithstanding, the existing system of Title IV regulation is plagued by a series of problems that inhibit effective regulation and reduce the impact that these regulations have on program accountability and integrity. The most significant of these problems include those delineated in what follows.

Lack of Clarity About Program Goals

One of the fundamental flaws of the three components of the program integrity system is that the purpose of none of them is explicitly described. Although accreditation, the SPRE program, and the federal eligibility and certification process each have their own functions, there is no reference in the law or regulations to the purposes to be achieved by each component. What are the goals of the program integrity triad? How can we measure those goals across the three areas? As a 1994 study of federal student aid regulations noted,

> Policies, or program goals, are not clearly defined in the current federal system. Instead, procedures for controlling the administrative aspects of programs have been substituted for measures of program effectiveness. The result is that there is no real way to know whether program performance has been improved by the regulatory process. (Merisotis, 1994, p. 9–10.)

For example, there appears to be a significant redundancy in the regulations with the more technical, administrative aspects of the student aid programs. Of the 7,000 sections in the Code of Federal Regulations that apply to student aid programs, more than 1,500 deal with the applications processes, 60 address definitions of "eligible institutions," and 38 are concerned with "eligible students." But none of these regulation addresses why such redundancy is necessary, or what it has to do with the overall effectiveness of the programs in promoting access to higher education.

The Department of Education's Administrative Process

Neither law nor regulations can substitute for effective management of the oversight process. Unfortunately, the department has been hampered by a series of long-standing problems, including understaffing, litigation pressures, and lack of fiscal resources. These problems have combined to seriously impede effective implementation of the law and regulations. Prior to the 1992 reauthorization, investigations by the U.S. Senate Government Operations Subcommittee (chaired by Senator Sam Nunn of Georgia) found that the number of institutions removed from Title IV participation was minuscule (Gold, 1990). However, since the 1992 reauthorization, the situation has improved somewhat: The number of institutions removed rose from 105 in 1991 to 213 in 1995 (U.S. Department of Education, 1995).

Disconnection Between Title IV and Other Regulations

Compounding the problems for institutions is the fact that there is no coordination between federal loan regulations and the various other federal regulations to which institutions are subjected. Regulations related to other education programs, such as those contained in other parts of the Higher

Education Act, and training programs emanating from the Department of Labor are not consistent with those that regulate student aid programs. Nor is there coordination between federal loan regulations and the numerous health and safety regulations that apply to higher education institutions. As Jane Wellman (1995) has pointed out, "The regulatory rubric has grown incrementally and has never been consistently rationalized, so many of these requirements work at cross-purposes with one another" (p. 7).

Financial Uncertainty

The effective elimination of the SPRE program in 1995 resulting from the program's defunding points to the fragile nature of the oversight process and to the critical role that federal resources play in this process. Critics of the SPRE program were successful in killing the program, but not by arguing against its merits as a matter of institutional rights or academic freedom issues; rather, they simply were able to block its implementation by eliminating the funds that states needed to meet the requirements imposed under the law.

PRIORITIES FOR A NEW OVERSIGHT AGENDA

There has been a great deal of controversy about the new federal regulations within the higher education community. Institutional concern about the cost and complexity of the regulations and fear of the incremental shift toward a federal "ministry of education" model have grown. There is also widespread belief that the Department of Education has gone beyond its regulatory authority with such detailed scrutiny not required by the law.

The available research does not support the conclusion that the regulations as yet exceed the statutory authority of the Department of Education. Rather, it appears that it is the law that is leading the department away from its traditional oversight functions. To fundamentally improve the regulations will require changes in the law. Whether such statutory changes will be pursued immediately in the next reauthorization or will be put on hold until some future date—perhaps the beginning of the new millennium—is unknown at this time. At such time that Congress does take up the issue of statutory change, several key issues should be part of the agenda:

Enforceability

In order for a regulatory apparatus to work properly, it must be consistently and effectively enforced. The range of new reporting requirements has inhibited the administrative capacity of the Department of Education to consistently and accurately monitor regulatory compliance. The information management systems do not exist that would ensure that information received by the federal government is properly reviewed, registered, and filed.

Coherence

The range of regulatory responsibilities that all institutions face is so bewildering that it is entirely possible for well-managed institutions to violate the regulations out of ignorance or confusion, rather than malfeasance. A more circumscribed list of requirements, coupled with more effective communication with institutions, would help ensure better institutional understanding of the regulations.

Clarification of Federal and State Roles

The law blurs distinctions between federal and state authority by delegating decision-making authority over Title IV programs to states, yet the structure under which the SPRE programs operate is clearly a federal program. Unless the ambiguity of state and federal roles is clarified, litigation will undoubtedly result as states attempt to administer the law.

In addition, private institutions are justly concerned about loss of institutional autonomy as the law attempts to enforce federal performance standards that go beyond accounting for legal use of Title IV funds into matters such as time-to-degree, job placement, and tuition and fees. This is also an issue for public institutions, many of which have a state mandate to provide access to undeserved student populations.

Limiting Federal Encroachment into Academic Policy Areas

In addition to deviating into matters of institutional policy and performance, the regulations of the standards of accreditation set a precedent for the department to dictate such areas as curriculum, faculty, and tuition and fees. In the past, federal statutes clearly prevented the Department of Education from regulating in these areas, but those restrictions were effectively erased in the 1992 amendments.

This new foray into the academic policy-making processes of institutions could have major consequences for higher education and its relationship with government in the future. It is imperative that the federal government and the higher education community reach some agreement about the limits of federal encroachment into what have heretofore been considered matters of academic policy.

CONCLUSION

The preliminary implementation of Part H has been controversial and has polarized the higher education community, making any compromise difficult to achieve. However, as funding for federal student aid has grown and placed the programs under increasing scrutiny, it is in the best interests of student financial aid and its supporters to foster program integrity. All of the players in the policy process must work together to solve the problems and pitfalls contained in Part H and to ensure that true accountability goals are achieved.

REFERENCES

College Board. (1995). *Trends in student aid: 1985 to 1995*. Washington, DC: Author.

Gold, L. (1990). How colleges and career schools become eligible to participate in federal programs. Unpublished paper prepared for the State Higher Education Executive Officers Association.

Lee, J., & Merisotis, J. (1990). *Proprietary schools: Programs, policies, and prospects*. ASHE-ERIC Higher Education Reports. Washington, DC: Association for the Study of Higher Education.

Merisotis, J. (1994). *Federal regulations affecting higher education*. Washington, DC: National Association of Independent Colleges and Universities.

Trivett, D. (1976). *Accreditation and institutional eligibility*. ERIC/Higher Education Research Report. Washington, DC: American Association for Higher Education.

U.S. Department of Education. (1995). Institutions Removed from Title IV Participation. Washington, DC: Author.

Wellman, J. (1995). Accreditation and state government: Developing organizational capacity on state institutional licensure, specialized accreditation and diploma mills. Unpublished paper prepared for the Regional Accrediting Association.

Zook, J., & Cordes, C. (1995, July 14). Education cuts reduced in GOP-White House compromise. *Chronicle of Higher Education, 42*, p. A24.

CHAPTER 6

How Do Loans Affect the Educational Decisions of Students?

ACCESS, ASPIRATIONS, COLLEGE CHOICE, AND PERSISTENCE

David A. Campaigne and Don Hossler

OVERVIEW

The original goals of student financial aid were to make higher education affordable and accessible for moderate- and low-income students who could benefit from postsecondary education, but who might not be able to matriculate for financial reasons. Since the original funding of the Higher Education Act of 1965, federal financial aid policy has shifted back and forth between a greater reliance on loans or grants as the most effective way to achieve the original goals. During the 1960s, loans were the principal mechanism for providing federal assistance to students. By 1970–71, however, grants comprised more than 65% of all federal student aid, and, by 1975–76, grants peaked at more than 80% of all federal aid (Gillespie & Carlson, 1983). The 1980s, however, marked the end of the dominance of grants, and loans once again became the principle vehicle for providing financial assistance to students. By 1992, various types of federal loans accounted for 52% of all federal student aid (College Board, 1992).

It would be appealing to report that changes in federal financial aid policy have been driven by data, rational planning, and clear policy objectives. However, Hearn (1993), in his analysis of federal policy, concludes that policies have not been rational or purposeful, and that no clear goals are evident from the decisions. Hearn concludes that Cohen and March's concept of organized anarchy is the most apt description of federal aid policy. Although we may yet see the day when federal aid policy swings back in the direction of student grants, at the moment, this is difficult to imagine. The large federal deficit and current political trends are likely to result in more reliance on student loans, not less. The lack of rational policy development with clear goals and the reality that federal financial aid policies change almost annually has made it difficult to assess the effects of federal policy on the college choices that students make.

Indeed, it is difficult to disaggregate the influence of federal student aid programs, and student loan programs in particular, for many reasons. Federal student loans are embedded in a larger system of direct and indirect educational costs as well as student subsidies that include federal financial aid, state financial aid, institutional financial aid, and family financial contributions. There have been dramatic increases in college costs and significant increases in institution-based financial aid, and, in recent years, median family incomes have remained flat or have actually declined. These trends affect the real and the perceived costs of higher education, and the effects are not uniform. The consequences of these economic, social, and public policy trends differentially affect students and families from different income groups. In addition, the types of educational options, their location, and their cost also influence the educational decisions that students and their families make. To further complicate efforts to study the effects of federal loans on access, institutional choice, and student persistence, perceptions and subjectivity cannot be ignored. Some families, and students, are simply more sensitive to costs and subsidies regardless of their income (Hossler & Vesper, 1993).

Although there have been many studies and essays written about the impact of student loans on student access and student persistence, little research has been done on the impact that current federal aid policy (especially student loans) has on how students actually choose a specific college or university. Furthermore, a systematic summary of the effects of student loans on the student college choice process and on students' subsequent decision to persist has yet to be written. Indeed, in many instances, we can only speculate about the effects of student loans in the context of all the other societal, economic, and policy trends that influence enrollment and persistence decisions in higher education. If in this chapter we can effectively outline extant research on this topic and frame key issues that merit further analysis, we will have achieved our goals.

We will examine here the effects of federal student financial assistance policy, especially Federal Family Education Loans, on the postsecondary education decisions of students and their families. We will focus exclusively on traditional-age, full-time students. We do this because there is sufficient research on this topic that we can at least arrive at some informed speculation about traditional-age students. If we attempt to include nontraditional and part-time students, we would be able to do little beyond reporting loan usage patterns among these groups of students.

We begin by outlining some trends in financial aid over the past decade and a half, devoting special attention to the college loan segment of federal assistance programs and the effect on loan volume of the 1992 amendments and reauthorization of the Higher Education Act. We then turn our examination to three specific postsecondary educational decisions: aspirations for college attendance (access), postsecondary destinations (college choice decisions), and student persistence (once enrolled). We conclude with speculations on current trend projections and their possible effect on postsecondary education decisions and pose a series of questions for further research. Throughout the chapter, we follow Hearn's (1993) conceptual lead and interweave various aspects of specific student financial assistance programs in an attempt to explore the question of whether *federal financial aid policy* is even a legitimate term for the current pastiche of goals, programs, strategies, incentives, and disincentives that have propelled the Office of Student Financial Aid to the prominent position that it occupies today on most college campuses.

OVERVIEW OF CURRENT FINANCIAL AID TRENDS

The deliberations of the 104th Congress focused debate on federal student assistance programs, which reverberated from Capitol Hill to college campuses and back again. Whereas the Pell Grant program remained at less than full funding levels ($3,100 authorized, $2,400 actual currently), which represents slightly less than $7 billion annually, the Federal Family Education Loan (FFEL) programs swelled to an annual volume of $18.7 billion for Fiscal Year (FY) 1994; and to a cumulative volume of $182 billion since the Higher Education Act of 1965 authorized the issuance of $73 million in guaranteed student loans (U.S. Department of Education [USDOE], 1994).

College students and their families showed dramatic increases in debt incurred for postsecondary education in the first half of the 1990s in both current and constant (1994) dollars. Table 6.1 illustrates that total borrowing (in current dollars) under all FFEL programs rose by 72.8% in the first half of the decade.

Although these increases in loan volume are impressive, other sources (e.g., Roche, 1994; The Education Resources Institute [TERI], 1995) showed even more startling increases, especially from FY 1993 to FY 1994. For purposes of comparison and consistency, however, we will employ data from the *Digest of Education Statistics 1994* (USDOE, 1994).

Loan Volume and Needs Analysis

In the 5 fiscal years prior to those in the table, 1985–1989, the annual FFEL volume in current dollars rose from $8.467 billion to $10.938 billion, a

TABLE 6.1. Borrowing Under FFEL Programs.

Year	Current $ (billions)	Percent Change	Constant $ (billions)
FY 1990	10.826		12.390
FY 1991	12.336	+13.9	13.512
FY 1992	13.658	+10.7	14.461
FY 1993	16.524	+21.0	16.982
FY 1994	18.705*	+13.2	18.705*

Note. *Digest of Education Statistics 1994*. USDOE, 1994.
*Includes initial Federal Direct Student Loans of $456 million.

comparatively modest increase of 29.2%. In the 5-year span prior to that, FFEL current dollar annual volume rose from $4.598 billion in FY 1980 to $7.520 billion in FY 1984, an increase of 63.5%. Thus, from 1980 to 1994, there has been an increase of some $14.1 billion annually in borrowing for education, a 300% increase in annual debt load.

The primary contributing factor to the rise in family borrowing for college in the 1990s appears to be the 1992 amendments and reauthorization of the Higher Education Act. The reauthorization raised the annual limits on (subsidized) Stafford loans from $2,625 to $3,500 for 1st and 2nd year undergraduates and from $4,000 to $5,500 for upper-division undergraduates. The aggregate Stafford loan limit (both subsidized and unsubsidized) for dependent undergraduate students was increased from $17,250 to $23,000, while the maximum cumulative loan amount permitted for graduate and professional school students rose from $74,750 to $138,500 (including outstanding undergraduate loans). Other provisions of the 1992 reauthorization included the elimination of dollar limits on PLUS loans to parents, creation of an unsubsidized component of the Stafford Loan program, and elimination of need-based Supplemental Loans for Students (SLS).

Perhaps more important, financial needs methodologies were modified to eliminate home and family farm equity from consideration for Stafford eligibility, and families with gross annual incomes of less than $50,000 were presented with a greatly simplified needs test for financial eligibility. Thus, in the 1990s, as new programs were created, old ones expanded, needs analysis simplified, eligibility requirements relaxed, and dollar limits increased, borrowing for college has resulted in record debt levels for postsecondary students and their families.

Loan Recipients

Although these dollar volume amounts are clearly very large, the individual indebtedness of American college students expresses the figures in a more personal way. More than 6 million students (approximately 40% of those enrolled in postsecondary institutions) participated in FFEL programs in FY 1994. A 1992 American Council on Education study looked at borrowing patterns of individual students and found that between 1985 and 1991, the mean cumulative per-student indebtedness from all federal student loan programs rose from $6,488 to $16,417, an increase of 153%. At the same time, mean annual repayment amounts rose from $987 in 1985 to $2,161 in 1991, an increase of 119%. Expressed as a percentage of respondents' annual gross income, the increase was from 6.23% in 1985 to 9.52% in 1991, whereas the average increase in annual gross income for the period was 5.5% (Andersen, 1992).

College Costs and Loans

In the 1990s, tuition and fee increases at public 4-year institutions have outpaced those at private four-year institutions nationally. From academic year (AY) 1990 to AY1994, tuition and fees increased by 34.7% at public 4-years and by 21.0% at private 4-years. Over the longer term, AY 1982 to AY 1992, public 4-year institutions increased tuition and fees by 133% on national average, whereas private 4-year colleges and universities increased tuition and fees by 138%. In the same time period, first-time freshmen fall enrollments at 4-year public institutions fell by 3.8%, whereas first-time freshmen fall enrollments at 4-year private institutions showed a moderate rise of 0.7%. From 1990 to 1993, debt levels for undergraduates attending public 4-year institutions rose by 13%, whereas borrowing by undergraduates at 4-year private colleges and universities rose by 2% (College Board, 1993).

From the institutional point of view, other current fund sources of revenue have been replaced by tuition and fees at public colleges and universities. From AY 1981 to AY 1992, current fund revenue at public institutions rose from $5.57 billion to $17.46 billion, an increase of 213%. Expressed as a percentage of current fund revenues for public institutions, tuition accounted for 12.9% in AY 1981 and grew to 17.1% in AY 1992 (USDOE, 1994). From these trends, it appears that federal student loans comprised a significant portion of the funds that students and their families used to pay increased tuition and fees at public institutions of higher education.

ACCESS, CHOICE, AND PERSISTENCE

The term *college choice* is often used to indicate a longitudinal process involving many decision-making points along a sort of continuum that culminates in an enrollment action. Hossler, Braxton, and Coopersmith (1989) define student college choice as "a complex, multistage process during which an individual develops aspirations to continue formal education beyond high school, followed later by a decision to attend a specific college, university, or institution of advanced vocational training" (p. 234). Edward P. St. John (1994) has suggested that "these three behaviors—deciding to attend a college (or other postsecondary schooling), choosing a college or university, and persisting—in combination are characterized as 'student choice behavior'" (p. 13). For this chapter, we rely on St. John's extended definition of student choice behavior as the organizational framework.

In the triad of postsecondary education decisions considered in this essay, access, choice, and persistence, access is normally given initial attention. This is true for a number of reasons, most commonly because of the emphasis given to access to higher education as the primary goal in the historical development of federal student financial aid programs. The GI Bill gave access to college to returning veterans as a reward for their national service and, partially, to encourage them not to try to explore the limited possibilities of the workforce immediately following separation. College choice was not originally a policy goal for federal financial aid programs, but it began to emerge as a priority because of the portability of federal loans and grants. Over time, federal financial aid came to be evaluated not only on the basis of its impact on access, but for its effects on students' choices of institutions as well. Only in recent years has the effect of federal loans and grants upon student persistence also come into question.

Access and Postsecondary Aspirations

Sociologists have studied the formation of postsecondary educational aspirations extensively. More recently, higher education scholars have also looked at the formation of aspirations, but from the framework of stage-based models of college choice (Hossler & Gallagher, 1987; Jackson, 1982; Litten, 1982). The work of sociologists and higher education researchers focuses on the role of family background, student ability, and educational experiences in facilitating the development of educational aspirations. The development of postsecondary educational aspirations takes place over various time spans for different students. Some report that they have "always known" that they were going to attend a college or university, whereas others are still undecided at the end of their senior year in high school. Most of the research on this process does not include measures of financial aid policies. Family income is included, but not federal, state, or institutional aid variables.

Without complex longitudinal research designs, it is impossible to assess the impact of federal loan policy on the development of postsecondary educational aspirations. It is likely (Bouse & Hossler, 1991) that most students do not begin to think seriously about how they will pay for college until after their sophomore year in high school; however, research also suggests that students have typically formulated their educational aspirations by the 9th or 10th grade (Hossler, Braxton, & Coopersmith, 1989; Paulsen, 1990). Thus, federal loan policy is unlikely to directly influence the educational aspirations of most students. Parents, however, exert considerable influence on both the aspirations and the college destinations of their children (Conklin & Dailey, 1981; Hossler, Schmit, Bouse, & Vesper, 1990; Stage & Hossler, 1989). Furthermore, Hossler, Schmit, Bouse, and Vesper (1990) found that although students do not become concerned about how they will pay for higher education until the 11th or 12th grade, parents express concern much earlier. Thus, federal loan policy may affect parents, and what they tell their children can in turn influence their children's aspirations.

There are no studies of the impact of loan policy on parents' attitudes toward the affordability and accessibility of higher education. Research on the knowledge level of parents about financial aid and tuition costs is mixed. Some studies indicate that parents are not well-informed (Olson & Rosenfeld, 1984). More recent studies suggest that low- and moderate-income parents are knowledgeable about financial aid programs (Flint, 1993; Hossler, Schmit, & Bouse, 1991). In addition, there is anecdotal evidence that when congressional threats to make large reductions in federal financial aid have been well publicized in the media, applications for student financial aid have subsequently declined.

If parents are knowledgeable about federal financial aid, then it is possible that trends in federal loan policy could indirectly influence the postsecondary aspirations of students. It is likely, however, that the causal links between loan policies and student aspirations are weak and that any effects are lagged over several years. Since the development of educational aspirations evolves over several years and is the result of parental encouragement, interaction with peers and other family members, student ability, and school experiences (Stage & Hossler, 1989), it is unlikely that shifts in federal loan policies have an immediate impact on the aspirations of students.

Access to higher education, typically measured by comparing postsecondary participation rates among various socioeconomic groups, is often used to examine the impact of federal financial aid policies (including loans). Although this is different from attempting to determine the impact of aid

TABLE 6.2. Changes in College Participation.

Family Income ($)	1979–93 Percent Change
less than 21,300	+4.1
21,300 to 38,700	+12.8
38,700 to 63,800	+16.0
more than 63, 800	+21.1

policies on aspirations, access (without consideration of college destinations) is also a useful frame of reference for considering the effects of federal loan policies. We highlight the use of a more tentative word such as *consider* here because of the difficulties we have already discussed in assessing the isolated impact of loan policy on aspirations, access, choice, or persistence.

It is well documented that there are significant differences in the willingness of students and families of diverse income levels to take on loans. Families and students from lower income groups are more averse to taking out loans (Hossler, Braxton & Coopersmith, 1989; Newman, 1985). Conversely, students from middle- and upper-income families are not opposed to taking out student loans. If this is true, we would expect federal loan policies that emphasize the use of loans over grants to have an adverse effect on access among students from low- to moderate-income groups.

As evidence of this adverse effect, if we examine postsecondary education participation rates for traditional-age students in light of family income, we see that enrollment by students from lower income families has actually lagged behind those better able to afford increased costs. Using data from the U.S. Census Bureau *Current Population Survey* for 1979 and 1993, we can compare college participation rates by family income quartiles over the past decade and a half. (See Table 6.2).

Thus, those students from families least affected by higher educational costs and federal financial aid policies have matriculated at higher rates than have those most affected by costs and financial aid over the past 15 years. In fact, as Mortenson (1995b) points out, this has resulted in the greatest inequality in the distribution of postsecondary education participation across family income levels since the data were first reported in 1970.

Mortenson (1995a) has also argued that current federal reliance on loans and failure to provide higher limits for Pell grants has resulted in low postsecondary participation rates among students from these family income groups. He suggests that access has been adversely affected by these policies.

Mortenson, however, may be not be correct, or at least the factors that influence access may be more complex. Rather than financial aid policies being the cause, it may be that youth from these income groups lack the social and cultural capital, the parental encouragement, and the requisite educational experiences in school to develop postsecondary aspirations, and that these are the real causes of low postsecondary participation rates among students from low- and moderate-income groups. These causes should also be of great concern for public policy makers and scholars, but would also mean that federal loan policy is not solely responsible for inadequate access. These issues again illustrate the difficulty of untangling the multiple causes of postsecondary participation rates.

There are a number of countervailing trends that make it difficult to determine the current effects of federal financial loan policy. The efforts of Congress to balance the budget and to reduce federal loans in the process has received considerable attention. This media attention might be expected to reduce demand for student loans, and thus reduce student access, because students and families might believe that they will not be able to afford to matriculate. On the other hand, during the past decade there has been a dramatic increase in the number of postsecondary encouragement programs in cities, regions, and states targeted at low- and moderate-income families (Hossler & Schmit, 1995). These programs appear to have increased knowledge about college costs and federal, state, and institutional financial aid programs among students and families in these income brackets. In addition, state aid programs, tuition policies at public and private institutions, and family background and educational experiences influence the development of educational aspirations and access to higher education.

Clearly, there is a need for additional research on the effects of federal loan policy on both the development of postsecondary aspirations and access. Such research, however, will not be easy. Longitudinal research that includes an emphasis on multiple interviews of students and parents over several years will be necessary to understand the effects of loan policies on aspirations and access. Making inferences on the basis of large financial aid data sets or short-term survey research is limited because of the difficulty of untangling the impact of social and economic trends, federal grant and loan policy, state financial aid polices, and institutional pricing and financial aid.

The College Choice Decision

Sociologists have devoted less attention to the college destinations of traditional-age students, but higher education researchers and economists have given this topic considerable attention. Institutional policy makers are interested in learning more about how financial aid policies can influence a student's selection of a specific college to attend. Public policy makers are also interested in the college choice decision for a variety of reasons. From an equity perspective, public policy makers have sought to insure that federal and state financial aid makes family income irrelevant in the process of deciding which college to attend. Ideally, student ability and aspirations should be the only relevant constraints on students' college matriculation decisions. In addition, financial aid policy can be used to more evenly distribute students across types of institutions of higher education and can be used to induce students into certain careers in times of labor market shortages (e.g., health care workers, scientists, teachers, etc.).

In their three-stage model of college choice, Hossler and Gallagher (1987) include the stages of predisposition (formation of aspirations), search, and choice. The search stage involves students discovering and evaluating possible colleges and universities in which to enroll. In the choice stage, students choose a school to attend from among a list of institutions that are being seriously considered. Hossler, Braxton, and Coopersmith (1989) note that for many students who plan to live at home and commute, the search and choice stages are combined. These students may only seriously consider one institution. For the purposes of this analysis of federal loan policy, both the search and choice stages are collapsed into St. John's (1994) framework of "choosing a college or university" (p. 13). We will further focus on how one environmental (or organizational) factor—education loans—influences the choice of one college or university over another.

In order to explore the effects of federal loan policy on students' choices of colleges, it is necessary to examine its effects on students from different income groups. In their extensive reviews of the literature on student college choice both Hossler, Braxton, and Coopersmith (1989) and Paulsen (1990) conclude that low- and moderate-income students are very price sensitive and averse to taking out loans. Middle-income students, and their parents, on the other hand, are not hesitant to take out loans, indeed they often view loans as a good investment, for they believe that higher education will enhance their employability and their income over time.

A study using data from the 1993 National Postsecondary Student Aid Survey (NPSAS) contained a profile of federal student loan recipients at the time that loan repayment was scheduled to begin (Dynarski, 1994). The sample of more than 7,300 respondents was drawn from 4-year, 2-year, and proprietary postsecondary institutions. The characteristics from the total sample show that 75.3% had completed their program of study, and the average amount borrowed was $4,269. Distribution of parental annual income for loan recipients showed 27.6% at less than $17,000, 31.3% in the range from $17,000–$30,000, and 41% at more than $30,000.

These data indicate that students from families with higher incomes tend to borrow more for education as a result of the 1992 need analysis formula, which allowed a shift from unsubsidized to subsidized loans. For example, a 1994 survey of all Pennsylvania 4-year institutions showed that in the last 6 months of 1993, students from families with gross annual incomes of more than $48,000 took out 64% more loans with a dollar value of 100% more than they did in the last 6 months of 1992 (Redd, 1994). At the same time, students from families with gross annual incomes of less than $18,000 took out 19% more loans with an increase in the amount borrowed of 51%.

In his recent study of enrollment trends, St. John (1994) points out that "changes in federal policy during the early 1980s improved middle-income enrollments at all types of institutions, but changes in federal *grant* policy influenced a shift of low-income enrollments from four-year colleges to two-year colleges or out of the higher education system altogether" (p. 19). Thus, the Middle Income Student Assistance Act of 1978 (MISAA) marked the beginning of a shift in federal financial aid policy from an accent on grants to an emphasis on loans. This shift, which continued over the next 15 years, had a serious negative effect on college choice for low-income and minority students. In addition, coming as it did during a period of high commercial interest rates, the MISAA provided a spread (of perhaps as much as 10 points) between guaranteed student loan rates and investment market rates of return, which made it economically attractive for higher-income families to overborrow for college costs and invest the difference in high-interest instruments.

The research literature tends to agree that college choice decisions are responsive to tuition discounts, financial aid packages, or both. Whether loans can be used as a lever to influence specific college choice remains problematic. However, some data exist that permit us to make broad inferences about choice.

Whereas college costs have escalated over the past 15 years, median household income has remained relatively flat (College Board, 1993; USDOE, 1994). As a result of this and other previously discussed factors, debt is a growing ingredient in the mix of methods of paying for postsecondary education. If we assume that a student has the academic ability and the aspiration to enroll at either, then let us further assume that the college choice decision is to be made between a public 4-year and a private 4-year institution.

From examination of data from *How Floridians Pay for College* (Human Capital, 1994) (see Table 6.3), it appears that loans are now being employed to leverage the public-versus-private choice decision across all household income groups.

Proportionately, the percentage of students from families with less than

TABLE 6.3. Loan Patterns for Public/Private Colleges by Family Income.

Family Income ($)	Percent of Students	Percent of Students Receiving Loans	Average Annual Loan Amount
Public 4-year:			
0–30,000	22	33	2900
30,000–60,000	38	33	3500
60,000+	40	15	4500
Private 4-year:			
0–30,000	27	67	5200
30,000–60,000	38	50	4800
60,000–	35	27	4800
Public 2-year:			
0–30,000	38	19	1600
30,000–60,000	36	12	1700
60,000+	26	5	1000

Note. From Exhibit 4 and Exhibit 57, Human Capital Research Corporation, 1994. For comparison, median family income for all families with college-age children was $45,000 in this survey.

$30,000 annual income enrolled in private 4-year colleges is slightly higher than in public 4-year schools, but they are incurring a great deal more debt to make that choice. Although this may seem to represent a contradiction of the previous assertion that low-income families are averse to borrowing, recall the caveat that low-income students may be forced by financial aid policy to shift their choices from 4-year to 2-year institutions or out of higher education altogether. In this example, note the greater proportion of below-median-income students enrolled in community colleges, the lesser percentage receiving loans, and the smaller amount borrowed. Thus, responsiveness to loans may offer a measure of choice to some students, whereas others may be marginalized. A similar study conducted in Minnesota also indicates that the median family income of students enrolled in the private sector is lower than that of students in the 4-year public sector. These findings suggest that the pattern in Florida is not unique.

Other research by St. John (1989, 1990b) and St. John and Noell (1989) established that low-income students' enrollment behavior is responsive to the amount of grant aid but not to the amount of loan aid. In addition, it was found that middle-income student enrollments are more responsive to loans than grants. The widening gap between available federal grant dollars and loan dollars would seem to exacerbate the negative effect that loans have on some first-time college students.

One plausible interpretation of the responsiveness of middle-income students to loans over grants involves two complex factors. The first is the very real marketing efforts placed behind the various loan programs over the years to make them not only available but also broadly encouraged. Banks and other commercial student lenders receive an allowance from the government that guarantees a rate of return above their cost of funds as well as a 98-cents-on-the-dollar guarantee against repayment default. Second, state agencies that administer the loan programs receive special cost allowances and interest-free loans from the government as an incentive to handle the paperwork and administration. Finally, student and family borrowers receive an interest rate set below market rates. When this broad marketing effort is coupled with the fact that most aspects of the student loan system are considered congressionally "off budget," loans are positioned to appear to be an attractive educational financing device to lenders, program administrators, borrowers, and taxpayers.

The other factor that may affect middle-income students' responsiveness to loans is the amount and readiness of credit available as opposed to the amount of grant aid available. Whereas the average Pell grant hovered around $1,500 per recipient in the early 1990s, the average Stafford loan amount was approximately twice that figure. Additionally, the actual maximum Pell grant is currently $2,400, whereas the FFEL cap is $3,500 annually for first- and second-year students and $5,500 annually for third- and fourth-year students. These loan amounts, in conjunction with federal, state, and institutional grants, represent substantial sums of money to undergraduates and, when presented as a "package" of financial aid, make it quite difficult to say no to a loan as a part of that package. It should scarcely come as a surprise that "financial aid refund day" can create a real sense of euphoria in many students.

In sum then, Federal Family Education Loans do seem to offer an added measure of flexibility in college destination choices for middle- and upper-income students, but this benefit appears to go hand in hand with a deleterious effect on the college choices of many lower-income and minority students.

Persistence

Persistence, the decision to remain enrolled in postsecondary education, is an issue for students at the end of each academic term (within year) as well as at the end of each school year (year to year). We will define persistence as the decision to remain enrolled for consecutive terms until a degree is awarded—a bachelor's degree from a 4-year institution or an associate's degree from a 2-year institution.

From the institution's financial point of view, a student who does not persist represents a substantial loss of income to the school. As the supply side of postsecondary education has grown, recruiting and admissions budgets have been increased in order to attract top students and fill allocated places. The loss of one student at the end of the first year means a loss of 3 years of tuition income as well of the cost of recruiting that student. For every student who drops out at the end of the first year, in effect, three additional students will have to be recruited to replace the lost income.

For the student's financial future, dropping out may mean forfeiting significant future earnings. And since one of the underlying assumptions of the college loan program is that college graduates' incomes are expected to exceed those of noncollege graduates in the long term, dropping out of school may have especially severe economic consequences for a student who has accumulated substantial education debt.

A number of models of student persistence (Bean, 1983; Pascarella & Terenzini, 1983; Tinto, 1987) have been postulated, but until recently little attention has been given to the effects of financial aid—especially student loans. Perhaps this is because the financial aid variable is difficult to isolate in the myriad of factors affecting persistence, or perhaps the effects of financial aid (especially loans) on persistence are unclear.

An early study by Alexander Astin (1975) found that loans were negatively associated with 1st- to 2nd-year persistence for male students but positively associated with that same persistence for females. Astin did find that loans were positively associated with 4-year persistence while pointing out that this phenomenon may be self-fulfilling, because 4-year persisters were more likely to have borrowed for education.

Whereas Astin's (1975) findings are occasionally cited as evidence of the negative influence that loans may have on persistence, both Leslie and Brinkman's (1988) review of the literature and Moline's (1987) review established a positive link between persistence and the receipt of financial aid in general. By the late 1980s, interest in the relationship between financial aid variables and persistence began to gather more attention. Cabrera and Nora, with the assistance of other colleagues, conducted a series of studies examining the effects of aid on persistence (Cabrera, Castenada, Nora, & Hengstler, 1992; Cabrera, Stampen & Hansen, 1990). St. John and others took this line of inquiry one step further and investigated the relationships between various types of aid and student persistence (St. John, 1990a, 1990b; St. John, Kirshstein, & Noell, 1991; St. John & Somers, in press).

In a 1991 study, Edward P. St. John found that financial aid in the form of loans only had a significant (.05 level) positive effect on first to second year persistence and had a significant (.01 level) positive effect on 3rd to 4th year persistence. He points out that "research on student aid consistently shows that students are more likely to receive loans as part of their aid packages the longer they stay in school" (p. 401). St. John concludes that financial aid is positively associated with persistence, and "when the increased likelihood that persisters will take out loans is controlled for, loans appear to have a positive impact on persistence" (p. 399).

In 1994, St. John and associates looked at the effect of various forms of student aid on within-year persistence by traditional college-age students in 4-year colleges. With respect to loans, their findings were complex and sometimes conflicting. For example, loans had a negative effect on within-year persistence, but it is possible that the amount of the loan, rather than the receipt of it, caused the negative association. However, they conclude that "both loans as the only form of aid and the amount of loans awarded are negatively associated with persistence" (p. 474). In another recent study using a sample of students from a single public institution, Somers (1995) concluded that loans did have a positive effect on student persistence, but that the effect was small in comparison with the effects of grants.

Overall, the results of research to date on the effects of loans on student persistence are mixed. Furthermore, as loans have become an even more common form of financing postsecondary education, and debt loads continue to increase, it remains to be seen if their effect on persistence is a positive one. It can be argued that 3rd- to 4th-year persistence is at least partially motivated by the desire to (1) postpone repayment or (2) complete the program of study in order to get a higher-paying job. Further, undertaking a program of graduate study may also be envisioned as a sort of "holding pattern" while repayment obligations are deferred.

SPECULATIONS AND IMPLICATIONS

Given the complexities of the relationships between federal loans and questions of postsecondary educational aspirations, access, college choice, and persistence as well as the dearth of research, we can only offer tentative conclusions and informed speculations about the effects of federal loan policy on students' postsecondary choices.

The effect of federal loans on postsecondary aspirations is probably weak and indirect, mediated through parents. Status attainment research and research in the higher education literature suggest that parental encouragement, family socioeconomic status, and student ability are the most important variables in the formation of aspirations. The role of federal loans is limited to its contribution to the overall parental perceived affordability of higher education, which is transmitted through parents to students in the degree of encouragement that the former provide for their children to aspire to continue their formal education after high school. Parents may also send more subtle messages about how realistic students' aspirations are on the basis of the extent to which parents believe that higher education will be affordable to them and their children.

The impact of federal loan policy on the college destinations of students is more discernible. As federal policy shifts from a reliance on grants to increased emphasis on loans, low- and moderate-income students are less likely to consider attending private colleges and universities. They may also be less likely to attend 4-year public institutions as residential students. Indeed, as previously indicated, St. John (1994) suggests that low income students are simply less likely to attend 4-year colleges of any type and more likely to attend public 2-year colleges as a result of federal loan policy.

Up to now, federal loan policy may have had a positive effect on the range of college choices considered by middle-income students. Without the increased availability of loans to such students, it is unlikely that students, and their parents, could have continued to consider private institutions or public flagship residential universities in the light of rising tuition costs and the flat growth of median family income. However, there is growing evidence (Breneman, 1994; McPherson & Shapiro, 1991) that middle-income students may have reached a price threshold in the private sector for which even the increased availability of federal loans cannot make the costs of private higher education affordable. These studies are not conclusive, but if current tuition policies and wage trends continue, the private sector may see a significant flight of middle-income students to the public sector. It is possible that students and parents have reached a threshold on the amount of debt they are willing to assume to attend private, or even out-of-state public, colleges and universities.

As we have already noted, there is a dearth of research of the effects of loans on persistence. The research that has been conducted presents a mixed picture, thus it is difficult to arrive at any definitive conclusions. That conducted by Cabrera, Stampen, and Hansen (1990) indicates that the overall effect of receiving financial aid is positive, but that aid has less impact on persistence decisions than have other variables such as measures of social and academic integration. Triangulating Cabrera's work with that of Leslie and Brinkman (1988), Moline (1987), Somers (1995), and St. John and his colleagues (St. John, 1990a, 1990b; St. John et al, 1991, in press), we offer a tentative conclusion that federal loans appear to have a very small, modest effect on persistence; however, much more research is needed on this topic.

At this writing, it remains to be seen if the increased student loan volume characteristic of the mid-1990s is a temporary spike or "blip" in the data trends caused by the new needs analysis methodology of the 1992 amendments and reauthorization, or if it portends similar future increases. For the moment, however, it appears that public policy makers as well as college students and their families can expect increased reliance on loans as a vehicle for financing postsecondary education.

Over the past 10 years, college costs have increased 133% for private and 138% for public 4-years. During this same period, median family income has risen 45.7% (in current dollars). Enrollments have continued to climb as well, by about 13% in all 4-year institutions. In this context, we offer another intriguing view of the effects of federal loan policy on access, choice, and persistence. If we assume that a portion of the spread between increased costs and median income has been covered by student financial aid, and about half of that is represented by loans, then institutions have captured more federal aid dollars; and a portion of these have been channeled back to the student in the form of tuition discounts. Loans for some students are transformed into grants for others. Given the truth of this assertion, student loans may have had a positive impact (albeit an indirect one) on access, choice, and persistence—but perhaps not only for the recipient.

We close with a call for more research on the impact of loans on aspirations, access, choice and persistence. To date, policy makers have made important decisions about federal student aid with very little sense of how these policies might affect students. As Hearn (1993) concludes, there are no clearly articulated goals for federal financial aid, and the stakeholders and beneficiaries are no longer clear. This leaves policy makers, institutions, families, and students operating in a vacuum. Students and their families are left to react to the incentives of current loan policies, and only when the negative effects on students are clearly evident from trend analyses are public policy makers likely to respond. Research is unlikely to completely change public policy discourse on federal loans, but it might at least make the discussion and some of the policies more informed.

REFERENCES

Andersen, C. J. (1992). *Student financial aid: The growth of academic credit's other meaning*. Washington, DC: American Council on Education.

Astin, A. W. (1975). *Preventing students from dropping out*. San Francisco: Jossey-Bass.

Bean, J. P. (1983). The application of a model of turnover in work organizations to the student attrition process. *Review of Higher Education, 6*, 129–148.

Bouse, G., & Hossler, D. (1991, Winter). A longitudinal study of college student choice: A progress report. *Journal of College Admissions*, 11–16.

Breneman, D. W. (1994). *Liberal arts colleges: Thriving, surviving, or endangered*. Washington, DC: The Brookings Institution.

Cabrera, A. F., Castenada, M. B., Nora, A., & Hengstler, D. (1992). The convergence of two theories of student persistence. *Journal of Higher Education*, 63(2), 143–164.

Cabrera, A. F., Stampen, J. O., & Hansen, W. L. (1990). Exploring the effects of ability to pay on persistence in college. *Review of Higher Education*, 13, 303–336.

College Board (1992). *Update: Trends in student aid: 1982–1992*. Washington, DC: Author.

College Board (1993). *Trends in student aid: 1983 to 1993*. Washington, DC: Author.

Conklin, M. E., & Dailey, A. R. (1981). Does consistency of parental encouragement matter for secondary students? *Sociology of Education*, 54, 254–262.

Dynarski, M. (1994). Who defaults on student loans? Findings from the national postsecondary student aid study. *Economics of Education Review*, 13(1), 55–68.

Flint, T. A. (1993). Early awareness of college financial aid: Does it expand choice? *Review of Higher Education*, 16(3), 309–328.

Gillespie, D. A., & Carlson, N. (1983). *Trends in student aid: 1963 to 1983*. Washington, DC: College Board.

Hearn, J. C. (1993). The paradox of growth in federal aid for college students, 1965–1990. In J. Smart (Ed.), *Higher education: Handbook of theory and research* (Vol. 9, pp. 94–153). New York: Agathon Press.

Hossler, D., Braxton, J., & Coopersmith, G. (1989). Understanding student college choice. In J. C. Smart (Ed.), *Higher education: Handbook of theory and research* (pp. 231–287) (Vol. 5.). New York: Agathon Press.

Hossler, D., & Gallagher, K. S. (1987). Studying student college choice: A three-phase model and the implications for policy-makers. *College and University*, 2(3), 201–221.

Hossler, D., & Schmit, J. (1995). Postsecondary encouragement programs: The Indiana experiment. In E. P. St John (Ed.), *Rethinking tuition and student aid strategies*. New Directions in Higher Education, No. 89. San Francisco: Jossey-Bass.

Hossler, D., Schmit, J. S., & Bouse, G. (1991). Family knowledge of postsecondary costs and financial aid. *Journal of Student Financial Aid*, 21(1), 4–17.

Hossler, D., Schmit, J., Bouse, G., & Vesper, N. (1990). Family knowledge of post-secondary costs and financial aid and their relationships with family savings behavior. *Proceedings of the seventh annual conference of the NASSGP/ NCHELP Research Network*. Trenton, NJ: New Jersey Higher Education Assistance Authority.

Hossler, D., & Vesper, N. (1993). An explanatory study of the factors associated with parental saving for postsecondary education. *Journal of Higher Education*, 64(2), 140–165.

Human Capital Research Corporation (1994). *How Floridians pay for college*. Tallahassee, FL: Florida Family Funding Study.

Jackson, G. A. (1982). Public efficiency and private choice in higher education. *Educational Evaluation and Policy Analysis 4*(2), 237–247.

Leslie, L. L., & Brinkman, P. T. (1988). *The economic value of higher education.* San Francisco: Jossey-Bass.

Litten, L. (1982). Different strokes in the applicant pool: Some refinements in a model of student college choice. *Journal of Higher Education, 53*(4), 83–402.

McPherson, M. S., & Shapiro, M. O. (1991). *Keeping college affordable: Government and educational opportunity.* Washington, DC: Brookings Institution.

Moline, A. E. (1987). The relationship of financial aid to student persistence in a commuter institution: A test of a causal model. Paper presented at Fourth Annual NASSGP/NCHELP Research Network Conference, St. Louis, MO.

Mortenson, T. G. (1995a, April). Anxiety about affordability. *Postsecondary Education Opportunity*, (34), 1–6.

Mortenson, T. G. (1995b, June). Student price response coefficients. *Postsecondary education opportunity*, (36), 1–6.

Newman, F. (1985). *Higher education and the American resurgence.* Princeton, NJ: Carnegie Foundation for the Advancement of Teaching.

Olson, L., & Rosenfeld, R. A. (1984). Parents and the process of gaining access to student financial aid. *Journal of Higher Education, 55*(4), 455–480.

Pascarella, E. T., & Terenzini, P. T. (1983). Predicting voluntary freshman year persistence/withdrawal behavior: A path analytic validation of Tinto's model. *Journal of Educational Psychology, 75*, 215–226.

Paulsen, M. B. (1990). *College choice: Understanding student enrollment behavior.* (ASHE-ERIC Higher Education Report no. 6). Washington, DC: Association for the Study of Higher Education.

Redd, K. E. (1994). *The effects of higher loan limits and need analysis changes on FFELP borrowing in Pennsylvania.* Harrisburg, PA: Pennsylvania Higher Education Assistance Agency.

Roche, G. C. (1994). *The fall of the ivory tower.* Washington, DC: Regnery.

St. John, E. P. (1989). The influence of student aid on persistence. *Journal of Student Financial Aid 19*,(3), 52–68.

St. John, E. P. (1990a). The impact of student financial aid: A review of recent research. Paper presented at Mid South Educational Research Association meeting, New Orleans, LA.

St. John, E. P. (1990b). Price response in persistence decisions: An analysis of the high school and beyond senior cohort. *Research in Higher Education, 31*(4), 387–403.

St. John, E. P. (1994). *Prices, productivity, and investment: Assessing financial strategies in higher education* (ASHE-ERIC Higher Education Report no. 3). Washington, DC: George Washington University, School of Education and Human Development.

St. John, E. P., Andrieu, S., Oescher, J., & Starkey, J. B. (1994). The influence of student aid on within-year persistence by traditional college-age students in four-year colleges. *Research in Higher Education, 35*(4), 455–480.

St. John, E. P., Kirshstein, R. J., & Noell, J. (1991). The effects of student financial aid on persistence: A sequential analysis. *Review of Higher Education 14*(3), 383–406.

St. John, E. P., & Noell, J. (1989). The impact of financial aid on access: An analysis of progress with special consideration of minority access. *Research in Higher Education, 30*(6), 563–582.

Somers, P. A., & St. John, E. P. (1997). Analyzing the role of financial aid in student persistence. In J. S. Davis (Ed.), *Student aid research: A manual for financial aid administrators* (pp. 127–138). Washington, DC: National Association of Student Financial Aid Administrators.

Somers, P. A. (1995). A comprehensive model for examining the impact of financial aid on enrollment and persistence. *Journal of Student Financial Aid, 25*(1), 13–27.

Stage, F. K., & Hossler, D. (1989). Differences in family influence on the college plans of high school males and females. *Research in Higher Education, 30*(3), 301–315.

The Education Resources Institute, (1995). *College debt and the American family.* Boston: Author.

Tinto, V. (1987). Leaving college: Rethinking the causes and cures of student attrition. Chicago: University of Chicago Press.

U.S. Census Bureau (1979 & 1993). *Current population survey.* Washington, DC: U.S. Government Printing Office.

U.S. Department of Education (1994). *Digest of education statistics 1994.* Washington, DC: National Center for Education Statistics.

CHAPTER 7

Who Defaults on Student Loans?

THE EFFECTS OF RACE, CLASS, AND GENDER
ON BORROWER BEHAVIOR

James Fredericks Volkwein and Alberto F. Cabrera

In this chapter, we review the evidence suggesting individual and institutional causes of student loan default. We contend that the student loan program is plagued by clashes between the competing values and goals of public subsidy, educational opportunity, cost effective investment, and institutional accountability. This policy and value conflict remains unresolved (Hearn, 1993) and is amplified by a relative lack of empirical evidence to validate the policies and claims advanced by the various financial aid stakeholders.

For 3 decades, public investment in higher education has been directed at removing economic barriers to attendance and persistence in college (Stampen & Cabrera, 1986). This commitment to educational opportunity produced growth in student financial aid from $557 million in 1963–64 to an astonishing $50 billion in 1995–96. Federal financial aid to college students has increasingly taken the form of publicly subsidized loans (Lewis, 1989). Since 1980, approximately half of all students attending 4-year colleges and more than 60% of students at proprietary schools have borrowed at one point in their education (College Board, 1992). These loans must be repaid, and there is public concern about the alarming trend in default rates. Knapp and Seaks (1992) have estimated that whereas federal loan volume grew by 58% during the 1980s, the dollar value of default claims grew by about 1,200%, accounting for over a fifth of total program costs.

Annual student loan delinquency rates, averaging between 17 and 21% through the early 1990s, compare unfavorably with other types of consumer loans, where the annual delinquency rates since 1980 have ranged from 1.5 to 3.6% for various types of personal consumer credit and automobile loans (American Bankers Association, 1994), and from 4.6 to 5.8% for various types of home mortgages (Mortgage Bankers Association of America, 1994).

Concomitant with the growth in student borrower default is the commonly held perception that institutions of higher education themselves contribute substantially to this problem. Despite the demise of in loco parentis, colleges and universities are widely believed to exert considerable influence on the personal actions of their students, not only while they are on campus pursuing their degree programs, but also after they cease attending the institution and leave the campus. Current student loan policy and national legislation is based substantially on this belief.

THE PUBLISHED RESEARCH ON STUDENT LOAN DEFAULT

Despite the importance of this national problem, the literature contains few empirical studies and only one national database of out-of-school borrowers—the 1987 *National Postsecondary Student Aid Study* (NPSAS-87) (NCES, 1989). We found fewer than 10 referenced journal articles and a handful of unpublished research reports and doctoral dissertations that describe the characteristics of defaulters. In the aggregate, these sources provide useful information about the characteristics of loan defaulters, but most of the published studies are limited to a particular state or particular type of institution, or have other data limitations. Stockham and Hesseldenz (1979) analyzed a variety of academic, demographic, and personality data collected between 1971 and 1974 from a sample of 878 borrowers at a single institution in Kentucky. Myers and Siera (1980) developed a default model on a New Mexico State University population of 107 borrowers. Gray (1985) used a population of 328 at the University of Missouri to develop a logistic regression model. Wilms, Moore, and Bolus (1987) limited their study to a population of borrowers at proprietary schools and 2-year colleges in the state of California. Greene (1989) studied 161 students who received Perkins loans at a school in North Carolina. In Texas, Lein, Rickards, and Webster (1993) compared 50 defaulters with 50 repayers among former vocational and proprietary students. A study by Knapp and Seaks (1992) examined borrowers in the state of Pennsylvania at 26 public and private 2- and 4-year institutions. Mortenson (1989) examined national survey data, summarized American attitudes toward borrowing, and reviewed the findings from several earlier studies, but did not himself present a new analysis of defaulters. More recently, Flint (1994) studied a cohort of borrowers at a multicampus 2-year institution in Illinois.

The NPSAS-87 is the only national database of postcollege borrowers. Although several publications have displayed descriptive statistics from NPSAS-87, only two analytical studies of borrowers have been published using NPSAS-87 data (Dynarski, 1994; Volkwein & Szelest, & 1995), and one other has been presented as a conference paper and is in press (Volkwein, Cabrera, Szelest, & Napierski-Prancl, 1998). The Dynarski study develops logit default models on 4,750 NPSAS-87 borrowers who were within two years of leaving college. The Volkwein and Szelest study takes the Dynarski analysis a step further by merging NPSAS with Integrated Postsecondary Education Data System (IPEDS) and College Board data, thus allowing them to examine repayment and default behavior in relation to a variety of campus organizational measures, as well as in relation to individual borrower characteristics. Volkwein and Szelest develop logistic regression models on 4,007 pre-1984 out-of-school borrowers with complete transcript and survey data. The Volkwein et al. paper (1998) advances the other two NPSAS-87 studies, first by capturing 6,087 complete cases, and second by analyzing the separate and combined results for Whites, Blacks, and Hispanics.[1]

WHAT ARE THE REAL CAUSES OF LOAN DEFAULT?

These studies collectively raise questions about the individual and institutional influences on borrower repayment and default behavior. Do the reasons for loan default have more to do with the characteristics and behaviors of individual borrowers or with the institutions that they attend? In addressing this question, we draw extensively on the evidence in the NPSAS-87 database, as well as on the relatively sparce research literature.

Studies by Astin (1993), Hearn (1984, 1991), Mow and Nettles (1990), and others suggest that student outcomes are associated with type of institution attended, but the literature contains only a few published investigations that compare the characteristics of defaulters with the characteristics of institutions they attend. For example, Wilms, Moore, and Bolus (1987) studied a population of California proprietary and 2-year college borrowers in selected fields of study and found that race, high school completion, annual income, and graduating with a degree or credential were significantly related to differences in default rates. The two institution types contributed little to their model once student characteristics were taken into account. Knapp and Seaks (1992) examined a population of borrowers at 26 Pennsylvania 2-year and 4-year campuses and also found that a group of institutional variables (including size, cost, highest degree, and institution type) had no impact on default rates compared to important borrower characteristics (such as race, parent income, and graduating with a degree). However, the NPSAS-87 studies by Dynarski (1994) and Volkwein et al. (1995) found that attending a 4-year institution, controlling for borrower characteristics, is independently associated with a significantly lower default rate. Dynarski believes that school type is an endogenous variable that is correlated with unobserved factors related to default, but Volkwein and Szelest (1995) concluded from their NPSAS-87 study that an array of institutional characteristics (reflecting mission, size, wealth, complexity, and selectivity) exhibit minor influences on default compared to individual borrower characteristics such as college major, college grades, degree earned, marital status, and dependent children.

Most empirical analyses of student loan default, including the three NPSAS-87 studies, have found that the characteristics of individual borrowers exert stronger influences on default and repayment behavior than do the characteristics of the institutions they attend. The higher loan default rates by racial minorities constitutes the most consistent and perhaps most troubling finding across these published studies. The 12 studies cited above report that being African American or American Indian and coming from a family of little education are characteristics that have default rates generally ranging from 30 to 50%. However, none of these studies examines the extent to which the patterns of default behavior may vary by ethnic group.

The research literature suggests the need for more carefully assessing the effects of personal, institutional, and socioeconomic characteristics on default behavior among separate ethnic groups. Astin (1982) found that minority group and socioeconomic status are significantly related to various educational outcomes. In particular, he found that the lower the family income, the lower the opportunities for minority students to perform well in college and to persist. Hearn (1984, 1991) examined the college destinations of a national sample and compared the role of ascriptive factors, such as race, to the role of academic factors and socioeconomic factors, such as high school achievement and parental income. Olivas (1985) found that Hispanics are more reluctant to go into debt to finance their college education. Mortenson (1989) reports that Hispanics, women, and students from lower economic backgrounds are less likely to have positive attitudes towards borrowing. St. John (1994) and St. John and Noell (1989) compare the college attendance behavior of White, Black, and Hispanic students and documents the importance of loans and other financial aid promoting college attendance by minorities. Several of the loan default studies have produced results that are consistent with Astin, Hearn, Mortenson, Olivas, and St. John. Wilms, Moore, and Bolus (1987) in California, Knapp and Seaks (1992) in Pennsylvania, and Flint (1994) in Illinois found race to be significantly related to differences in default rates. An early study commissioned by the U.S. Department of Education (1978) found that being Black and from a low-income family are strong predictors of student loan default. More recently, the three NPSAS-87 studies (Dynarski, 1994; Volkwein & Szelest, 1995; Volkwein et al., 1998) report that the ethnicity of the student is strongly associated with default and repayment behavior.

Using NPSAS-87, we explored for this chapter the interaction between

FIGURE 7.1. Student Loan Default Rates by Racial Group and Institution Type.

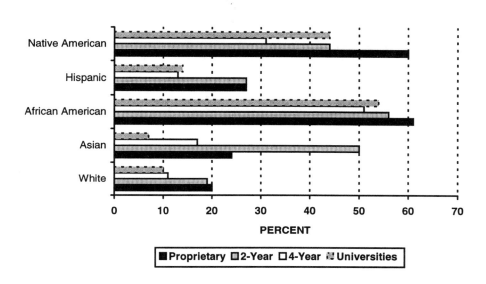

institution type and race as factors in default. From what we had been told by the popular press, we expected to find that loan default would be concentrated among minority borrowers at proprietary institutions. Figure 7.1 shows that African and Native American borrowers from all institution types have high default rates. Moreover, Whites, Asians, and Hispanics from 2-year colleges have default rates that are as high as those from proprietary schools. Among Whites, Asians, and Hispanics, over two thirds of defaulters are located at proprietary and 2-year institutions. Indeed, the loan default "problem" at universities and 4-year colleges appears to be concentrated among African and Native American borrowers. At any rate, it is evident that default rates vary significantly both by institution type and by race, thus suggesting the need for research on each, even if they both are endogenous variables.

We also need to be concerned about why it is that student borrowers default at such high levels. Recognizing the limitations of self-reported information, in Table 7.1 we show the reasons for default rated as "very important" on the NPSAS survey by the 1,191 responding defaulters. The inability to pay would seem to be the most obvious explanation, and this is confirmed by the large number indicating that the most important reasons for default are being unemployed (58.9%) and working at low wages (49.1%). Interference from personal problems (32.7%) is a distant third factor. Most students

TABLE 7.1. Reasons for Default Reported by Each Racial/Ethnic Group (%) (N = 1191).

Reasons for Default Rated As "Very Important"	Total Sample	White	Asian	American Indian	Black	Hispanic	Level of Significant Diff. Among Groups
Unemployed and w/out income	58.9	52.7	33.3	54.5	70.3	70.3	.001
Working but had insufficient funds for repayment	49.1	51.7	41.7	36.4	45.7	43.2	n/s
Repaying more import loans than GSL	20.7	21.3	41.7	27.3	19.1	10.8	.05
Dissatisfied w/ Educ. Program	12.0	9.2	0	9.1	17.6	13.5	.01
Had interfering personal problems	32.7	27.6	8.3	31.8	41.1	54.1	.001
Confused by repayment process	24.1	23.7	33.3	27.3	24.8	21.6	n/s
Didn't realize loan had to be repaid	7.2	5.5	0	9.1	10.3	10.8	n/s
Were you aware of deferment options (% Yes)	26.4	27.0	50.0	27.3	23.8	37.8	n/s
Begun making payments since default (% Yes)	66.0	72.5	91.7	54.5	54.0	62.2	.001

realize that the loan has to be repaid (93%), so ignorance and misinformation do not seem to be significant factors in loan default. However, one out of four (24.1%) are confused by the repayment process, and almost three out of four are not aware of loan deferment options as an alternative to default.

We find significant differences in the reasons for default reported by each ethnic group. African American and Hispanic defaulters are significantly more likely to be unemployed, to be dissatisfied with their educational programs, and to have personal problems that interfere with repayment. Whites and Asians are significantly more likely to report resuming loan repayment after default.

With the high level of student loan default, the resumption of payments after default is an important object of study. Two out of three defaulters report making payments since the official default first occurred. Figure 7.2, drawn from data in NPSAS-87, shows not only that 66% of defaulters have resumed payment, but that 31% have completed repayment. This may occur because the NPSAS database covers a dozen years, and many earlier default-

FIGURE 7.2. Repayment Status of Student Loan Defaulters (N = 1191).

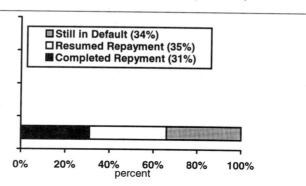

ers had time to improve their circumstances enough to repay. This finding suggests that the actual costs of loan default may be substantially lower than what is publicly discussed.

Most Prominent Multivariate Results for Default Behavior in NPSAS-87

The findings from the most recent analysis of NPSAS-87 are especially intriguing, not only because the Volkwein et al. (1998) study captures a greater number of cases from that database, but also because it concentrates our attention on the dominant influence of three interacting factors on loan default: degree completion, marital status, and dependent children.

Because race and ethnicity exert such a strong effect on the findings in previous studies noted above, we wanted to explore the possibility of differences in the patterns of default for each racial group. Moreover, the research literature suggests the need for investigating variable default behavior among different ethnic groups. We are limited by the low number of borrowers in the data set for Asians and Native Americans. However, the Volkwein et al. (1998) study did capture enough cases for us to carry out separate logistic regressions for Whites, African Americans, and Hispanics.

The logistic regression model for White borrowers produced results that are largely similar to those for the entire sample. On the other hand, the regression models for the African American and Hispanic populations produced fewer significant Delta-p values, but the magnitudes are much greater. Black and Hispanic females (compared to males) have about a 13% lower default rate—three times the effect for White females. Having a parent who attended college is associated with 27.7% lower default for Blacks—eight times the size of the effect on Whites. For both Whites and Blacks, degree completion has a dramatic influence on lowering the rate of loan default, but the impact of each credential through bachelor's degree attainment is two to three times more important for Black borrowers than for Whites. Married Black and Hispanic borrowers exhibit default rates that are 14 to 15% lower than for those who are single—an effect that is over three times the size as for Whites. Among African American borrowers, each dependent child increases the probability of default by about 5%. Again, this is substantially greater than the 3.6% increase for White borrowers with dependent children (Volkwein et al., 1998).

In developing this chapter, we went back to the NPSAS-87 database and developed additional logistic regression models to test the influence of institution type and organizational characteristics. Since we have IPEDS and College Board data for the research universities and 4-year colleges, we first developed a model for these institutions that contains eight measures reflecting their size, wealth, selectivity, diversity, and complexity. To our surprise, we found that there are no significant influences on loan default exerted by any of these variables. Instead, this logistic regression model produced results that are almost identical to the one produced by Volkwein et al. (1995): Substantially increasing default probability are the same variables reflecting race and dependent children; significantly decreasing default probability are the same variables reflecting gender, parent's income, major, grades, degree attainment, and being married.

We also developed separate regression models for each of four institution types to see if the patterns of default behavior in NPSAS-87 are substantially different for proprietary institutions, 2-year colleges, 4-year colleges, and research universities. We found few notable differences in the patterns of default probability among the four institution types. Again, we found that the factors of African American race and dependent children exert both large and consistent influences on increased loan default across all four types, controlling for all other variables. Completing the appropriate level of education for each institution type is strongly associated with reduced default in all four models. Being female, parent education, and high college GPA reduce default probability in three of the four institution types.

Thus, we find that student loan repayment and default behavior can be substantially predicted by the characteristics of individual borrowers. While there is wide variation in default rates among racial and ethnic groups, the factors that contribute to loan default among Whites, African Americans, and Hispanics differ more in degree than in kind. Moreover, the type of institution attended, the grades earned, and the choice of major appear to be less important than completing a degree, being married, and not having dependent children.

We find little evidence that the organizational characteristics of institutions have an impact on student loan default. Even the effects of institution type appear to be outweighed by the level of degree earned by the borrower. The 1998 Volkwein et al. study reports that default rates range from greater than 29% at proprietary schools to below 14% at most doctoral granting universities. However, once the individual borrower characteristics are entered into a logistic regression model, these significant differences across institutions are greatly reduced for 4-year institutions and disappear completely for 2-year schools. Indeed, the impact of institution type appears important only for White borrowers, and not for Blacks or Hispanics. These results appear consistent with studies by Hearn (1984, 1991, 1992) that found significant linkages between the background characteristics of students and their college destinations. Overall, the evidence suggests that these default rate differences are based more substantially on the nature of the borrowers and their achievements than on the types of institutions that the borrowers attend.

We conclude from our various analyses of the data sets that we created from NPSAS-87 that loan repayment and default behavior appear to be less a function of the institutions themselves and more a function of the nature of the students, their performance in college, their choice of major, their degrees earned, and their subsequent postcollege achievement and behavior. In nearly all racial groups and institution types, we find that two measures (sex and marital status) exert consistent influences on default behavior, but being female and being married lowers the default rate even more dramatically for Black and Hispanic borrowers than it does for Whites. Similarly, although having a parent who attended college, completing a degree, being married, and not having dependent children are all factors that lower the likelihood of default and increase the likelihood of repayment, these effects have the strongest impact on the population with the highest default rates—African American borrowers. Thus, the magnitude of the effect (reflected in default probability) is generally larger for the Black and Hispanic populations than for Whites in this study. For example, the benefit to a Black borrower of earning a degree is two or three times greater than the benefit to a White borrower. This suggests the power of public and personal investment in the education of minority groups, and supports the effectiveness of the student loan program.

We were interested in conducting this research because of the strong connection between race and loan default in the earlier studies. Blacks and Hispanics in this study, compared to Whites, have lower levels of degree attainment, lower levels of academic achievement, almost twice the number of dependent children, and almost twice the rate of separation and divorce. We find that having dependent children and being separated or divorced increase the probability of default enormously. Conversely, being female and

TABLE **7.2**. Income and Default Rates for Each Ethnic Groups Separated According to Differences in Marital Status, Dependent Children, and Degree Attainment.

Borrower Characteristics	1986 Taxable Income	Default Rate
Married with No Dependents and Bachelors Degree or Higher:		
Asian American	$44,067	08%
African American	$45,625	10%
Native American	$44,311	07%
Hispanic	$43,911	08%
White	$40,985	07%
Unmarried (includes Single/Sep/Wid/Div) with One or More Dependents and No College Degree:		
Asian American	$22,350	37%
African American	$22,350	43%
Native American	$22,325	37%
Hispanic	$24,875	38%
White	$21,604	35%

married, and completing a degree program significantly decrease the probability of default. Thus, the regression results indicate not only that these factors play strong roles in loan repayment behavior, but also that they outweigh the effects of most other variables, including parent education and income, type of institution attended, transfer status, financial aid mix, and borrower's income.

The highest default rates in NPSAS-87 are among single parents with no degree or certificate. Having dependent children combined with being single, separated, or divorced produces default rates above 40%, regardless of income. The lowest default rates occur among those with bachelors or graduate degrees, those with higher loan amounts (perhaps indicating more years of schooling and borrowing), and those married without children. Table 7.2 shows that three variables—degree completion, marital status, and dependent children—are the great equalizers among the races. Borrowers in similar circumstances, especially with respect to earned degrees, marital status, and family size, exhibit generally similar levels of income and loan default, regardless of race or ethnic group. These findings are consistent with human capital and ability to pay theories and have rich implications for national policy makers, campus managers, researchers, parents, and students alike.

DISCUSSIONS AND POLICY IMPLICATIONS

We began our work by considering five theoretical perspectives and found support for the relevance of some of them. Human capital theory and the value of public subsidy is best demonstrated by the significant linkage between earned degrees and lower default rates in most analyses that we and other researchers have conducted. The ability to pay model is supported by the role of parent income and support during college, but even more strongly by the significant influences of marital status, income, and dependent children after college. Most loan default studies do not contain measures of student–institution fit, so we have used college grades and college major as proxies and found that they are influential, especially among White borrowers at 4-year colleges and universities in NPSAS-87. The relevance of perspectives from the organizational literature is less clear. The recent analyses of NPSAS-87 data cast doubt on the importance of institution type and other structural measures as independent influences on loan default (Volkwein & Szelest 1995, Volkwein et al. 1998).

The empirical literature on this topic contains only three previous published investigations that compare the characteristics of defaulters with the characteristics of institutions they attend, and they produced results that are in some important respects consistent with our own. Wilms, Moore, and Bolus (1987) studied a population of California proprietary and 2-year college borrowers in selected fields of study and found that race, high school completion, annual income, and graduating with a degree or credential were significantly related to differences in default rates. The two institution types contributed little to their model once student characteristics were taken into account. Knapp and Seaks (1992) examined a population of borrowers at 26 Pennsylvania 2-year and 4-year campuses and also found that a group of institutional variables (including size, cost, highest degree, and institution type) had no impact on default rates compared to important borrower characteristics (such as race, parent income, and graduating with a degree). Volkwein and Szelest (1995) analyzed a national sample of 2,600 borrowers and concluded that an array of institutional characteristics (reflecting mission, size, wealth, complexity, and selectivity) exhibited minor influences on default compared to borrower characteristics, such as college grades, major, degree earned, marital status, and dependent children. Our larger national database (Volkwein et al., 1998) containing more than 6,000 borrowers and 1,000 institutions, strengthens their conclusions considerably. As in the other studies, we find only scant support for the hypothesis that institutional characteristics have a direct impact on student loan default among ethnic minorities.

We find that college GPA is a strong predictor of loan default and repayment behavior among Whites but not minorities. Among minorities, especially Blacks, degree completion is more important than grades earned. Most investigations of loan default have not included measures of academic ability or performance. The earlier single-institution studies by Dyl and McGann (1977), Stockham and Hesseldenz (1979), Myers and Siera (1980), and Gray (1985) concluded that college GPA is positively associated with repayment. More recently, Flint (1994) analyzed a population of over 1,000 borrowers at a 2-year institution in Illinois and also found, as we did, that college GPA is an especially powerful predictor of loan repayment. We suspect that, though less important for minorities, academic ability and performance in high school and college are early indicators of the characteristics that eventually lead to loan repayment and default behavior.

Low academic performance may have several detrimental influences. First, it may encourage (or even require) students to withdraw before degree completion. Second, poor performance may leave students dissatisfied with their college experience. Third, a low GPA makes it difficult for students to continue their education and earn additional degrees. Each of these possibilities will lower the likelihood of repayment. We introduced college GPA as one indicator of student–institution fit, but it may serve also as a proxy for student ability, conscientiousness, and motivation—traits associated with success in later life, as well as in college.

We also find that a college major in a scientific, engineering, or agricultural discipline lowers the default probability by over 4% among White borrowers but not among Blacks or Hispanics. Although this result may be due substantially to differences in sample size among the three populations, degree completion among minorities appears to be more important than grades earned or major field of study, especially among Blacks. Among White borrowers, earning good grades and majoring in a scientific or technological field generally lowers the probability of default substantially, although completing a degree is even more influential than these in lowering default among Whites and minorities alike. These findings are consistent with the economics literature indicating that the American labor market is very degree sensitive.

We expected, but did not find in NPSAS-87, that the amount of loan indebtedness would have a negative influence on repayment, at least by minorities, if not Whites. This is one of many studies showing that the amount borrowed has either no effect or a beneficial effect on student loan repayment and default. Sanford (1980), Myers and Siera (1980), Gray (1985), Flint (1994), and Volkwein and Szelest (1995) have all found that higher student loan indebtedness is not detrimental to repayment behavior. The explanation may rest in economic and human capital theory. Higher levels of indebtedness result from additional years of schooling and degree attainment. Those with higher levels of training and degree credentials, regardless of race, are able to compete more successfully in the labor market for jobs and income. It is quite clear from the finance literature that additional years of schooling and additional degrees yield greater rates of return (Leslie and Brinkman, 1988). Thus, even though student borrowers with advanced degrees emerge from college with higher levels of debt, their investment generally enables them to enter careers that yield higher levels of income and make loan repayment more likely.

Recent research by Duncan (1994) found that family income differences eliminate most of the gap in years of schooling between Blacks and Whites. Thus, we anticipated that parent income and family support would be influential in our models of minority borrowers, but they are not. Whereas higher levels of parent education are associated with lower default rates for all three populations, parent income and family support while in college are not significant predictors of default behavior among African American nor among Hispanic borrowers. Parent education may be a more powerful variable than parent income, because education reflects certain values that transcend income (Coleman, 1988).

An ability to pay perspective also suggests that personal income levels would be highly significant in our models for minority groups, as well as for Whites, but they are not. We expected that 1986 income would be an influential variable, but we were surprised by its relative weakness. Since the database includes borrowers who left college beginning in the 1970s up through the mid-1980s, and since many of these loan defaults occurred during the 1970s, we suspect that 1986 income has a low relationship to the income at the time of default for many borrowers in the sample.

Our suspicion is confirmed by one of the more interesting and perhaps hopeful findings in this study: Two out of three defaulters had resumed payment at the time of the 1987 survey, and almost one third had completely repaid. This indicates that many earlier defaulters, especially those in the 1970s, had improved their situations and by 1987 were able to repay. Repayment after default strikes us as a phenomenon for fruitful additional study, especially since we observed the same racial/ethnic differences in loan repayment after default that we observed in the original default behavior. Asians are most likely to resume payment after default, followed by Whites. Blacks and Native Americans are least likely, followed by Hispanics.

We remain surprised that parent income does not have a more significant effect in explaining the default differences among racial groups. This result may be created by minority borrowers having both lower average parental incomes and smaller standard deviations in income compared to Whites. Nearly three fourths of the Black and Hispanic borrowers in this study come from families at the two lowest levels of income, compared to less than 50% of White borrowers. These significant differences suppress the mediating influence of parental income between models, especially with the smaller sample sizes. Another problem with parent income is that it may not be reported accurately by students. For example, there is some evidence that low-income Hispanics and other disadvantaged minorities are least likely to report parent income accurately (Olivas, 1986).

The literature also suggests that parent income, especially for minorities, does not sufficiently capture significant differences in family wealth and access to beneficial social and occupational networks. For example, Blau and Graham (1990) found that young Black families hold only about 18% of the wealth of young White families, even controlling for current income and other demographic variables. In addition, Coleman (1988) indicates that occupational and economic attainment is also a function of the cultural and social capital of the family. A strong family support system provides the student with an advantage in educational and occupational attainment, and Black, Hispanic, and American Indian families may lack these connections to a greater extent than Whites and Asians. The research evidence suggests that prejudice and segregation and separatism, both inside and outside minority group communities, acts to reduce the cultural and information networks that provide access to occupational opportunities (Coleman, 1988). In his longitudinal panel study, Duncan (1994) found that both neighborhood and family characteristics are significant contributors to differences in years of schooling among racial groups. With networks that are less rich and diverse, African American and Hispanic (and, for that matter, Native American) borrowers may have constricted educational and career opportunities, and therefore, a higher propensity to default, regardless of ability and parent income. Thus, colleges and universities that serve these students should consider the need for additional career counseling and placement services to fill gaps in their social and occupational networks, and to lower their default rates.

IMPLICATIONS FOR POLICY AND PRACTICE

The practical and policy implications of our study are complex because they reveal paradoxical clashes between the values, goals, and policies of public subsidy, educational opportunity, cost-effective investment, and institutional accountability. On the one hand, our models provide ample evidence that important aspects of the current system are functioning as they were designed. Students from low-income families are able to borrow, and if they earn good grades and stay in school to degree completion, the research suggests, they are likely to repay their loans and avoid default. Thus, the cycle of poverty is broken. On the other hand, if students do not perform well academically, and, worse, if they do not complete their degree programs, the return on their investment drops and they are less likely to be able to repay their loans. In fact, the additional indebtedness may be a heavy burden. The federal government gives the campus a keen interest in how this all turns out for the student by holding institutions accountable for their former students who default.

Campus enrollment management and financial aid programs appear to be in a struggle for the right balance between survival and accountability. Here's the enrollment management dilemma: On the one hand, campuses need student enrollments (and the revenue that comes with them) in a competitive system where about 3,000 accredited institutions of higher education (and thousands more proprietary schools) admit over 80% of their applicants (Volkwein, 1994). Thus, most students have a choice of institutions to attend because most, though not all, campuses have an economic self-interest in admitting a huge proportion of their applicants as a matter of simple survival.

On the other hand, many applicants have poor records of prior achievement and are not good risks for acceptable academic performance and graduation. Poor academic performance is the number one reason for student departure, and departure before degree completion is the number one reason for loan default. Depending on the year, the correlation coefficients between the percent of freshman applicants admitted and the retention and graduation rates are in the −.61 to −.75 range (the lower the proportion admitted, the higher the graduation rate). Retention and graduation correlations with average SAT scores are even higher, in the .71 to .85 range (Volkwein, 1994). Maintaining selective admissions standards, therefore, is a viable enrollment management and loan default reduction strategy, since it generally produces higher persistence and graduation rates. Moreover, faculty have concerns about academic standards that are usually reflected in pressures for selective admissions. Colleges and universities thus experience Janusian pressures both to admit more students and to become more selective.

The federal government is a paradoxical partner in this enterprise because it not only allows but encourages institutions, in the name of educational opportunity and human capital investment, to give loans to students who are poor risks (both educationally and economically), while simultaneously putting accountability pressure on the very institutions that serve these risky borrowers. Concerns about high levels of default have led the federal government to include high default rates as "triggers" for loss of federal grant and loan programs. Accordingly, default rates above 40% in 1 year or 25% over 3 years exclude institutions from qualifying for federal aid. This national policy assumes that default rates are under institutional control, but our results show that personal factors substantially outweigh institutional ones. Thus, financial aid officers and enrollment managers find themselves caught in a national clash of values between public subsidy and accountability.

The current federal obsession with graduation rates and student loan defaults as performance measures under "Student Right to Know" legislation seems rather crude, but it may work if it encourages campuses to improve academically and to become more thoughtful and selective in admissions. Institutions obviously have more influence upon the academic achievement and persistence of their borrowers than they do upon their race or sex or family size or marriages. Our models suggest that campuses can best assist their student borrowers by creating a climate that promotes good academic performance, encourages study in both pure and applied scientific disciplines, and ensures student degree completion. To the extent that colleges and universities can foster behavior that leads to student learning and skill attainment (reflected in good grades), and to student degree completion, they are likely to observe higher repayment and lower default rates among their former students. This may require campuses to strengthen academic degree programs and support services, including child care, that are responsive to the labor market and that give students needed skills (Volkwein & Szelest, 1995).

Although admissions selectivity and academic support services may be improvements leading to higher graduation and loan repayment rates, the frustrating fact is that a great deal of loan default behavior results from factors that are clearly beyond campus control, such as broken marriages and dependent children. Thus, another public paradox: Institutions are held accountable for loan default behavior, some proportion of which is a consequence of both educational openness and government encouragement, and a large proportion of which is related to factors for which individual borrowers rather than institutions should be held accountable, especially when it occurs years after students have left the campus.

The banking industry protects investors' money by using criteria to screen out risky borrowers, but the student aid program does the opposite by using tax revenue largely to serve risky borrowers. This is a delicate problem, because if hospital trauma centers were penalized for having higher than average death rates, they would likely reduce or eliminate the admission of trauma-injury patients (Volkwein and Szelest, 1995). Since it is illegal to deny federal loans (or even to vary the amount) to students based on such factors as sex or race or academic ability, the admissions decision (rather than the student loan decision) is likely to be the point at which institutions attempt to predict and control graduation rates and loan repayment prospects. The danger is that campuses will begin to search for overly simplistic admissions indicators, such as race and poverty, that may predict and screen out likely dropouts and loan defaulters. Such understandable campus action would diminish educational opportunity for many deserving students and would contradict the central purpose of the student loan program, which is to increase access to higher education, not deny it. Thus, one government policy, aimed at holding campuses responsible for loan default, may have the unintended consequence of undermining another government policy, aimed at interrupting the cycle of poverty in America.

NOTE

1. The 1987 NPSAS database includes over 11,000 nationally representative borrowers who began attending a higher education institution between 1973 and 1985 and who participated in the Guaranteed Student Loan (now Stafford) program. NPSAS-87 contains data from the Student Loan Recipient Survey (SLRS), as well as transcript and financial information; but not all data is available for every case (a requirement for logistic regression analysis).

We found relatively complete transcript and survey data in NPSAS on 6,338 out-of-school student aid recipients. This database includes information about student personal, demographic, and family characteristics, data reflecting financial and occupational information, and academic records from college transcripts. The borrowers attended over 1,400 different institutions of higher education ranging from private for-profit institutions and community colleges to professional schools and research universities. Of the 6,338 "good cases" in our NPSAS-87 data set, 1,219 (19.2%) officially defaulted on their loans and 5,119 either paid in full or were in repayment with their loans in good standing. We were able to find 6,087 cases with complete information for every variable. (A more detailed description of the NPSAS-87 population and methodology is available in the User's Manual [National Center for Educational Statistics, 1989].)

REFERENCES

American Bankers Association. (1994). *Consumer credit delinquency bulletin*, Washington, DC: American Bankers Association.
Astin, A. W. (1982). *Minorities in American higher education*, San Francisco: Jossey-Bass.

Astin, A. W. (1993). *What matters in college: Four critical years revisited.* San Francisco, CA: Jossey-Bass.

Bean, J. (1980). Dropouts and turnover: The synthesis and test of a causal model of student attrition. *Research in higher education 12*(2), 155–187.

Bean, J. (1985). Interaction effects based on class level in an explanatory model of college student dropout syndrome. *American Educational Research Journal, 22* (1), 35–64.

Becker, G. (1964). *Human capital: A theoretical and empirical analysis with special references to education.* New York: Colombia University Press.

Biglan, A. (1973a). The characteristics of subject matter in different academic areas. *Journal of Applied Psychology 57*(3), 195–203.

Biglan, A. (1973b). Relationships between subject matter characteristics and the structure and output of university departments. *Journal of Applied Psychology 57*(3), 204–213.

Blau, F. D., & Graham, J. W. (1990). Black–White differences in wealth and asset composition. *Quarterly Journal of Economics, 104,* 321–339.

Cabrera, A. F. (1994). Logistic regression analysis in higher education: An applied perspective. In J. C. Smart (Ed.), *Higher education: Handbook of theory and research,* (Volume X). New York: Agathon Press.

Cabrera, A. F., Stampen, O. J. & Hansen, W. L. (1990). Exploring the effects of ability to pay on persistence in college. *Review of Higher Education 13*(3), 303–336.

Cabrera, A. F., Castañeda, M. B., Nora, A. & Hengstler, D. (1992). The convergence between two theories of college persistence. *The Journal of Higher Education 63*(2), 143–164.

Cabrera, A. F., Nora, A. & Castañeda, M. B. (1993). College persistence: Structural equations modeling test of an integrated model of student retention. *The Journal of Higher Education 64*(2), 123–139.

Cabrera, A. F., Nora, A. & Castañeda, M. B. (1992). The role of finances in the persistence process: A structural model. *Research in Higher Education 33*(5), 571–593.

Coleman, J. S. (1988). Social capital in the creation of human capital. *American Journal of Sociology, 94* (Suppl.), 95–120.

College Board (1995). *Trends in student aid 1985 to 1995.* Washington, DC: Author.

College Board (1992). *Washington research report* (No. 2). Washington, DC: Author.

Duncan, G. T. (1994). Families and neighbors as sources of disadvantage in the schooling decisions of white and black adolescents. *American Journal of Education, 103,* 20–53.

Dyl, E. A., & McGann, F. (1977). Discriminant analysis of student loan applications. *Journal of Student Financial Aid, 7*(3), 35–40.

Dynarski, M. (1994). Who defaults on student loans? Findings from the National Postsecondary Student Aid Study. *Economics of Education, 13*(1), 55–68.

Feinberg, S. E. (1983). *The analysis of cross-classified categorical data* (rev. ed.). Cambridge, MA: Massachusetts Institute of Technology.

Flint, T. A. (1994). The federal student loan default cohort: A case study. *Journal of Student Financial Aid, 24*(1), 13–30.

Freeman, R. (1976). *The over-educated American*. Orlando, FL: Academic Press.

Gray, K. S. (1985). Can student loan default be forecast accurately? *Journal of Student Financial Aid, 15*(1), 31–41.

Greene, L. L. (1989). An economic analysis of student loan default. *Educational Evaluation and Policy Analysis, 11*, 61–68.

Hall, R. H. (1991). *Organizations: Structures, processes and outcomes* (5th ed.). Englewood, NJ: Prentice-Hall, Inc.

Hearn, J. C. (1984). The relative roles of academic, ascribed, socioeconomic characteristics in college destination. *Sociology of Education, 57*, 22–30.

Hearn, J. C. (1991). Academic and non-academic influences on the college destinations of 1980 high-school graduates. *Sociology of Education, 63*(4), 158–171.

Hearn, J. C. (1992). Emerging variations in postsecondary attendance patterns. *Research in Higher Education, 33*(6), 657–688.

Hearn, J. C. (1993). The paradox of growth in federal aid for college students, 1965–1990. In J. C. Smart, (Ed.), *Higher Education Handbook of Theory and Research*, Vol. IX (pp. 94–153). New York: Agathon Press.

Kerr, C. (1966). *The uses of the university*. New York: Harper & Row.

Knapp, L. G., & Seaks, T. G. (1992). An analysis of the probability of default on federally guaranteed student loans. *Review of Economics and Statistics, 74*, 404–411.

Lein, L., Rickards, R., & Webster, J. (1993). Student loan defaulters compared with repayers: A Texas case study. *Journal of Student Financial Aid, 23*(1), 29–39.

Leslie, L. L., & Brinkman, P. T. (1988). *The economic value of higher education*. San Francisco: Jossey-Bass.

Lewis, G. L. (1989). Trends in student aid: 1963–64 to 1988–89. *Research in Higher Education, 30*(6), 547–561.

Manski, C. F. & Wise, D. A. (1983). *College choice in America*. Cambridge, MA.: Harvard University Press.

Mortenson, T. (1989). Attitudes toward educational loans. *Journal of Student Financial Aid, 19*(3), 38–51.

Mortimer, K. P. (1972). *Accountability in higher education*. Washington, DC: American Association for Higher Education. ASHE/ERIC Report #1.

Mortgage Bankers Association of America. (1994). *National delinquency survey*, Washington, DC: Author.

Mow, S. L., & Nettles, M. T. (1990). Minority student access to, and persistence and performance in, college: A review of the trends and research literature. In J. C. Smart, (Ed.), *Higher Education Handbook of Theory and Research*, Vol. VI, (pp. 35–105). New York: Agathon Press.

Myers G. & Siera, S. (1980). Development and validation of discriminant analysis models for student loan defaultees. *Journal of Student Financial Aid, 10*(1), 9–17.

National Center for Education Statistics (1989). *1987 National postsecondary student aid study: Data file user's manual*. Washington, DC: Westat.

Nettles, M. T., Thoeny, A. R., & Gosman, E. J. (1986). Comparative and predictive analyses of black and white students' college achievement and experiences. *Journal of Higher Education, 57*(3), 289–318.

Nora, A. (1987). Determinants of retention among Chicano students: A structural model. *Research in Higher Education, 26*(1), 31–59.

Nora, A., Attinasi, L. C. & Matonack, A. (1990). Testing qualitative indicators of college factors in Tinto's attrition model: A community college student population. *Review of Higher Education, 13*(3), 337–356.

Olivas, M. A. (1985). Financial aid packaging policies: Access and ideology. *Journal of Higher Education, 56*, 462–475.

Olivas, M. A. (1986). Financial aid self-reports by disadvantaged students: The importance of being earnest. *Research in Higher Education, 25*(3), 245–252.

Pascarella, E. T., & Terenzini, P. T. (1982). Contextual analysis as A method for assessing residence group effects. *Journal of College Student Personnel, 23*, 108–114.

Pascarella, E. T., & Terenzini, P. T. (1991). *How college affects students: Findings and insights from twenty years of research,* San Francisco: Jossey-Bass.

Pedhazur, E. (1982). *Multiple regression in behavioral research: Explanation and prediction* (2nd ed.). New York: Holt, Rinehart & Winston.

St. John, E. P. (1992). Workable models for institutional research on the impact of student financial aid. *Journal of Student Financial Aid, 22*(3), 13–26.

St. John, E. P. (1994). What really influences minority attendance? Sequential analyses of the high school and beyond sophomore cohort. *Research in Higher Education, 32*(2), 141–158.

St. John, E. P., & Noell, J. (1989). The effects of student financial aid on access to higher education: An analysis of progress with special consideration of minority enrollment. *Research in Higher Education, 30*(6), 563–582.

Sanford, T. R. (1980). The effects of student aid on recent college graduates. *Research in Higher Education, 12*(3), 227–243.

Sewell, W., & Shah, V. P. (1978). Social class, parental encouragement, and educational aspirations. *American Journal of Sociology, 3*, 559–572.

Stage, F. K. (1990). LISREL: An introduction and applications in higher education. In J. C. Smart (Ed.). *Higher education: Handbook of theory and research,* VI (pp. 427–466). New York: Agathon Press.

Stampen, J. O., & Cabrera, A. F. (1986). Exploring the effects of student aid on attrition. *Journal of Financial Aid, 2*, 28–39.

Stockham, D. H., & Hesseldenz, J. S. (1979). Predicting national direct student loan defaults: Role of personality data. *Research in Higher Education, 10*(3), 195–205.

Stoecker, J. L. (1993). The Biglan classification revisited. *Research in Higher Education, 34*(4), 451–464.

Terenzini, P. T., Theophildes, C., & Lorang, W. G. (1984). Influences on students' perceptions of their academic skill development during college. *Journal of Higher Education, 55*(5), 621–636.

Terenzini, P. T. & Wright, T. M. (1987). Influences on students' academic growth during four years of college. *Research in Higher Education, 26*(2), 161–170.

Tinto, V. (1975). Dropout from higher education A theoretical synthesis of recent research. *Review of Educational Research, 45,* 89–125.

Tinto, V. (1987). *Leaving college: Rethinking the causes and cures of student attrition.* Chicago: University of Chicago Press.

Trusheim, D. (1994). How valid is self-reported financial aid information? *Research in Higher Education, 35*(3), 335–348.

U.S. Department of Education (1978). *Predicting default and bankruptcy: Factors affecting the repayment status of student loans.* Washington, DC: U.S. Government Printing Office.

Volkwein, J. F. (1991). Improved measures of academic and social integration and their association with measures of student growth. Paper presented at the Annual Meeting for the Association for the Study of Higher Education, Boston, MA.

Volkwein, J. F. (1994). Campus culture and politics. Workshop materials prepared for the AIR Summer Institute, University at Albany, State University of New York.

Volkwein, J. F., & Carbone, D. A. (1994). The impact of departmental research and teaching climates on undergraduate growth and satisfaction. *Journal of Higher Education, 65*(2), 147–167.

Volkwein, J. F., Cabrera, A. F., Szelest, B. P., and Napierski-Prancl, M. R. (1998). Factors associated with student loan default among different racial and ethnic groups. *Journal of Higher Education, 69*(2) (March/April).

Volkwein, J. F., King, M. C., & Terenzini, P. T. (1986). Student-Faculty Relationships and Intellectual Growth Among Transfer Students. *Journal of Higher Education, 57*(4), 413–430.

Volkwein, J. F., & Szelest, B. P. (1995). Individual and campus characteristics associated with student loan default. *Research in Higher Education, 36*(1), 41–72.

Volkwein, J. F., Szelest, B. P., & Lizotte, A. J. (1995). The relationship of campus crime to campus and student Characteristics. *Research in Higher Education, 36*(6), 647–670.

Wilcox, L. (1991). Evaluating the impact of financial aid on student recruitment and retention. In D. Hossler (Ed.), *New Directions For Institutional Research No. 70* (pp. 47–60). San Francisco: Jossey-Bass.

Wilms, W. W., Moore, R. W., & Bolus, R. E. (1987). Whose fault is default? *Educational Evaluation and Policy Analysis, 9*(1), 41–54.

Yates, D. (1982). *Bureaucratic democracy: The search for democracy and efficiency in American government.* Cambridge, MA: Harvard University Press.

CHAPTER 8

Trade School Defaults: Proprietary Schools and the Federal Family Educational Loan Program

Michael D. Coomes

The Subcommittee investigation uncovered overwhelming evidence that the GSLP [Guaranteed Student Loan Program], as it relates to proprietary schools, is riddled with fraud, waste, and abuse, and is plagued by substantial misman-agment and incompetence. Despite the acknowledged contributions of well-intentioned, competent, and honest individuals and institutions comprising the large majority of GSLP participants, unscrupulous, inept, and dishonest elements among them have flourished throughout the 1980s.

(S. Rep. No. 102-58, 1991)

Perhaps more than any other single event, the investigation of fraud and abuse in the Guaranteed Student Loan (GSL) program by the Senate Permanent Subcommittee on Investigations of the Committee on Governmental Affairs under the direction of Senator Sam Nunn brought to light problems facing the GSL program and participation in that program by proprietary schools. Although numerous federal and state agencies had issued reports noting a similar finding, the attention paid to the program by a Senate Committee not normally charged with the oversight of student aid added substantial weight to claims that the GSL program was in serious trouble and that many of the problems with the program were directly linked to the participation of proprietary schools. That watershed event was to set in motion a series of government interventions that would, by 1996, result in significant changes in the GSL program, changes that would enable the U.S. Department of Education ([USDOE], 1996a) to report that

U.S. Secretary of Education Richard W. Riley today announced that the national student loan default rate has been cut almost in half, from 22.4% three years ago to 11.6% in the most recent year, due in part, he said, to the U.S. Department of Education's aggressive accountability and collection efforts.

The new rate released today marks the greatest one-year percentage drop since official student loan default reporting began with the fiscal year (FY) 1988 rate. (p. 1)

Although not all of the reductions to the nation's Federal Family Education Loan Program (FFELP) default rate could be attributable to changes in the ways loans were made and managed by proprietary schools, a significant portion of those reductions could be directly tied to reductions in defaults by the proprietary sector. In this chapter, I will examine the changes in the FFELP that resulted in "the greatest one-year percentage drop since official student loan default reporting began," with particular emphasis on the status of proprietary education in the FFELP. To help in an understanding of the issues relevant to proprietary school participation in the FFELP, a brief overview of proprietary education will be offered, and the status of proprietary school participation in the FFELP during the late 1980s will be examined. Changes that have been instituted to address the issues raised by the Senate Permanent Subcommittee on Investigations and other critics of proprietary school participation in the FFELP will be discussed, and the impact of those changes on the viability of the FFELP will be explored. The chapter will conclude with recommendations intended to address continuing programmatic issues related to proprietary school participation in the FFELP. Two notes of clarification should be offered at the outset: (1) A number of terms have been used interchangeably to describe the proprietary institutions in American higher education, including for-profit occupational and trade schools, private career schools, and private vocational schools. For the sake of simplicity, in this chapter, I will refer to all private, for-profit schools as proprietary institutions or schools. (2) This paper will be addressed to issues related to the FFELP and not to the newer William D. Ford Direct Loan Program. Although many of the issues related to the operation of the two programs are similar, it is beyond the scope of this chapter to address them at any great length.

THE CONTEXT OF PROPRIETARY EDUCATION

A Short History of Proprietary Education

Described by Moore (1994) as "hardy weeds in the garden of academia" (p. 15), proprietary institutions have been in existence for nearly 300 years. As Lee and Merisotis (1990) pointed out, the first proprietary, or for-profit, trade school in the nation was probably a home study course in shorthand offered by Caleb Phil in Boston in 1728. Early proprietary education expanded quickly in the early 1800s as the need for trained clerks and bookkeepers grew in a rapidly expanding industrial and entrepreneurial nation. Cincinnati, Philadelphia, Pittsburgh, New York, and St. Louis all saw the development of private business schools in the early 1800s (Lee & Merisotis, 1990). Increases in the numbers of schools and enrolled students continued through the 1920s with an estimated post–World War I enrollment high of 336,032 (Lee & Merisotis, 1990).

Proprietary school growth would accelerate significantly at the end of World War II with the passage of the Serviceman's Readjustment Act of 1944 (GI Bill). That legislation would lead to extensive enrollment increases at both traditional colleges and at proprietary institutions. As Lee and Merisotis (1990) have noted:

> Nearly twice as many veterans chose enrollment in a vocational school than in a college or university. . . . The number of schools approved [for participation under the GI Bill] during this period [the 20 years following the end of World War II] rose from just over 3,000 to almost 9,000 with nearly all of the growth attributed to private career schools. (p. 10)

This rapid growth in the proprietary sector greatly assisted thousands of students who were able to secure better jobs as a result of the training they received. However, that rapid growth was also to reveal a pattern of abuse of governmental programs, in this case of the GI Bill. Uncontrolled and rapid growth was accompanied by falsified student records, programs that trained students for nonexistent careers, inflated materials charges, and programs that were purposefully lengthened to keep veterans enrolled (Fraas, 1990a; Lee & Merisotis, 1990). Many of these abuses would reemerge in the proprietary sector in the 1980s as it once again expanded in size through the use of the Guaranteed Student Loan Program as its primary fiscal engine.

Additional impetus would be added to the expansion of the proprietary sector with the passage of the National Vocational Student Loan Insurance (NSVLI) Act of 1965. The NSVLI, (P.L. 89–287) "established a program of Federal loan guarantees and direct loans for students to attend postsecondary business, trade, technical and other schools" (Fraas, 1990a, p. CRS-51). As others have noted (Fraas, 1990a; Lee & Merisotis, 1990) the conditions of the NSVLI program were very similar to those of the Guaranteed Student Loan Program, which had been created that same year through the Higher Education Act. By 1968, an estimated 262,000 students had received loans under the program and an estimated 4,000 schools were accredited for program participation (Fraas, 1990a). Although the program appeared to be working, in 1968 it was merged with the GSL program through the Higher Education Amendments of 1968 (P.L. 90–575). Those amendments enabled students attending proprietary institutions to participate in the National Defense Student Loan Program (NDSL; currently the Federal Perkins Loan Program) and the College Work Study program (CWS). In an attempt to address concerns about abusive practices of the GI Bill by proprietary schools, Congress included in the legislation requirements that proprietary schools could not admit non–high school graduates, had to be in existence for a minimum of 2 years prior to program participation, and "had to be accredited either by a nationally recognized accrediting body or by alternative accrediting organizations" (Fraas, 1990a, p. CRS-55).

The passage of the Education Amendments of 1972 (P.L. 92–318), legislation characterized as "a measure of staggering comprehensiveness, easily the longest federal education statute in history" (Gladieux & Wolanin, 1976, p. 230) would further expand the federal student aid programs through the creation of the Basic Educational Opportunity Grant program (BEOG; currently the Federal Pell Grant Program). This "entitlement" program of federal need-based grants was intended to serve as the foundation for a student's financial aid award. In addition to the creation of the BEOG program, the Education Amendments of 1972 created the State Student Incentive Grant program, expanded the GSL program to include students from middle-class families, created the Student Loan Marketing Association (Sallie Mae), and created a program of direct aid to institutions (a program that was authorized but never funded) (Coomes, 1994; Federal Education Programs, 1973; Moore, 1983). Of particular importance to this discussion, the Education Amendments of 1972 made proprietary institutions "full partners with traditional higher education institutions in the receipt of student aid" (Lee & Merisotis, 1990, p. 13).

Following passage of the Education Amendments of 1972, subsequent legislation would influence proprietary schools in a variety of ways. In 1978, nonhigh school graduates who could demonstrate an ability to benefit from a postsecondary education were made eligible for all federal student aid programs. This provision greatly benefited the proprietary sector, for it traditionally enrolled more ability-to-benefit students than did other types of institutions (Fraas, 1990a). In 1987, proprietary school students became eligible to participate in the Supplemental Loans for Students (SLS) program. In 1989, following concerns that the SLS program had grown to quickly and was not meeting its original policy goals, changes were enacted to prohibit students from participating in the program if their institutions demonstrated high cohort default rates. Many of the institutions barred from participating in the SLS program were proprietary schools (Fraas, 1990a). The SLS program was subsequently merged with the unsubsidized Stafford Loan program (USDOE, 1995).

Current Status of Proprietary Education

The proprietary sector is better described by qualitative descriptors than by quantitative statistics. The former provide insight into to the purpose and unique characteristics of proprietary education, the latter, in all likelihood, provide only a rough approximation of the sector's size and complexity. Although this section will focus on qualitatively describing proprietary education, it will also offer some quantitative data on the sector as a whole.

Moore (1994) has identified a number of common characteristics of proprietary schools and the proprietary sector. The first of these is the dual mission of educational institution and profit-making business. Because of the need to be profitable, proprietary schools tend to be much more flexible than traditional colleges in their ability to respond to changes in the external environment:

> The sector as a whole is perpetually in flux. Just getting an accurate count of schools is close to impossible. Schools open and close daily. They enter and leave the student aid system constantly. Schools and entire chains are bought and sold on a brisk market. Schools branch, merge with others and close rapidly, new programs are added, and existing programs are dropped frequently, all in response to market demand. (p. 15)

Other factors that distinguish proprietary schools are their high degree of decentralization, a commitment to efficiency that results in increased profitability, and a strong reliance on federal student aid as a source of important revenue (Moore, 1994). The emphasis on decentralization means that even in schools that are part of larger chains, local administrators (who frequently are school owners) have significant autonomy to structure curriculum, determine resource allocation, and make institutional policy decisions in response to changes in the local labor market (Lee & Merisotis, 1990). The bottom line for proprietary schools is the bottom line. Considerations that shape the missions of other sectors of higher education (e.g., preservation and transmission of culture, basic research, the centrality of learning as evidenced in the liberal arts) play only a secondary role, if any role at all, in the proprietary sector. Proprietary schools are about training, and not education. Students have traditionally sought out proprietary schools to seek training for specific careers and not for an education that leads to such lofty, and frequently nebulous, goals as lifelong learning, critical thinking, or community involvement. These are the responsibilities of the 4-year college, not the proprietary school.

As Moore (1994) pointed out, the proprietary sector is highly dynamic, making any assessment of its size and scope problematic. For the 1993 academic year, the National Center for Education Statistics estimated that there were 10,601 postsecondary institutions in the United States (USDOE, 1994). Of that number, 5,529 (52.2%) were classified as private, for-profit institutions. Estimated numbers of proprietary schools at other points in time are 6,512 in 1974, 5,676 in 1980, 5,509 in 1982, and 6,200 in 1989 (Apling & Aleman, 1990). Of the 5,529 proprietary schools in existence in 1992–93, 146 (2.6%) were classified as having programs 4 years or longer in duration, 740 (13.4%) were classified as 2 years but less than 4 years in length, and 4,643 (80.7%) were classified as having programs of less than 2 years in length.

As noted above, proprietary schools are primarily involved with occupational training. Data from the 1988–89 *Institutional Characteristics Survey* (ICS) of the Integrated Postsecondary Education Data System (IPEDS88) indicated that 91% of all surveyed proprietary schools offered occupational programs. An examination of the types of training offered by proprietary schools discloses that personal services (e.g., cosmetology, barbering/hairstyling) accounted for 40% of all programs, followed by business and marketing (24%), technology (8%), health care (7%); trade and industry (7%); and transportation (5%). Nine percent of the programs could not be classified into any of the aforementioned program areas (Apling & Aleman, 1990). Examination of the programs by enrollment, reveals a different pattern. The largest proportion of students (42%) were enrolled in business and marketing programs, followed by technology (25%), personal services (14%), health (7%), other (5%), and transportation (<1%) (Apling & Aleman, 1990).

Because they receive no direct state or federal financial support, proprietary schools must be revenue driven. This results in high program costs when compared with other similar types of institutions. A 1988 study (Carroll, 1988) of proprietary schools disclosed that 76.8% of surveyed proprietary school students paid $1,500 or more in tuition and fees. That compared with 70.5% of the students attending private not-for-profit institutions, 27.9% of students at public, less-than-2-year institutions, and 7.2% at public 2-year colleges. Similarly, Apling and Aleman, (1990) reported on data collected from the National Postsecondary Student Aid Study (NPSAS) that the average full-year tuition and fees for students receiving student aid at proprietary schools was $3,700. Tuition and fee charges for vocational students attending public community colleges were $400. Net costs (i.e., total cost less all grant aid received) of the two student groups also differed substantially. Net costs for proprietary school students were $6,900; for vocational students attending public community colleges, those costs were $4,400, or 36% less (Apling & Aleman, 1990).

Establishing accurate enrollment data for proprietary schools is also problematic. The fluid nature of the proprietary sector and the short duration of programs results in a situation where making accurate counts of student populations is difficult. For the fall of 1993, the National Center for Education Statistics (Snyder & Hoffman, 1995) estimated, through the use of its Integrated Postsecondary Education Data System (IPEDS), that 747,957 students attended proprietary schools. This represented 4.8% of the 15,333,371 students enrolled in postsecondary education that fall. The IPEDS enrollment data for proprietary students in all likelihood is an underestimate of the number of students enrolled in proprietary schools in any given year. As Apling and Aleman (1990) noted:

> Fall enrollment underestimates the number of undergraduates who were ever enrolled during the school year. . . . This is particularly a problem in estimating students attending proprietary schools because these schools usually operate year round and more than one cohort of students often begins and completes a program during the year. (p. CRS-21)

Estimates of the numbers of students attending proprietary schools may not be totally accurate, but a rather complete picture of the characteristics of those students emerges from a number of reports (e.g., Apling & Aleman, 1990; Carroll, 1988; Lee & Merisotis, 1990; Tuma, Gifford, & Choy, 1989). Using data drawn from the High School and Beyond data base, Carroll characterized students attending proprietary schools as female (70.3%), primarily White (78.8%), and from high school vocational programs (48.4%). When compared with students at other types of institutions (i.e., private not-for-profit schools, public 2-year colleges, and public institutions offering less-than-2-year programs) some difference did emerge that distinguished the proprietary school student. Whereas the proportion of students of color at all institutions was basically the same (it ranged from 21.2% at proprietary schools to a low of 15.3% at private not-for-profit schools), the proportion of African American students, 15.2%, was highest at proprietary schools. This compares with 11.7% at not-for-profit private schools, 11.1% at public, less-than-2-year schools, and 9.1% at public 2-year institutions (Carroll, 1988).

Similar findings are presented by Apling and Aleman (1990) through an analysis of the National Postsecondary Student Aid Study (NPSAS). According to fall 1986 NPSAS data, proprietary school students were predominately women (65%), financially independent (54%), poor (24% of dependent students came from families with incomes under $10,000; 56% of independent students earned less than $10,000), and more likely to be members of a minority group (39%) than their counterparts nationally (22%). However, Apling and Aleman also pointed out that although the proprietary sector tends to enroll larger numbers of minority students, it enrolls a "relatively modest proportion of all minority and low income students attending postsecondary institutions" (p. CRS-22). For example, fall 1986 enrollment nationwide was estimated at 11,186,000; of these students approximately 22% were classified as minorities. Proprietary schools for that same period enrolled an estimated 9% of the total number of minority students enrolled nationally (Apling & Aleman, 1990).

With regard to financial aid, the 1986 NPSAS data set disclosed that 84% of proprietary school students received some type of financial aid (grants or loans). This compares with 56% of students at all postsecondary institutions; 65% of students at 4-year private colleges, 54% at 4-year public colleges, and 28% of students at 2-year public colleges (Tuma, Gifford, & Choy, 1989). The two primary types of assistance for proprietary schools students were guaranteed student loans and Pell grants. Sixty-seven percent of proprietary school students received a GSL compared with 20% of students at all postsecondary institutions, 35% of students at 4-year private colleges, 21% at 4-year public colleges, and 6% of students at 2-year public colleges. Among proprietary school students, 47% participated in the Pell Grant program. Participation rates for students at other institutions for the same time period were all postsecondary institutions, 17%; 4-year private colleges, 16%; 4-year public colleges, 19%; and 2-year public colleges, 12% (Tuma, Gifford, & Choy, 1989). Analyses of both the NPSAS data base (Tuma, Gifford, & Choy, 1989) and the High School and Beyond (HSB) data set (Carroll, 1988) disclosed that proprietary students not only participated to a greater extent in the GSL program than did students at other types of institutions, they also tended to secure larger average loans to finance their education. According the 1986 NPSAS data, proprietary schools students borrowed an average of $2,347 under the GSL program; this was the highest average loan amount for students at any type of postsecondary institution. The next highest average amount was $2,283 for students at 4-year private colleges. Students at 2-year, public, vocational institutions had the lowest average GSL—$1,958. Using data contained in the HSB data set, Carroll found that nearly one quarter (24.9%) of all proprietary school students secured student loans in excess of $2,500. This compares with 20.8% for students at private not-for-profit schools, 12.1% for students attending public less than two year institutions, and 4.1% for public 2-year students. A partial explanation for the strong dependence on loans by proprietary schools students may be the increased cost of attendance at these institutions (Carroll, 1988).

The picture that emerges of proprietary student is that of a low-income female student, highly dependent on federal sources of aid for assistance in meeting educational cost, and who, in substantial numbers, is a member of a minority group. As will be established shortly, all of these factors will play a role in explaining the high default rates of proprietary school students.

PROPRIETARY EDUCATION AND FFELP:
NATURE OF THE ISSUES

The viability of proprietary education became a significant policy problem in the 1980s as a result of three issues: (1) the growing levels of defaulted guaranteed student loans incurred by students attending proprietary schools, (2) prominently reported cases of fraud and abuse by owners and managers of proprietary schools, and (3) underregulation of the proprietary sector by accrediting agencies, state coordinating boards, and the Department of Education. The primary focus of this section will be on the nature of borrowing and default patterns in the GSL program during the 1980s. However, since the other two issues are related to, and perhaps partial causes of increases in defaults at proprietary schools in the 1980s, they will be briefly discussed as well.

GSL Defaults and Proprietary Students

A number of factors converged in the 1970s and 1980s to bring the issue of the costs of the guaranteed student loan program, and specifically default costs incurred by proprietary school students, to the attention of policy makers and the public. Briefly, some of those issues included

1. The modification of the goals of the GSL program from a program originally intended to assist middle-income students to one that became open to all students, thus making it a primary source of assistance for lower-income students.
2. The steady state of funding for the federal grant programs (most specifically the Pell Grant program) coupled with rapidly increasing college costs resulting in a growing need gap that could only be filled for many students through increased reliance on the GSL program.
3. The creation of a loan industry consisting of lenders, institutions, state guarantee agencies, and secondary markets (such as the Higher Education Assistance Foundation and Sally Mae) that all had an important stake in seeing the GSL program expand.
4. The entitlement nature of the program, whereby any student who meets the eligibility requirements is "'entitled,' to all program benefits au-

thorized by the law. The program's statutory authorization constitutes a binding obligation for the Federal Government to pay the beneficiary full benefits." (Fraas, 1988, p. CRS-21)

5. The passage of the Education Amendments of 1972, which authorized full participation by proprietary schools in the federal Title IV student aid program.

All of these factors converged to ensure that the GSL program would experience significant growth during the decade of the 1980s. Some of those factors, particularly the last one, would lead to a concomitant increase in defaults during that same time period. In Fiscal Year (FY) 1980, total loan volume for the then–Guaranteed Student Loan Program totaled $4.8 billion, by FY 1989 total loan volume reached an estimated $12.2 billion (Fraas, 1989). During that same period, annual costs for defaulted loans increased from $263 million to $1.91 billion (Fraas, 1990b). For FY 1991, it was estimated that defaulted student loans would cost the government $2.4 billion. An examination of the proportion of loans in default, as opposed to the dollar amount defaulted, yields a slightly different picture. Traditionally, the Department of Education has utilized two different default measures: gross default rate and net default rate.

> The gross default rate is the cumulative dollar amount of default claims paid to lenders since the inception of GSLs divided by the cumulative dollar amount of loans that ever entered repayment, or "matured." The net default rate reduces the cumulative default claims paid by any funds recovered through collections, and this number is divided by cumulative matured loans. (Fraas, 1990b)

An examination of gross default rates indicates a steady increase from FY 1966 (7.1%) to FY 1980, when the rate reached 12.5%. During the early 1980s, the gross default rate hovered around the 12% figure, but began to inch up slowly as the total federal obligation for defaults increased. By FY 1990, when obligations for defaults reached an all-time high of $2.4 billion, the gross default rate also reached an all-time high of 14.9%. Fiscal Year 1990 also represented the highest level of net defaults (10%) since the previous high of 10.1% in FY 1980 (Fraas, 1990b).

Since publication of default reduction regulations in 1989, the primary vehicle for reporting defaults under the FFELP has been the cohort default rate. "The cohort default rate for a given year is the ratio of the number of borrowers in default to the number of borrowers in repayment" (USDOE, 1996b, p. 3). Borrowers in default are defined as borrowers who "entered repayment in an applicable fiscal year (October 1 through September 30) and defaulted on their loans either that year *or the subsequent year*" (p. 2). Borrowers in repayment include all borrowers who entered repayment during the applicable fiscal year. Utilizing the cohort default rate has allowed policy makers to (1) be able to make effective comparisons across different fiscal years, (2) make comparisons between different types of institutions, and (3) establish benchmarks for continued participation in the FFELP.

As did federal obligations for defaulted loans and gross and net default rates, the total cohort default rate saw substantial increases during the late 1980s. The total cohort default rate was calculated at 17.2% in FY 1988, rose to 21.4% in FY 1989, and peaked at 22.4% in FY 1990. Since FY 1990, the cohort default rate has decreased steadily to 17.8% in FY 1991, 15.0% in FY 1992, and 11.6% in FY 1993, the most current year for cohort default rate calculations (USDOE, n.d., 1996b). Table 8.1 presents detailed information on cohort default rates for Fiscal Years 1990, 1991, 1992, and 1993. Factors that led to the moderation of defaults since 1990 will be explored in a subsequent section.

As noted earlier, a major contributing factor to the increases in defaulted loans during the late 1980s was increased participation by proprietary schools in the Guaranteed Student Loan Program. Although the total number of proprietary programs participating in the GSL program is open to conjecture, one fact is clear. Defaulted loans by proprietary school students constituted, and still constitute, a significant proportion of total defaults. According to Fraas (1990a) approximately 40% of proprietary school borrowers default, compared with 25% of borrowers at public community colleges and 10% of borrowers attending 4-year institutions. The U.S. General Accounting Office (GAO) in a series of reports issued between 1988 and 1991 consistently found proprietary schools and proprietary school students to have higher default rates than other institutions and students. For example, a 1989 GAO report indicated that 39% of borrowers at proprietary schools were in default on their loans. This compared with 25% of borrowers at 2-year public colleges, 20% of borrowers at 2-year private colleges, and 10% of borrowers at 4-year both public and private colleges. The scope of defaults at proprietary schools is particularly problematic when one realizes that, when compared with 4-year institutions, there are fewer proprietary schools.

Table 8.2 presents a summary of nine different studies that have attempted to identify factors related to default within the Federal Family Education Loan Program. These studies, which utilize a wide range of statistical analyses as well as a number of different data bases, present some remarkably consistent findings. Factors that are consistently related to, or are predictive of, default are

(1) proprietary/vocational school attendance (9 studies);
(2) failure to persist in a designated course of study (7 studies);
(3) low income, either the student's or in the case of dependent students, the student's parents (7 studies);
(4) the students race (4 studies); and
(5) small loan amounts (3 studies).

These findings are supported by a 1991 GAO meta-analysis that reviewed 12 previously published default studies (only one of those studies, Wilms, Moore, and Bolus [1987] is included in the analysis presented in Table 8.2). The GAO report noted nine characteristics of students likely to default:

(1) attendance at vocational/proprietary institutions (12 studies),
(2) low income status (11 studies),
(3) little or no financial support from others (8 studies),
(4) borrowing small amounts (7 studies),
(5) failure to complete required program of study (6 studies),
(6) attending academic programs of less than one year in duration (6 studies),
(7) minority background of borrower (3 studies),
(8) unemployed at the time of default (2 studies), and
(9) lack of a high school diploma (1 study).

The GAO (1991) noted that the reviewed studies found default rates for students attending proprietary schools that ranged from 29% to 62%.

Obviously, a number of the factors associated with the high rate of default among proprietary school students are interrelated. As noted above in the discussion of the characteristics of proprietary school students, proprietary schools enroll higher percentages of women, racial minorities, and low-income students. In addition, proprietary schools, by their very nature, emphasize short program lengths (frequently under one year), and have traditionally enrolled large numbers of ability-to-benefit students (i.e., students who have not earned a high school diploma or GED certificate, but who have been deemed by the institution as demonstrating the ability to benefit from a postsecondary education). When these characteristics of proprietary schools and their students are taken into consideration, what emerges is a complex interplay of variables that makes predicting default quite difficult. As a matter of fact, the authors of two of the studies summarized in Table 8.2 have suggested that individual student characteristics are more predictive of default than are institutional characteristics. Wilms, Moore, and Bolus (1987) concluded:

TABLE 8.1. Federal Family Educational Loan Program Cohort Default Rates.

Type of Institution	Fiscal Year 1990					Fiscal Year 1991			
	Schools (n)	Borrowers Defaulted(n)	Borrowers Entered Repayment (n)	Borrower Default Rate (%)	Schools (n)	Borrowers Defaulted (n)	Borrowers Entered Repayment (n)	Borrower Default Rate (%)
Public 4-year	649	44,255	633,746	7.0	640	42,224	644,544	6.6
Public 2-year	1,465	35,620	207,405	17.2	1,429	30,629	207,283	14.8
Private 4-year	1,545	33,709	521,748	6.5	1,516	28,479	481,525	5.9
Private 2-year	859	9,556	51,617	18.5	826	6,703	45,098	14.9
Proprietary (all)	3,750	427,497	1,038,829	41.2	3,770	271,306	749,267	36.2
4-year +	48	6,486	40,453	16.0	65	7,118	39,248	18.1
2-4 years	452	61,161	196,728	31.1	483	45,803	161,565	28.3
< 2 years	3,250	359,850	801,648	44.9	3,222	218,387	548,454	39.8
Foreign	442	424	4,314	9.8	446	161	3,630	4.4
Unclassified	78	147	2,443	6.0	37	842	4,238	19.9
Total	8,788	551,208	2,460,102	22.4	8,664	380,346	2,135,595	17.8

Source: U.S. Department of Education (n.d., 1996b)

TABLE 8.1. Continued.

Type of Institution	Schools (n)	Fiscal Year 1992			Schools (n)	Fiscal Year 1993		
		Borrowers Defaulted (n)	Borrowers Entered Repayment (n)	Borrower Default Rate (%)		Borrowers Defaulted (n)	Borrowers Entered Repayment (n)	Borrower Default Rate (%)
Public 4-year	626	44,714	638,163	7.0	693	45,743	666,264	6.9
Public 2-year	1,397	30,474	209,660	14.5	1,407	31,309	215,991	14.5
Private 4-year	1,504	30,231	474,916	6.4	1,576	30,174	484,046	6.2
Private 2-year	779	6,444	44,963	14.3	753	5,800	42,957	13.5
Proprietary (all)	3,760	187,739	621,412	30.2	3,575	98,869	414,237	23.9
4-year +	70	8,630	44,021	19.6	80	7,312	39,858	18.3
2-4 years	496	39,646	156,847	25.3	419	24,654	112,034	22.0
< 2 years	3,194	139,463	420,544	33.2	3,076	66,903	262,345	25.5
Foreign	409	162	2,926	5.5	423	145	2,835	5.1
Unclassified	29	117	2,885	4.1	7	12	295	4.1
Total	8,504	299,881	1,994,925	15.0	8,434	212,052	1,826,625	11.6

Source: U.S. Department of Education (n.d., 1996b)

TABLE 8.2. A Comparison of Studies Examining Factors Associated with Default in the FFELP.

Study	Data Source	Unit of analysis	Sample size	Statistics	Factors Associated with Default	Relationship to Default
Wilms, Moore, & Bolus (1987)	Self-generated survey/California Student Aid Commission Records	Student borrowers	4,617	Descriptive/ Multivariate (Descriptive Function)	• Completed postsecondary program	-
					• Family income	-
					• Not US citizen	-
					• High school graduate	-
					• Program: Other	+
					• Ethnicity: Black	+
					• Proprietary school attendance	+
Brooks (1988)	Virginia State Education Assistance Authority (1982-1987)	Number of student loans originated	Varied by year	Descriptive	• Low loan amount (<$2,500)	+
					• Failure to persist is program of study	+
					• Low post-employment income (<$10,000)	+
					• Public institution attendance	+
					• Proprietary school attendance	+
					• Vocational school attendance	+
GAO (1988)	GSL Tape Dump (1987)	Student borrowers	1,182,000	Descriptive	• Independent student categorization	+
					• Short-term attendance	+
					• Family income <$10,000	+

TABLE 8.2. Continued.

Study	Data Source	Unit of analysis	Sample size	Statistics	Factors Associated with Default	Relationship to Default
Merisotis (1988)	Guarantee Agency Data (CA, IL, MA, NJ, PA) (1986-1987)	Institutions	n/a	Descriptive	• Proprietary and 2-year college attendance	+
Beanblossom & Rodriguez (1989)	GSL Tape Dump (1987)	Student borrowers	7,394	Descriptive/ Multivariate (Regression Analysis)	• Adjusted gross income • Year in school • Nonproprietary school attendance • Withdrawal from program • Independent borrower	- - - + +
GAO (1989)	GSL Tape Dump (1987)	Institutions	7,849	Descriptive	• Proprietary school attendance • 2-year college attendance	+ +
Stowe & Zimbler (1990)	NPSAS (1987)	Student borrowers	8,223	Descriptive	• For-profit school attendance • Vocational education program • Failure to complete program of study • Low income • Higher percentage of income needed for loan repayment	+ + + + +

TABLE 8.2. Continued.

Study	Data Source	Unit of analysis	Sample size	Statistics	Factors Associated with Default	Relationship to Default
GAO (1991)	Meta-analysis of 12 previously published default studies	Varied	Varied	Descriptive	• Vocational/trade school attendance	+
					• Low-income level	+
					• Limited financial support	+
					• Minority background	+
					• No high school diploma	+
					• Failure to complete educational program	+
					• Attendance in program of less than one year	+
					• Unemployment during repayment period	+
					• Low loan amount	+
Dynarski (1991)	NPSAS Student Loan Recipient Survey (1987)	Student borrowers	4,304	Descriptive/ Multivariate (Linear Regression)	• Earnings	−
					• Married	−
					• Race: Black	+
					• No HS diploma	+
					• Failure to complete postsecondary program	+
					• Race: Hispanic	+
					• Parental income <$17,000	+
					• Size of monthly payment	+
					• Proprietary school attendance	+
					• 2-year college attendance	+
Knapp & Seaks (1992)	Pennsylvania Higher Education Assistance Authority (1986)	Student borrowers	1,834	Descriptive/ Multivariate (Probit model)	• Parent's income	−
					• Two-parent home	−
					• Graduation	−
					• Race: Black	+

Two key themes emerge from these finding. . . . The first is that student characteristics are of overwhelming importance in correctly predicting defaulters, in
contrast to the institutions they attend, or the administrative practices those institutions use to try to curb student defaults. (p. 50)

In their study, Wilms, Moore, and Bolus (1987) found that student characteristics (e.g., persistence in a program of study, family income, race) were
the primary determinants of default. When student characteristics were controlled in the prediction equation, the only institutional characteristic related
to default was attendance at a proprietary school. However, the addition of
this factor to the equation "did not substantially increase the model's power
to explain the variation" (p. 50). Until more extensive research has been
conducted, the fact that students attending proprietary institutions exhibit
higher defaults than do students attending institutions in the collegiate sector should not be interpreted as being solely a function of the institution the
student attends.

Acknowledging that students who attend proprietary schools default at
greater rates than do students at other types of institutions, even though that
finding may be confounded by other considerations, leads one to the question: Why do these students default? Some (e.g., Dynarski, 1994) have attempted to explain the incidence of default by examining the characteristics
of proprietary school borrowers, whereas others have examined the operation of the proprietary schools and regulations for monitoring the proprietary sector (e.g., McCormick, 1989, 1991). Dynarski (1994) compared the
reasons offered by proprietary school students for defaulting on their student loans with the reasons offered by defaulters who had attended 2-year
and 4-year schools. For students who had attended proprietary schools, the
most prevalent reasons (scored as either "very" or "somewhat" important
reasons for defaulting) were unemployment (83%) and intervening personal
problems (62%). For students from 2-year schools, the most important reasons were unemployment (74%) and, though working, earning insufficient
funds (62%). Those were the same two factors cited by students from 4-
year institutions, but in this case, working but earning insufficient funds was
offered as the primary reason for default (69% of the survey students indicated this was a "very" or "somewhat" important reason) whereas unemployment was offered as the secondary reason (64%). These factors lend
support to the conclusions offered earlier, that personal factors may be more
important in determining default than the type of institutions attended.
Careful analysis of the types of employment secured by students from various postsecondary sectors, as well as their ability to support themselves once
they have completed their program of study, needs to be conducted before

conclusions should be offered directly linking postsecondary attendance to default on FFELP loans.

Fraud and Abuse in the Proprietary Sector

Reports with such titles as *School or scandal? Schools with unscrupulous practices that invade and abuse the Guaranteed Student Loan Program* (McCormick, 1989) and newspaper articles with such headlines as "Guess Who Pays for School Scam?" (Royko, cited in McCormick, 1989) brought general public attention to the issue of fraudulent practices by some proprietary schools. These practices included the accumulation of excess profits by proprietary school owners, the reasons were fraudulent claims for employability upon graduation, the recruitment of students from the ranks of the unemployed, the admission of unqualified students, the failure to refund tuition payments to students who have withdrawn from programs, and the closure of schools or elimination of programs prior to program completion by enrolled students (Fraas, 1990a; McCormick, 1989). Many of these practices gave the impression that abuses within the proprietary sector were motivated more by the desire to maximize institutional profits than by a wish to aid students in securing needed training. Significant concerns were raised, in addition to those about abuses of students, over issues of institutional integrity. These issues include financial instability, branching, and changing ownership. Since institutions are approved for participation in the student aid programs, the latter two issues become particularly vexing. Starting up programs in new locations as branches of existing institutions enabled some institutions to utilize a single program-participation agreement to certify student aid awards to students at multiple locations. During the 1980s, it was a relatively common practice for proprietary schools to "sell" USDOE identification numbers (McCormick, 1991). Existing regulations required schools to be in existence for 2 years prior to becoming eligible to participate in the Title IV programs. "In practice, the two year rule is not a factor. . . . A purchaser can buy a school, change its name and location, and even type of educational program, and still be considered the same institution by the Department of Education" (p. 13).

Many of the incidents reported in the popular press and in investigative reports by government agencies were anecdotal in nature, but they painted a picture of a postsecondary education sector that was rife with fraud and abuse, that placed the need for institutional profit ahead of the needs of students, and that was willing to utilize federal student aid as the primary means of financing operations. These images, whether accurate or not, were certainly detrimental to the status of proprietary education, and that image was further tarnished by a system of government and agency oversight that seemed inadequate to the task of reigning in abusive programs.

Failures of the Regulatory "Triad"

Some policy analysts have suggested that the substantial rate of default among proprietary schools and the prevalence of unscrupulous practices were partially the result of ineffective regulatory oversight. The regulatory structure for monitoring efficiency and effectiveness in the federal student aid programs is frequently referred to as the "triad" (Schenet, 1990). This triad has traditionally consisted of (1) accrediting agencies, approved by the secretary of education; (2) state licensing boards; and (3) the Department of Education. Each of these entities has a role in establishing institutional eligibility for participation in the student aid programs, but each organization frequently supports different goals and utilizes different process to establish institutional eligibility. As Schenet noted:

> Of the three components of the "triad"—accreditation, State licensing, and eligibility and certification—two of these components developed independently of any Federal program needs to serve purposes related to quality assurance and consumer protection, but not necessarily from the Federal perspective. (p. CRS-7)

Accreditation of proprietary schools, like proprietary schools themselves, is a frequently changing landscape consisting of multiple organizations representing different institutional types. Lee and Merisotis (1990) summarized the issues related to proprietary school accreditation. These issues included

1. Multiple sources of accreditation for the proprietary sector;
2. The viability of the standards used by accrediting agencies for accrediting schools and colleges;
3. Establishing consistent and normative standards for accreditation;
4. Links between accrediting agencies and professional and trade associations; and
5. Length of time between accrediting site visits. (Lee & Merisotis, 1990)

The second leg of the triad, state licensing boards, have their own set of problems when faced with assuring quality programs. By 1985, all states and the District of Columbia had established laws requiring proprietary institutions to secure a license in order to operate in the state. In the past, a significant problem has been the number of state agencies that were responsible for licensing the operation of schools within a state (Schenet, 1990, Lee & Merisotis, 1990, McCormick, 1991). These multiple agencies "may have little contact or coordination with each other. . . . [and] are likely to be completely excluded from any participation in higher education coordination or planning in the State" (Schenet, 1990, p. CRS-14). Many critics of state licensing boards suggest that the major problem isn't a lack of effective regulations for directing the operation of proprietary schools, but rather the failure of those boards to diligently and regularly enforce existing regulations.

The final leg of the triad is the federal government, most specifically the Department of Education. In its Committee Report, the Senate Permanent Subcommittee on Investigations of the Committee on Governmental Affairs saved some of its most scathing criticism for the Department of Education (1991):

> The Subcommittee found that through gross mismanagement, ineptitude, and neglect in carrying out its regulatory and oversight functions, the Department of Education had all but abdicated its responsibility to the students it is supposed to service and the taxpayers whose interests it is charged with protecting. (p. 33)

The Department of Education has a number of oversight responsibilities relative to the student aid programs. These include certifying accrediting agencies, certifying institutions to participate in the Title IV programs, and monitoring compliance with program agreements, legislative statues, and agency regulations. To fulfill the latter requirement, institutions must provide USDOE with the results of biennial independent audits and are subject to institutional program review by USDOE personnel. A major problem for USDOE has been a shortage of resources to conduct program reviews. "Between 1982 and 1989, ED [USDOE] conducted an average of approximately 600 reviews annually, about one quarter of the number that would be needed each year to ensure that every school was reviewed every 3 years" (Schenet, 1990, p. CRS-23). During this same time period, USDOE failed to carefully assess the viability of institutions for participation in the Title IV programs (McCormick, 1991). "Looking only for proof of accreditation and state license, the ED blindly rubber-stamped schools' eligibility applications. From October 1985 to September 1988, ED approved 97 percent of the 2,087 schools which applied for eligibility" (p. 16). Careless certification coupled with infrequent program review would result in the failure to detect and prevent many of the questionable practices outlined above, and those practices would, in direct and indirect ways, influence the rapid growth of defaults in the Guaranteed Student Loan Program.

Whether the condition of proprietary education at the end of the 1980s was sufficiently weak to warrant being called a crisis is unclear. What is clear is that there were significant problems with the sector, that those problems were a function of institutional mismanagement as well as inadequate oversight, and that the result was unacceptable levels of default in the Guaranteed Student Loan Program. In the next section of this chapter, I will outline a number of policy initiatives implemented at the federal level to address many of the issues noted here.

DEPARTMENT OF EDUCATION DEFAULT INITIATIVES

In an attempt to address many of its critics and rectify many of the problems plaguing the Guaranteed Student Loan Program, the Department of Education, under the leadership of Secretaries of Education William Bennett and Lauro Cavazos, proposed a number of initiatives intended to address the issue of default in the Guaranteed Student Loan Program (Fraas, 1989, USDOE, 1990). Those initiatives consisted of regulatory, administrative, and legislative proposals that were formally unveiled as final and proposed regulations on June 5, 1989 (Fraas, 1989). Subsequently, the plan was modified by passage of The Higher Education Amendments of 1992 (USDOE, 1995).

The linchpin of the department's initiatives was the establishment of maximum cohort default rates that would trigger institutional disqualification from participation in the Guaranteed Student Loan program, all Title IV student aid programs or both. Although changes have been made in how the cohort default rate is calculated and in the levels of default that trigger various sanctions since the original 1989 regulations, the basic concept has remained unchanged. For purposes of this discussion, the current regulations guiding the calculation of cohort default rates (originally called the fiscal year default rate) and the implications of those rates for institutions will be reviewed. Readers seeking additional information on the process that led to the establishment of the cohort default rate as a yardstick of institutional viability and seeking details on the original legislative requirements are directed to Fraas (1989). Elaboration on the Department of Education's proposed default reduction plans can be found in USDOE (1990).

Cohort default rates are produced annually by the Department of Education and are used to determine whether a program is eligible for continued participation in the FFELP. Institutions with cohort default rates of 25% or higher for FY 1991, FY 1992, and FY 1993 are subject to loss of participation in the FFELP (historically Black colleges, tribally controlled community colleges, and Navaho community colleges are exempt from this requirement until July 1, 1998) (USDOE, 1996d). Schools with more than 30 borrowers that have official default cohort rates that exceed 40% are subject to even more stringent measures. These institutions may be subject to limitation, suspension, or termination of participation in all Title IV student aid programs (USDOE, 1996e).

The establishment of maximum cohort default has been the major policy initiative developed by the Department of Education to address the issue of high defaults. However a number of other regulations and administrative practices have been implemented to reduce the level of default in the program and to address questions of institutional viability. These include

1. Requiring trade and technical schools to provide clear and extensive consumer information to students;
2. Requiring that all schools participating in the FFELP develop a default management plan that must be approved by USDOE as part of either the institution's initial application for participation or recertification to participate in the program;
3. Mandating that schools who admit students without a high school diploma make available to those students a General Education Development (GED) program;
4. Establishing conditions for the disbursement of loan proceeds to students including multiple disbursements and delayed disbursements for students entering their first year of an undergraduate program; and
5. Requiring that all schools develop fair and equitable refund policies (USDOE, 1995).

OUTCOMES OF ED DEFAULT INITIATIVES

The initiatives just outlined were intended to reduce the amount of defaults in the FFELP by making schools with high default rates more accountable and by increasing the oversight and program review responsibilities of the regulatory triad. Many of those initiatives were implemented in 1990, and, at the time of this writing, 3 years of cohort default data are available to determine if the initiatives have been effective. In this section, I will evaluate the effectiveness of the Department of Education's default reduction initiatives by examining the status of defaults within the FFELP as of Fiscal Year 1993, and by examining the status of institutions with a record of high defaults.

The data for this section are drawn from two primary sources: the *Secretary's Federal Family Education Loan Program institutional default reduction comparison of FY 1990, FY 1991, FY 1992 cohort default rates* (U.S. Department of Education, n.d.), and the *Federal Family Education Loan*

Program: FY 1991, FY 1992, and FY 1993 cohort default rates for schools (USDOE, 1996b). Table 8.3 presents a comparison of default data for the 1990 and 1993 fiscal years. Two primary conclusions stem from the data presented in Table 8.3. The first of these is that the default initiatives instituted by the Department of Education do appear to have effectively reduced defaults nationally. The national cohort default rate decreased from 22.4% in FY 1990 to 11.6% in FY 1993; a decrease of 48.2%. The second conclusion is that the most impressive changes have been made by proprietary schools. The data contained in Table 8.3 show that proprietary schools are making significantly fewer loans and are making fewer bad loans, thus resulting in a lower cohort default rate. A comparison of the number of borrowers who entered repayment in FY 1990 and FY 1993 discloses a reduction of 624,592 fewer borrowers. This represents a reduction of 60.1%. Nationally, the number of borrowers who entered repayment during that same time period declined by 633,477 (a decrease of 25.8%); meaning that the largest proportion (98.6%) of the decline in borrowers entering repayment is attributable to changes in the proprietary sector. Similar changes are evident when examining the data on borrowers in default during that same time period. Nationally, the number of defaulted borrowers declined by 339,156, or 61.5%. Of those 339,156 fewer defaulted borrowers, 328,626 (96.9%) were accounted for by changes in the proprietary sector. The substantial decrease in the number of defaulted borrowers resulted in a significant decline in the borrower default rate for proprietary schools. During FY 1990 the borrower default rate for all proprietary schools was 41.2%; by FY 1993 that rate had declined by 30.2%. Although the default rate for proprietary schools still exceeded the rates for all other types of institutions, the magnitude of the reduction from FY 1990 to FY 1993 was also greatest for proprietary schools.

Decreases in default rates, defaulted borrowers and borrowers who have entered repayment were uniform across all institutional types with the exception of public 4-year institutions and 4-year proprietary schools. In the case of the former, modest increases in defaulted borrowers accompanied by much larger increases in borrowers entering repayment yielded a rather stable default rate when comparing FY 1990 (7.0%) and FY 1993 (6.9%). For 4-year proprietary schools, the increase in the default rate from 16% in FY 1990 to 18.3% (a change of 14.4%) represents only a modest increase of 826 defaulted borrowers, a number that is greatly overshadowed by the significant decreases in the number defaulted borrowers at other types of proprietary schools. However, an interesting phenomenon is the rather large (66.7%) increase in 4-year proprietary institutions during the time period in question. The actual number of new 4-year proprietary schools (32) is small, but in light of concerns that some proprietary schools have padded their

TABLE 8.3. Changes in the Number of Participating Institutions, Borrowers in Default and Repayment, and the Borrower Default Rate from FY 1990–1993.

Sector	Schools (n)	Borrowers Defaulted (n)	Borrowers Entered Repayment (n)	Borrower Default Rate (%)
Fiscal Year 1990				
Public 4-year	649	44,255	633,746	7.0
Public 2-year	1,465	35,620	207,405	17.2
Private 4-year	1,545	33,709	521,758	6.5
Private 2-year	859	9,556	51,617	18.5
Proprietary All	3,750	427,497	1,038,828	41.2
4-year+	48	6,486	40,453	16.0
2-4 year	452	61,161	196,728	31.1
<2 years	3,250	359,850	801,648	44.9
Foreign	442	424	4,314	9.8
Unclassified	78	147	2,443	6.0
Total	8,788	551,208	2,460,102	22.4
Fiscal Year 1993				
Public 4-year	693	45,743	666,264	6.9
Public 2-year	1,407	31,309	215,991	14.5
Private 4-year	1,576	30,174	484,046	6.2
Private 2-year	753	5,800	42,957	13.5
Proprietary All	3,575	98,869	414,237	23.9
4-year+	80	7,312	39,858	18.3
2-4 year	419	24,654	112,034	22.0
<2 years	3,076	66,903	262,345	25.5
Foreign	423	145	2,835	5.1
Unclassified	7	12	295	4.1
Total	8,434	212,052	1,826,625	11.6

educational calendars to ensure compliance with regulatory program length requirements, this trend warrants close monitoring in the future.

Finally, one other piece of information from Table 8.3, the significant

TABLE 8.3. Continued.

Sector	Schools (n)	Borrowers Defaulted (n)	Borrowers Entered Repayment (n)	Borrower Default Rate (%)
Change: FY 1990–1993				
Public 4-year	+44 (+6.8%)	+1,488 (+3.4%)	+32,518 (+5.1%)	-.1% (1.4%)
Public 2-year	-58 (-3.9%)	-4,311 (-12.1%)	8,586 (+4.1%)	-2.7% (-15.7%)
Private 4-year	+31 (+2%)	-3,535 (-10.5%)	-37,702 (-7.2%)	-.3% (-4.6%)
Private 2-year	-106 (-12.3%)	-3,756 (-39.3%)	-8,660 (-16.8%)	-5% (-27%)
Proprietary All	-175 (-4.7%)	-328,628 (-76.9%)	-624,592 (-60.1%)	-17.3% (-41.9%)
4-year+	+32 (+66.7%)	+826 (+12.7%)	-595 (-1.5%)	+2.3% (+14.4%)
2-4 year	-33 (-7.3%)	-36,507 (-59.7%)	-84,694 (-43.1%)	-9.1% (-29.3%)
<2 years	-174 (-5.4%)	-292,947 (-81.4%)	-539,303 (-67.3%)	-19.4% (-43.2%)
Foreign	-19 (-4.3%)	-279 (-65.8%)	-1,479 (-34.3%)	-4.7% (-47.9%)
Unclassified	-71 (-91%)	-135 (-91.8%)	-2,148 (-87.9%)	-1.9% (-31.7%)
Total	-354 (-4%)	-339,156 (-61.5%)	-633,477 (-25.8%)	-10.8% (-48.21%)

decrease in the number of new borrowers entering repayment, warrants additional examination. 633,477 fewer borrowers entered repayment in FY 1993 than entered repayment in FY 1990. Although this reduction contributed to the decline in overall default rates, one must question whether the elimination of nearly two thirds of a million borrowers meets the policy goals of the FFELP program. As Goodwin (1991) pointed out, the use of default data to make decisions about institutional viability presents a number of problems, not the least of which is the problem of confounding institutional characteristics that may lead to default with student characteristics that may be more effective measures of default. The elimination of programs that have sizable default rates "could penalize those schools that enroll students with a higher propensity to default: minorities, economically disadvantaged students, and students whose training is in low-wage fields" (p. 15). In many cases, these are exactly the types of students the Title IV student aid programs were intended to assist. With a focus on institutional defaults as a measure of institutional effectiveness, it is possible that students who should be receiving assistance are being eliminated from the programs and are being denied the opportunity to seek a postsecondary education.

Tables 8.4, 8.5, and 8.6 were created from data drawn from three Department of Education reports (1996b, 1996c, 1996d) that identify the current status of institutions by their cohort default rates. Table 8.4 lists the number of schools participating in the FFELP program as of February 1996; the number of schools that may be subject to loss of eligibility to participate in the FFELP due to cohort default rates that are 25% or higher; schools that have had their "participation in the FFELP Program ended in the past, and their loss of participation is now being extended for an additional year due to their FY 1993 cohort default rates" (USDOE, 1996d, p. 1); and schools with more than 30 borrowers that have official default cohort rates that exceed 40% for FY 1993 and therefore may be subject to limitation, suspension, or termination of participation in all Title IV student aid programs. In addition Table 8.4 includes a synthetic category, "problematic programs," that consists of the total of the programs in the previous three categories (i.e., schools with defaults in excess of 25%; schools with extended loss of eligibility, and schools subject to LS&T). Table 8.4 discloses that the vast majority of programs categorized as problematic (87%) are proprietary schools. These data would indicate that although the problem of defaults is still an important issue at proprietary schools, it is being addressed under the Department of Education's default initiatives and that significant numbers of proprietary schools are being carefully monitored to ensure compliance with default reduction regulations.

The data in Tables 8.5 and 8.6 were developed to determine if particular states are more susceptible to problems in the FFELP program. Table 8.5 lists all states whose percentage of problematic programs exceeds the national average. Nationally, 654 programs have default rates of 25% or higher, are subject to extended loss, or may be subject to limitation, suspension, or ter-

TABLE **8.4.** Family Education Loan Program Participation Status by Type of Institution.

Type of Institution	Total Schools Participating in FFELP (n)	(%)	Schools Subject to Loss of Eligibility[1] (n)	(%)	Schools with Extended Loss[2] (n)	(%)	Schools Subject to LS & T[3] (n)	(%)	Problematic Programs[4] (n)	(%)
Public Institutions	1,785	31.0	11	4.6	20	10.5	25	11.3	56	8.6
Private Institutions	1,925	33.3	8	3.3	6	3.1	15	6.8	29	4.4
Proprietary Institutions	2,066	35.8	222	92.1	165	86.4	182	82.0	569	87.0
Totals	5,776	100.0	241	100.0	191	100.0	222	100.0	654	100.0

Sources: U.S. Department of Education (1996b, 1996c, 1996d)
1. Data in this column include schools who may be subject to loss of eligibility to participate in the FFELP due to cohort default rates that are 24% or higher. This column lists schools whose participation in FFELP will end as a result of their FY 1991, FY 1992, and FY 1993 cohort default rates.
2. Data in this column include schools whose "participation in the FFELP Program ended in the past, and their loss of participation is now being extended for an additional year due to their FY 1993 cohort default rates" (U.S. Department of Education, 1996d, p.1).
3. Data in this column include schools with more than 30 borrowers that have official default cohort rates that exceed 40% for FY 1993 and therefore may be subject to limitation, suspension, or termination of participation in all Title IV student aid programs.
4. Data in this column are the sum of the data in the preceding three columns.

mination of participation in the Title IV student aid programs. This number represents 11.3% of all the programs (5,776) currently participating in the FFELP. The percentage of problematic programs in 15 states and the District of Columbia currently exceeds the national average. The percentage of problematic programs ranges from a high of 45.1% in Louisiana (46 of 102 programs) to a low of 0% for a number of states and territories (e.g., Maine, Nebraska, Guam). Additional analysis needs to be conducted to determine why some states exceed the national average. Possible reasons might include a higher than average number of proprietary schools in those states, significant numbers of borrowers with characteristics correlated with default (e.g., low-income college students, low-wage earners, racial minorities), or a lack of careful oversight of participating programs by state agencies.

The latter is a particularly interesting conjecture when Table 8.6 is ex-

TABLE 8.5. Problematic States I: States with Problematic FFELP Programs in Excess of the National Average for FY 1993.

State	Total FFELP Programs (n)	Number of FFELP Programs Classified as Problematic	Percentage of FFELP Programs Classified as Problematic
Louisiana	102	46	45.1
Texas	287	94	32.8
Florida	202	62	30.7
Nevada	20	5	25.0
Michigan	165	34	20.6
District of Columbia	20	4	20.0
Arkansas	78	14	17.9
Mississippi	57	10	17.5
Oklahoma	86	15	17.4
California	516	86	16.6
Alabama	63	9	14.3
South Carolina	72	10	13.9
Virginia	127	17	13.4
Kentucky	154	20	12.9
Ohio	264	41	12.5
Illinois	250	29	11.6
Total: All Other States	3,313	158	4.8
National Totals	5,776	654	11.3

amined. This table presents information on FFELP participation through calculation of the percentage of programs within a state that have been classified as problematic (this differs from the data in Table 8.5, which looked at each state as a proportion of the national total). Examining which states have the highest percentage of state programs that qualify as problematic yields a slightly different pattern. Texas, with 14.4% of its programs classified as programmatic, becomes the most problematic state. This finding is particularly interesting in light of the efforts by the Texas Guaranteed Student Loan Corporation (TGSLC) to bring to the nation's attention the problems of unscrupulous practices in the FFELP and to design standards that would limit the number of school employing those practices (McCormick, 1989, 1991). These standards, many of which were approved by the Texas

TABLE 8.6. Problematic States II: States with a Substantial Percentage of Problematic Programs: FY 1993.

State	Number of FFELP Programs	Number of Problematic Programs	Percentage of Total Programs	Percentage of Problematic Programs
Texas	287	94	5.0	14.4
California	516	86	8.9	13.1
Florida	202	62	3.5	9.4
Louisiana	102	46	1.8	7.0
New York	443	41	7.7	6.3
Michigan	165	34	2.9	5.2
Ohio	264	33	4.6	5.0
Total: All Other States	3,797	258	65.7	39.4
National Totals	5,776	654	100.0	100.0

Note: From U.S. Department of Education (1996b, 1996c, 1996d).

state legislature in 1989 included recognizing the TGSLC as the state agency responsible for coordinating student loan default prevention efforts in the state; establishing maximum acceptable default rates for institutions participating in the FFELP and intervening with institutions if their rates exceed those acceptable levels; and focusing on schools with high levels of default (above 15% and 30%) that are owned by out-of-state corporations (McCormick, 1989). In defense of the Texas efforts, it should be noted that the data contained in Tables 8.5 and 8.6 are from programs that are still participating in the FFELP; they do not contain data on schools that have been eliminated from the program. A better indicator of the success of the Texas initiatives would be data on the number of programs in Texas that have been barred from participation in the FFELP or other Title IV student aid programs or both as a result of both Texas and federal default initiatives. However, the data in Tables 8.4 and 8.5 do offer policy makers insight into states that should be the target of intense scrutiny and analysis.

CONCLUSIONS

Important changes have been made in the way proprietary schools are monitored and certified for participation in the FFELP as a result of the Department of Education's 1989 default reduction initiatives and the Higher Education Act of 1992. An analysis of the data on defaults in the FFELP since the implementation of those initiatives indicates that those initiatives are working. The number of proprietary schools participating in the FFELP program has declined, proprietary schools are making fewer FFELP loans, and a smaller proportion of those loans are going into default each year. Although the total cohort default rate of the proprietary sector still exceeds the rates for all the other sectors by a sizable margin, it has experienced considerable moderation since implementation of the Department of Education's default initiatives. The most recent cohort default rates suggest that an additional 569 proprietary schools have sufficient default rates to warrant suspension from the FFELP, all Title IV student aid programs, or both. The use of cohort default rates and the establishment of a reasonable standard of default appears to have significantly rectified many of the problems the FFELP program faced in the 1980s.

However, defaults are only one indicator of program quality. As some policy analysts (Goodwin, 1991; Lee & Merisotis, 1990) have suggested it may now be time to look beyond defaults and begin to examine other determinants of institutional quality when examining proprietary education. For example, Goodwin has offered compelling arguments that single measures of program quality (such as defaults) are inadequate for evaluating proprietary schools effectiveness and that policy makers must begin to employ multiple measures for that purpose. Measures suggested by Goodwin include labor market outcomes (e.g., job retention rates, entry level salaries, and employer satisfaction with proprietary school graduates), learning outcomes, (e.g., rates at which program graduates demonstrate occupational knowledge, passage rates on state certification examinations) and program completion outcomes (e.g., student persistence rates).

The literature on higher education outcomes is rich and sophisticated (see, for example, Pascarella & Terenzini, 1991). The research on educational outcomes of proprietary education is much less well developed. Although some evidence exists (see Carroll, 1988 on educational attainment—particularly attainment of a vocational license or certificate) that many proprietary school students fair quite well in terms of their occupation training when compared with students trained by other types of institutions (e.g., community college or state-supported vocational institutions) much more research needs to be conducted on the outcomes of proprietary education.

One caution is warranted in examining the outcomes of proprietary education. Comparisons should not be made with institutions in the collegiate sector. Proprietary schools have different missions from colleges and universities. A clear understanding of those missions is necessary before any meaningful research on the outcomes of proprietary training should be conducted.

Proprietary education is not without its challenges and problems. Unscrupulous owners will still continue to take advantage of the largess of the federal government and the naïveté of poorly prepared students. However, in all likelihood, such cases represent a minority of schools and their owners and their fraudulent practices should not overshadow the positive contributions that proprietary schools make to educational and training needs of the nation. Because of their lean management structures and refined environmental scanning mechanisms, proprietary schools are frequently much more flexible and agile, and thus much more readily adaptable to the changing demands of a rapidly changing, global economic environment. In addition, this flexibility, coupled with their small size, makes many proprietary schools more responsive to student needs. The changing nature of proprietary school programs, a frequently criticized aspect of proprietary education, may be seen as a strength if program changes are implemented to meet changing occupational demands and student needs. Finally, proprietary education has a solid record of openness. It frequently offers programs in locations that traditional colleges are unwilling to serve, to students who are inadmissible to many traditional colleges.

The federal student aid programs, including the FFELP, were created to assure educational opportunity and choice. These should still be the primary goals of the federal student aid programs. Although program efficiency must never be ignored, an overemphasis on efficiency at the risk of eliminating needy students from the opportunity to earn the education and training they seek should be diligently resisted. As long as proprietary schools can demonstrate, as many can, that they provide useful and usable training for significant numbers of students, they should be allowed to participate in all the Title IV student aid programs.

REFERENCES

Apling, R. N., & Aleman, S. R. (1990). *Proprietary schools: A description of institutions and students.* (CRS Report for Congress No. 90-428 EPW). Washington, DC: Congressional Research Service.

Beanblossom, G., & Rodriguez, B. R. (1989). *Characteristics of Stafford Loan program defaulters: A national sample.* Washington, DC: U.S. Department of Education.

Brooks, N. (1988). Examining Guaranteed Student Loan defaulter characteristics. *The VASFAA Journal, 6,* 13–18.

Carroll, C. D. (1988, September). *Postsecondary institutions offering vocational/*

technical programs: Analysis findings from High School & Beyond (1980–1986). (National Center for Educational Statistics, Data Series: DR-HSB-80/84. CS 88-432). Washington, DC: U.S. Department of Education.

Coomes, M. D. (1994). A history of federal involvement in the lives of students. In M. D. Coomes & D. D. Gehring (Eds.), *Student services in a changing federal climate. (New Directions for Student Services, No. 68,* pp. 5–27). San Francisco: Jossey-Bass.

Dynarski, M. (1991, April). *National Postsecondary Student Aid Survey: Task 3: Analysis of factors related to default—final report.* Princeton, NJ: Mathematica Policy Research.

Dynarski, M. (1994). Who defaults on student loans? Findings from the National Postsecondary Student Aid Study. *Economics of Education Review, 13*(1), 55–68.

Federal Education Programs. (1973). *Congress and the nation: A review of government and politics, Volume 3, 1969–1972* (pp. 581–604). Washington, DC: Congressional Quarterly Service.

Fraas, C. J. (1988, November 18). *The Guaranteed Student Loan Program: Current status and issues.* (CRS Report for Congress No. 88-727 EPW). Washington, DC: Congressional Research Service.

Fraas, C. J. (1989, July 31). *The U.S. Department of Education's student loan default reduction initiative: Background and analysis.* (CRS Report for Congress No. 89-454 EPW). Washington, DC: Congressional Research Service.

Fraas, C. J. (1990a, August 31). *Proprietary schools and student financial aid programs: Background and policy issues.* (CRS Report for Congress No. 90-427 EPW). Washington, DC: Congressional Research Service.

Fraas, C. J. (1990b, November 13). *Guaranteed student loans: Defaults.* (CRS Issue Brief No. IB88050). Washington, DC: Congressional Research Service.

Gladieux, L. E., & Wolanin, T. R. (1976). *Congress and the colleges.* Lexington, MA: Lexington Books.

Goodwin, D. (1991, August). *Beyond defaults: Indicators for assessing proprietary school quality.* Washington, DC: U.S. Department of Education.

Knapp, L. G., & Seaks, T. G. (1992). An analysis of the probability of default on federally guaranteed student loans. *Review of Economics and Statistics, 74,* 404–411.

Lee, J. B., & Merisotis, J. P. (1990). *Proprietary schools: Programs, policies, and prospects* (ASHE-ERIC Higher Education Report No. 5). Washington, DC: George Washington University.

McCormick, J. L. (1989, July). *School or scandal? Schools with unscrupulous practices that invade and abuse the Guaranteed Student Loan Program.* Austin: Texas Guaranteed Student Loan Corporation.

McCormick, J. L. (1991, September). *Back to basics: Stricter standards for school eligibility can restore public confidence in the Title IV programs.* Austin: Texas Guaranteed Student Loan Corporation.

Merisotis, J. P. (1988, Winter). Default trends in major postsecondary education sectors. *The Journal of Student Financial Aid, 18*(1), 18–28.

Moore, J. W. (1983). Purposes and provisions of federal programs. In R. H. Fenske, R. P. Huff, & Associates, *Handbook of student financial aid: Programs, procedures and policies* (pp. 27–54). San Francisco: Jossey-Bass.

Moore, R. W. (1994). Proprietary schools and direct loans. In M. Kramer, R. W. Moore, P. Keitel, A. M. Hauptman, R. Haines, S. Baum, & E. B. Hicks, *Selected issues in the Federal Direct Loan Program: A collection of commissioned papers.* Washington, DC: U.S. Department of Education.

Pascarella, E. T., & Terenzini, P. T. (1991). *How college affects students.* San Francisco: Jossey-Bass.

Rodenhouse, M. P. (Ed.). (1996). *1996 higher education directory.* Falls Church, VA: Higher Education Publications.

Schenet, M. A. (1990, August 31). *Proprietary schools: The regulatory structure.* (CRS Report for Congress No. 90-424 EPW). Washington, DC: Congressional Research Service.

Snyder, T. D., & Hoffman, C. M. (1995). *Digest of education statistics; 1995.* (National Center for Education Statistics No. NCES 95-029). Washington, DC: U.S. Department of Education.

S. Rep. No. 102-58, 102d Cong., 1st Sess. (1991, May 17). *Abuses in the federal student aid programs: Report made by the Permanent Subcommittee on Investigations of the Committee on Governmental Affairs; United States Senate.* Washington, DC: U.S. Government Printing Office.

Stowe, P., & Zimbler, L. (1990). *Characteristics of Stafford Loan recipients, 1988.* (National Center for Education Statistics, no NCES 90-349). Washington, DC: U.S. Department of Education.

Tuma, J., Gifford, A., & Choy, S. (1989). *Student financial aid and postsecondary vocational education.* Berkeley, CA: MPR Associates.

U.S. Department of Education. (n.d.). *Secretary's Federal Family Education Loan Program institutional default reduction comparison of FY 1990, FY 1991, FY 1992 cohort default rates.* Washington, DC: Author.

U.S. Department of Education. (1990). *Reducing student loan defaults: A plan for action.* Washington, DC: Author.

U.S. Department of Education. (1995). *The federal student financial aid handbook.* Washington, DC: U.S. Government Printing Office.

U.S. Department of Education. (1996a, January 22). *News: National student loan default rate hits all-time low.* Washington, DC: Author.

U.S. Department of Education. (1996b, February). *Federal Family Education Loan Program: FY 1991, FY 1992, and FY 1993 cohort default rates for schools.* (Office of Postsecondary Education, Report No. DMS020). Washington, DC: Author.

U.S. Department of Education. (1996c, February). *Schools subject to limitation, suspension, or termination. Action of all Title IV programs due to excessive FY 1993 cohort default rates.* (Office of Postsecondary Education, Report No. DMS002). Washington, DC: Author.

U.S. Department of Education. (1996d, February). *Schools subject to the loss of eligibility to participate in the Federal Family Education Loan Program due to FY*

1991, FY 1992, and FY 1993 cohort default rates of 25.0% or greater. Schools with extended loss listed separately. (Office of Postsecondary Education, Report No. DMS001). Washington, DC: Author.

U.S. Department of Education, Office of Educational Research and Improvement, National Center for Educational Statistics. (1994, February). *E.D. Tabs: Characteristics of the nation's postsecondary institutions: Academic Year 1992–93.* Washington, DC: Author.

U.S. General Accounting Office. (1988, June). *Defaulted student loans: Preliminary analysis of student loan borrowers and default.* (Briefing report to the Chairman, Subcommittee on Postsecondary Education, Committee on Education and Labor, House of Representatives, No. GAO/HRD-88-112BR). Washington, DC: Author.

U.S. General Accounting Office. (1989, July). *Guaranteed Student Loans: Analysis of default rates at 7,800 postsecondary schools* (Briefing report to the Congressional Requesters, no GAO/HRD-89-63BR). Washington, DC: Author.

U.S. General Accounting Office. (1991, April). *Student loans: Characteristics of defaulted borrowers in the Stafford Student Loan Program.* (Briefing report to the Chairman, Subcommittee on Education, Arts, and the Humanities, Committee on Labor and Human Resources, U.S. Senate, No. GAO/HRD-91-82BR). Washington, DC: Author.

Wilms, W. W., Moore, R. W., & Bolus, R. E. (1987). Whose fault is default? A study of student characteristics and institutional practices on Guaranteed Student Loan default rates in California. *Educational Evaluation and Policy Analysis, 9*(1), 41–54.

CHAPTER 9

Are Bankruptcy Courts Creating "the Certainty of Hopelessness" for Student Loan Debtors?

EXAMINING THE "UNDUE HARDSHIP" RULE

Richard Fossey

Every year, millions of students take out federally guaranteed loans to finance their college or trade school education, and every year thousands of these debtors default on their loan obligations. In 1991 alone, the total cost of defaulted student loans amounted to $3.5 billion, enough to finance the U.S. Department of Education's entire Head Start budget (Winerip, 1994a).

Congress has been concerned about student loan defaults since the 1970s. Based on a belief that some students were abusing the federal loan program by shedding their education debts in bankruptcy, Congress passed legislation in 1978 that substantially limited a debtor's ability to discharge student loan obligations in a bankruptcy proceeding. Unless they could show "undue hardship," debtors were precluded from discharging their educational loans in bankruptcy for 5 years after they become due. In 1990, the 5-year limitation was raised to 7 years.

Congress did not define undue hardship, but most bankruptcy courts have interpreted the phrase quite harshly. Some courts have ruled that debtors cannot discharge their educational loans within the 7 year period unless they can show "the certainty of hopelessness" about their long-term financial prospects.

Harsh measures against student loan defaulters are popular with the public and would be justified if the defaulters were middle-class college graduates who obtained good value from their education and then refused to pay for it. However, most student loan defaulters do not fit this popular stereotype. Research has shown that a typical defaulter is a low-income minority member (African American or American Indian) who incurred educational loan debts at a proprietary institutions or low-quality college. In addition, single parents are prominently represented among former students who default on educational loans.

In fact, a review of federal cases reveals few instances in which recent college graduates with good job prospects filed for bankruptcy for the primary purpose of shedding student loans. Instead, most of the cases involve individuals who encountered difficult life circumstances and whose economic situations were made more precarious by the burden of their educational loans. Single mothers, unemployed persons, and individuals with mild but not totally debilitating illnesses are often represented in these cases.

Often, the defaulters had assumed student loans in good faith but had received no value from their educational experience. For these students and their families, the decision to borrow money to pursue postsecondary education may have worsened their life chances instead of improving them.

In this chapter, I argue that most courts have interpreted the Bankruptcy Code's "undue hardship" provision too harshly and without compassion. Provision can be made for stopping bad faith bankruptcy filings without refusing bankruptcy relief to individuals who are truly overburdened by their educational loans. The undue hardship clause in the Bankruptcy Code should be interpreted in such a way that individuals who are overburdened by their student loans can discharge their debts in bankruptcy without the necessity of showing the certainty of hopelessness in their economic future.

AN OVERVIEW OF THE FEDERAL STUDENT LOAN PROGRAM

Government guaranteed student loans were first authorized by Congress in the Higher Education Act of 1965 (HEA). Congress determined that the national interest required greater access to higher education and created the Guaranteed Student Loan Program to meet that need.

Originally, the federal student loan program was intended as a program of last resort for college and university students who needed funds to pay for their education. Over time, however, student loans have assumed a larger and larger role in higher education finance, and now constitute one of the largest sources of funds for postsecondary students. By 1986, half of the students graduating from 4-year colleges had some student loan debt (Edelson, 1992).

Guaranteed student loans (GSLs) are funded by private and governmental lenders, but the amounts of the loans are guaranteed by the federal government. Most federally guaranteed educational loans are awarded based on financial need; students can only borrow in excess of other financial aid and parental contributions. Students must begin repaying the loans when they complete their education or when they cease being at least a half-time student.

THE ALARMING INCREASE IN GSL DEFAULT RATES

When the GSL program began in 1965, it was relatively small. Only $214 million was made available for all forms of student assistance (Edelson, 1992, p. 477). Over time, the program grew tremendously, eventually loaning students more than $30 billion a year.

As the GSL program grew, so did the rate of defaults by student debtors. During the 1980s, volume of guaranteed loans increased by about 58%, but the dollar value of default claims grew by about 1,200% (Volkwein & Cabrera, Chapter 7, citing Knapp & Seaks, 1992; also see Chapter 7). By 1994, $22 billion had been lost to defaults over the life of the program, with $14 billion lost during the 5-year period of 1988–1993 (Cohn, 1994). By 1989, loan defaults was the fourth largest item in the Department of Education's budget (Johnson, 1989). And in 1991, the worst year for defaults, $3.5 billion was lost (Winerip, 1994a).

CONGRESSIONAL RESPONSE: LIMITED RELIEF FOR BANKRUPT BORROWERS

Congress has been concerned about the growing default rate for over 20 years; hearings on the problem were held in 1975. To many in Congress, a major cause of the problem was a tactic by some students of taking out GSLs while they attended college and then discharging their debts in bankruptcy shortly after graduation.

In 1978, Congress addressed this perceived problem by amending the U.S. Bankruptcy Code. Under the amended law, GSL debtors were prohibited from discharging their student loans through bankruptcy until at least 5 years after the debt became due, unless the debtor could show "undue hardship" (11 U.S.C. § 523[a][8][B]). In 1990, the waiting period was extended to 7 years.

Congress enacted this special provision for student debtors out of concern that students, "on the brink of lucrative careers," were filing for bankruptcy to avoid paying their student loans (*In re Pelkowski,* 1993, p. 742). In the public view, individuals who used this tactic were generally graduates of 4-year colleges who could expect to benefit financially from their higher

education experience (Kosol, 1981). As one congressperson put it, student
loan debtors, not having assets to pledge, obtained student loans by pledging
their future earning power. "Having pledged that future earning power, if,
shortly after graduation and before having an opportunity to get assets to
repay the debt, [they seek] to discharge that obligation, I say that is tanta-
mount to fraud" (*In re Pelkowski*, 1993, p.743, quoting 124 Congressional
Record 1793).

By restricting student loan debtors' access to the bankruptcy courts,
Congress undermined a central purpose of bankruptcy: providing a "fresh
start" for overburdened debtors (Hallinan, 1986). As the Supreme Court
stated more than 60 years ago, the bankruptcy laws are intended to give "the
honest but unfortunate debtor . . . a new opportunity in life and a clear
field for future effort, unhampered by the pressure and discouragement of
preexisting debt" (*Local Loan Company v. Hunt,* 1934, p. 244). By passing
the undue hardship provision, Congress excluded student loan debtors from
the full benefits of bankruptcy protection.

Indeed, by making student loan debts harder to discharge, Congress
placed them in a class of debts arising from deliberate misconduct or moral
turpitude. For example, debts arising from fraud, embezzlement, or breaches
of fiduciary duty are also nondischargeable under the same Bankruptcy
Code provision that limits the dischargeability of student loans.

NO SOLID EVIDENCE OF BANKRUPTCY ABUSE

In retrospect, congressional fears about abuse of the bankruptcy laws by
student borrowers were not justified. As Janice Kosol pointed out (1981),
only $17 million had been paid out by the federal government on GSL bank-
ruptcy claims from 1969 to 1975, which represented only three tenths of
one percent of the $7 billion that had been loaned.

Moreover, there was virtually no evidence that the student borrowers who
had filed for bankruptcy had been acting in bad faith. No data existed on the
circumstances of the debtors who had discharged their educational loans. For
example, it was not known how many were employed at the time of filing, how
many were working in their chosen field, or how many of the bankrupts had
taken out more loans than they realistically needed (Kosol, 1981).

THE BANKRUPTCY COURTS INTERPRET UNDUE HARDSHIP

Congress did not define undue hardship when it amended the Bankruptcy
Code in 1978, but over the years, the bankruptcy courts have developed tests

for determining when undue hardship exists. In the vast majority of cases, the courts have interpreted the phrase in such a way as to virtually preclude student borrowers from discharging their educational loans until more than 7 years after they become due.

Many courts have applied the so-called *Johnson* test, a three-pronged test for determining whether a debtor is entitled to discharge student loans because of undue hardship (*In re Johnson*, 1979; Dunham & Buch, 1992; Rieder, 1989). Courts using this approach conduct (a) a mechanical test, (b) a good faith test, and (c) a public policy test.

Under the first prong—"the mechanical test," the court examines whether the debtor has sufficient resources to pay the debt (including present and future earning capacity) while maintaining a minimal standard of living. Debtors who have sufficient resources to service their loans while maintaining a minimal lifestyle are not discharged.

If the court determines that a debtor will have insufficient resources to pay the debt while maintaining a minimum standard of living, that is not the end of the matter. The court then applies the second prong: the "good faith" test. Even if the debtor cannot reasonably pay the debt, it will not be discharged in bankruptcy unless the court finds that the debtor made good-faith attempts to pay the debt. Here the court asks whether the student loan debtor was negligent or irresponsible in managing his or her finances and whether these actions were the cause of the debtor's undue hardship. If the answer to these questions is yes, then the court will not relieve the debtor of the student loan obligation.

Assuming the debtor successfully passes the mechanical test and the good faith test, the court then applies the "policy test." In essence, the court asks whether discharging the student loan is in keeping with the Bankruptcy Code's policy of restricted dischargeability of educational loans. At this stage, the court looks at the debtor's motive. If the main purpose of the bankruptcy filing was to discharge educational loans, the discharge will not be granted.

Other courts have rejected the *Johnson* undue hardship test in favor of another three-pronged inquiry, the *Brunner* test (*Brunner v. New York State Higher Education Services Corp.*, 1987). The first *Brunner* prong looks at the debtor's financial condition to determine whether paying back student loans would put the debtor below a minimum standard of living. Second, *Brunner* asks whether the debtor's impecunious position is likely to persist for the foreseeable future. The third prong of the *Brunner* test examines the debtor's good faith. To obtain bankruptcy relief, the debtor's default must result, not from negligence, but from circumstances beyond the debtor's control (*In re Faish*, 1995).

Not all courts use these three-prong tests. Another test—a "poverty level" test—has also been developed. Under this test, a bankrupt debtor's educational loans will not be discharged if the debtor's income is substantially above the federal government's poverty level guidelines (Dunham & Buch, 1992; *Bryant v. Pennsylvania Higher Education Assistance Authority*, 1987).

Some commentators have noted that it may not matter which test a bankruptcy court uses to establish undue hardship, since in most cases the debtor's educational loans are not discharged (Collins, 1990; Kosol, 1981). Indeed, one commentary concluded that in most of the cases, the courts have implicitly converted undue hardship to "extreme and unbearable hardship" (Dunham & Buch, p. 705).

Perhaps no cases demonstrate the bankruptcy courts' hostility to GSL defaulters more than those that require debtors to show "the certainty of hopelessness" concerning their economic future before their educational loans will be discharged. This chilling phrase appears in numerous federal cases, including *In re Mathews* (1994), in which a bankruptcy court refused to discharge a woman from $29,000 in student loans, in spite of the fact that the court acknowledged that her current income was inadequate to maintain even a minimum standard of living.

In the *Mathews* case, the debtor had incurred her debt attending Wichita State University, where she had obtained a bachelor's degree in fine arts, with an emphasis on printmaking. From the time she left the university until she filed for bankruptcy 4 or 5 years later, she had never worked in the print making field, finding employment instead in a series of short-term jobs. Her poor employment record and a history of mental depression were insufficient to convince the bankruptcy court that she deserved a fresh start, free of her student loans.

Likewise, the Seventh Circuit Court of Appeals invoked the certainty of hopelessness phrase when it denied a debtor's application for the discharge of $9,700 in student loans (*In re Roberson*, 1993). The debtor had obtained a bachelor of science degree in industrial technology in 1986 and had held a good job as an automobile assembler. However, he had been laid off at the automobile assembly plant; and at the time of the bankruptcy filing, he was unemployed, recently divorced, and living in a one-room apartment with no kitchen or toilet. Although this situation convinced a federal district court that he met the undue hardship exception for discharging educational loans, the Seventh Circuit reversed and reinstated the debt. Whether the debtor had received any value from his college education the court found to be immaterial.

Mathews and *Roberson* are just two of a series of bankruptcy court decisions in which courts refused to discharge educational loans, in spite of strong evidence that the student loan debtors were in dire financial straits. For example, in *Myers v. Pennsylvania Higher Education Assistance Agency* (1993), a Pennsylvania bankruptcy court refused to discharge a 50-year-old woman of loans taken out to acquire a bachelor of science degree in public administration from Slippery Rock University. The woman, who had been trained as a nurse prior to receiving her degree, was unable to find a job in public administration and resumed her nursing career. Although the woman represented that her expenses exceeded her income, the court was not convinced that her circumstances constituted undue hardship.

More than "mere unpleasantness" or "garden variety" hardship was required, the court said. The court questioned whether the woman should spend money on telephone calls to her daughter or whether it was necessary to incur expenses for mental health treatment. After concluding that the woman had not done enough to minimize her expenses, it ruled that she had failed not only the mechanical test but the good faith test as well.

In general, one of two underlying assumptions account for the bankruptcy courts' harsh decisions regarding the discharge of educational loans. First, the bankruptcy courts often assume that individuals who procured student loans received an education that is of substantial economic value and that it is unfair to benefit from a valuable education without paying for it. These courts hold the view that well-educated debtors are "armed with sufficient capabilities to earn their way out of whatever hole they dug with student debt" (*In re Mathews,* 1994, p. 945). For example, a court refused to discharge the student loans of a healthy debtor who held law and master's degrees, even though he did not have the present ability to pay the loans at his current income (*In re Woodcock,* 1993).

Alternatively, the bankruptcy courts often assume that debtors entered into their loan obligations with their eyes wide open and with full knowledge that they may not receive any economic benefit from their educational experience. Thus, bankruptcy courts have refused to discharge student loans even when debtors could show they received little financial gain from their postsecondary education (*In re Coveney,* 1996, p. 143). As one court observed:

> The loan program grants aid regardless of the financial stability of the debtor or the wisdom of his or her individual choice to pursue further education. Consideration of the "value" of the education in making a decision to discharge turns the government into an insurer of educational value. Those students who make wise choices prosper; those who do not seek to discharge their debts in bankruptcy. This is wholly improper. (*In re Brunner,* 1985, p. 755, footnote 3)

The Seventh Circuit, expressing the same sentiment, put it this way:

> The government is not twisting the arms of potential students. The decision of whether or not to borrow for a college education lies with the individual; absent an expression to the contrary, the government does not guarantee the student's future financial success. If the leveraged investment of an education does not generate the return the borrower anticipated, the student, not the taxpayers, must accept the consequences of the decision to borrow. (*In re Roberson,* 1993, p. 1137)

TYPICAL STUDENT LOAN DEFAULTERS: LITTLE EVIDENCE OF BAD FAITH

Unfortunately, the bankruptcy courts' hostility toward GSL debtors may not be based on accurate information. Over the years, considerable research has been conducted regarding the types of students who finance their postsecondary education with student loans, the types of students who default, and the reasons for their defaults. Taken together, this research refutes some of the bankruptcy courts' assumptions about GSL debtors. When this research is examined, it becomes clear that the courts have constructed a definition of undue hardship that is harsher than necessary to prevent student debtors from abusing bankruptcy protection.

Typical Borrowers: Minority, Proprietary School, and Low-Income Students

Students from Low-Income Families. First of all, the typical student who relies on student loans is not a middle-class individual attending a 4-year college. Not surprisingly, students from low-income homes are particularly reliant on educational loans. During the 1989–90 academic year, 32% of students from homes with annual incomes of less than $10,000 received loans to pursue postsecondary education. In contrast, only 3.1% of students from families with $100,000 or more in household income took out educational loans (National Center For Educational Statistics, 1993, p. 27).

Independent Students. Independent students—those not relying on family income—are also heavily dependent on loans to finance their postsecondary education. Thirty-two percent of independent students with $5,000 or less in annual income took out loans to pay for college.

Minority students. Minority students are also disproportionately reliant on student loans. Twenty-nine percent of the African American student population received loans during the 1989–90 academic year, compared to 17.7% in the White student population.

Students attending proprietary schools. Finally, students who attend short-term programs—less than 2 years—are more reliant on loans than are students who attend traditional 4-year institutions. According to the U.S. General Accounting Office (GAO), 25% of students attending 4-year institutions take out educational loans; whereas 46.5% of the students attending schools with short-term programs take out loans (GAO, 1988). For the most part, these short-term programs are operated by proprietary schools.

Typical Defaulters: Low-Income, Minority, and Proprietary School Students

In the popular imagination, individuals who default on their educational loans are "deadbeats"—persons who financed their college education with GSLs, received substantial economic benefits from their education, and then reneged on their loan obligations. However, research studies paint a very different picture of the typical GSL defaulter.

Vocational school students. First, most student loan defaulters attended proprietary trade schools, not 4-year institutions. According to a 1988 GAO report, 35% of vocational students defaulted on their GSLs. Overall default rates for students attending 2- or 4-year institutions was only about one third the rate of vocational students. The percentage of defaulting vocational students ranged from a low of 13% for students living with their families and whose families had incomes of $30,000 or more to a high of 53% for independent students with family income of $10,000 or less.

A 1993 GAO report also confirmed that students attending proprietary trade schools had disproportionately high default rates. According to that report, proprietary schools accounted for 28.3% of student loan disbursements in Fiscal Year 1990 but 69% of the defaults (GAO, 1993, p. 6).

Similarly, a 1994 *New York Times* article reported that only 5% of the nation's 15 million postsecondary students attend trade schools. Yet over a 3-year period, students attending these schools received about 25% of federal loan money and accounted for 76% of total student loan defaults (Winerip, 1994c).

Low-income students. Second, students from low-income families defaulted at higher rates than did students from more affluent families. Whether they were dependent or independent, students from low-income families defaulted at high rates. Thirty percent of students with family income of $10,000 or less defaulted on their GSLs. Only 6% of students with family income of $30,000 or more defaulted on their loans (GAO, 1988, p. 12).

Short-time students. Third, short-time students defaulted more than did students who attend school for a year or more. Among students attending school for one year or less, the default rate was about 30%, whereas the rate for students who stayed through a 2nd year or beyond had a default rate of 10 percent. Short-termers who attended vocational schools had the highest default rate—almost 40%. Students who attended higher education institutions for one year or less defaulted at about half that rate.

Independent students. Fourth, independent students dependent on their own resources defaulted more than students who were financially dependent on their families. Independent students defaulted on their loans at an overall rate of 28%, compared to a 15% rate for dependent students. The default rate for independent students was lowest among those with family incomes of $30,000 or more and highest among those with family incomes of less than $10,000; but the default rate for independent students was higher than the rate for dependent students at all income levels.

In short, the GAO concluded that many defaulters are poor, attended trade schools, dropped out of their studies, and have little or no means to repay their loans. Often these students received little or no educational value for their tuition dollars and were either unwilling or unable to pay back their student loans.

Racial minorities and single parents. Elsewhere in this volume, James F. Volkwein and Alberto F. Cabrera expand on GAO reports regarding the types of students who become defaulters. After reviewing the empirical literature on the topic, they concluded that higher default rates among racial minorities "constitutes the most consistent and perhaps the most troubling finding across the published studies." Indeed, the studies reported that African Americans and American Indians who came from families with little education had default rates ranging from 30 to 60%. Volkwein and Cabrera's own research found that African Americans had a 37% higher default rate than had White Americans, even after controlling for other important variables.

In addition, Volkwein and Cabrera found the highest default rates among single individuals with dependent children. In fact, default rates for such individuals was quite high in all racial groups. Single White individuals with one or more dependents had a 35% default rate. The corresponding figure for African Americans was 43% and for Hispanics, 38%.

Many Proprietary School Defaulters Receive Worthless Training

According to recent GAO reports, many proprietary school students receive training that has little value (1997a); and some borrow money to pay for training in oversupplied occupations (1997b). Indeed, some proprietary school programs are virtually worthless. As the GAO (1997a) pointed out:

> Some proprietary school operators have enriched themselves at the expense of economically disadvantaged students while providing little or no education in return. Faced with large debts and no new marketable skills, these students often defaulted on their loans. In fact, default rates for proprietary school students peaked at around 41 percent in 1990 at a time when the student loan default rate for all postsecondary students averaged around 22 percent. (p. 25)

Hearings conducted by the Senate Permanent Subcommittee on Investigations in 1993 confirm the GAO's observations. According to students, investigators, and employees who testified at the Senate hearings, one proprietary school apparently existed for the sole purpose of collecting student aid money. Testimony was received that the school had only 23 instructors but employed 70 loan processors. In addition, it was reported that the school had over 100 commissioned salespeople who recruited students at such locations as welfare and food stamp offices (Winerip, 1994b). The Senate subcommittee members heard testimony that only 10 to 20% of the proprietary school's students received jobs in their fields.

Representative Maxine Waters of California, a critic of the federal student aid program, has said these kinds of cases are all too common. According to Representative Waters, the poor are often victimized by trade schools that rake in student loan money while offering worthless courses, leaving their students with no jobs and with educational loan debts that they are unable to pay (Winerip, 1994c).

Few Student Loan Debtors Use Bankruptcy Courts in Bad Faith

In addition to other research findings, a review of reported bankruptcy cases over a 4-year period (1990 to 1993) helps develop a clearer picture of the kinds of individuals who attempt to cancel their student loans in bankruptcy.

This review reveals few cases in which student loan debtors filed for bankruptcy in bad faith.

During the years 1990 through 1993, West's *Bankruptcy Digest* published 44 cases involving efforts to discharge student loans. Courts discharged these loans in bankruptcy in only nine cases. In the other 35 cases, the courts either refused to nullify the debt or only granted a partial discharge.

This review revealed little evidence that student loan debtors had filed for bankruptcy in bad faith. Instead, most of the cases involve individuals who encountered difficult life circumstances and whose economic situations were made more precarious by the burden of their educational loans.

Only a handful of the published cases involve the kind of abuse Congress was concerned about when it passed the undue hardship provision in 1978. For example, *In re Woodcock* (1993) involved a male debtor who was in good health and had no dependents. Although the debtor had a law degree and an MBA degree, he had chosen to become a writer. The court refused to discharge the student loans, based on the debtor's past employment and the court's conclusion that the debtor's expenses were excessive. Similarly, an Ohio bankruptcy court refused to discharge a relatively small debt (less than $2,000) that an unemployed debtor had incurred to attend bartending school. The debtor, who was single, without dependents, and in good health, had by his own admission made insufficient efforts to obtain work. Not surprisingly, the court concluded that the debtor would not suffer undue hardship if he were required to pay back the loan (*In re Phillips,* 1993).

In other cases, debtors often were experiencing true hardships, although perhaps not so severe as to bring about the "certainty of hopelessness." Student loan defaulters were often unemployed or underemployed (*In re Roberson,* 1993), single parents scraping by on an inadequate income (*In re Johnson,* 1990; *In re Evans,* 1991), or in ill health (*In re Wardlow,* 1993; *In re Kline,* 1993). In several instances, the debtors had received little value for their educational experiences (*In re Law,* 1993; *In re Kraft,* 1993) or had failed to complete their studies (*In re Malloy,* 1993). Had the debtors borrowed money for any legitimate purpose other than to pay for education, most would have seen their debts fully discharged in the bankruptcy process.

Interestingly enough, only a few of the student loan debtors who filed for bankruptcy had incurred their debts at proprietary schools. Although most student loan defaulters are former proprietary school students, only about a quarter of the published bankruptcy cases involved this type of student. It seems likely that many of the proprietary school students who default on their student loans are judgment proof and so devoid of assets that it is not worth the trouble for them to file a bankruptcy petition.

A MORE REASONABLE INTERPRETATION
OF UNDUE HARDSHIP:
In re Correll

As we have seen, many bankruptcy courts have treated student loan debtors as if they were high-income professionals intent on getting something for nothing by filing for bankruptcy to shed themselves of their educational loan obligations. And even in cases where it was apparent that the bankrupt student received little of value from an educational experience, many bankruptcy courts have shown no sympathy.

Research suggests, however, that the courts are wrong to treat bankrupt student debtors so harshly. Many students who default on their educational loans are from low-income families, attended low-quality proprietary schools, and received little or no value from their education. A disproportionate share of defaulters are low-income African Americans. Moreover, many had inadequate information before assuming their loan obligation; and some were defrauded by their chosen educational institution.

A few bankruptcy courts have recognized that not every defaulting student debtor is an upwardly mobile "yuppie" intent on abusing the GSL program. In particular, *In re Correll* (1989), a Pennsylvania bankruptcy court decision, challenged the proposition that bankruptcy rules designed to prevent abuse by high-income professionals should apply to defaulting student debtors who were living at the poverty line.

> It is apparent that judicially developed rules defining circumstances which indicate "abuse" of the bankruptcy system were developed to apply to high income professionals, but have come in recent years to be applied to poverty line wage earners. We conclude that the key word in the legislative history is "abuse" and that is inappropriate to apply the same standards to poverty line wage earners as is applied to high income professionals and other college graduates. (p. 304)

The *In re Correll* court rejected the view that student loan debtors must show that they are living at or below the poverty line in order to discharge their educational loans in bankruptcy.

> We do not believe, however, that Congress intended a fresh start under the Bankruptcy code to mean that families must live at poverty level in order to repay educational loans. Where a family earns a modest income and the family budget, which shows no unnecessary or frivolous expenditures, is still unbalanced, a hardship exists from which a debtor may be discharged of his student loan obligations. Use by the Bankruptcy Court of poverty level or minimal standard of living guidelines is not necessary to meet the congressional purpose of correcting

a few abuses of the bankruptcy laws by debtors with large amounts of educational loans, few other debts, and well-paying jobs, who have filed bankruptcy shortly after leaving school. (p. 306)

With these observations as a prelude, the *In re Correll* court examined five bankruptcy cases involving petitions to discharge educational loans. Although it applied the three-prong test for determining undue hardship in all five cases, the court exhibited considerably more compassion than most federal courts had shown in similar situations. The court decided each case as follows:

The Correll case. In this case, the debtor had borrowed money to attend a state university but had withdrawn before graduating. Since that time, he had been employed in unskilled positions and had not benefited from his college coursework. At the time of the bankruptcy, the debtor was married and had a small child. The court decided that the debtor's income was not sufficient to meet even a minimum standard of living, that his circumstances were not likely to change soon, and that the added expense of paying back student loans would violate the fresh start policy of the Bankruptcy Code. Accordingly, the court discharged the educational loans.

The Rugh case. In this case, the debtors, a married couple, sought to discharge a student loan obtained by the husband to obtain a "doctor of motors" degree from a vocational school. The husband had enrolled in the school after being laid off from his steelworker's job, hoping to improve his skills enough to find better employment. The degree was of almost no value, and the husband was forced to take a laborer's job at $6.25 per hour. In ruling on this case, the court commented:

> Far too many school operators are exploiting America's neediest people and their dreams for a new start in life. They promise education and jobs which students never receive, leaving them deep in debt. (p. 307)

According to the court, the husband-debtor's doctor of motors degree exemplified this problem. The vocational school had not provided the husband with the necessary skills to obtain a job. All he received was debt. In their present circumstances, the court concluded, the couple could not pay back the educational loan and maintain even a minimal standard of living for themselves and their children. This student loan, too, was discharged.

The Gravante case. In this case, a woman had taken out a loan to enroll in a medical office assistant training program. At the time, she was a single mother with two children. She interrupted the program due a child's illness.

Later, the woman married and had two more children. Her husband was employed as a field engineer and earned, in the court's words, a "substantial" income, but there was a history of family illnesses (p. 308).

The court discharged this loan, too. It ruled that in light of the family's tight budget, the obligation to pay back the loan might disrupt family stability "and cast all six members on the public welfare rolls."

The Ledgerton case. The debtor in this case was a divorced woman with a 3-month-old child. She had incurred an educational debt to pursue nursing studies and additional debt to train as a travel agent. She was unable to work as a nurse due to an injury, and she was only able to obtain a minimum wage job in the travel industry.

"This is not a case," the court ruled, "where the debtor obtained a superior education and then filed for bankruptcy to avoid paying her student loans" (p. 309). Since completing her education, she had been unable to maintain even a poverty level of living. To force her to pay back the student loans would cause undue hardship.

The Miles case. In this case, a woman had obtained a student loan to attend a proprietary business school. She completed the program and was employed part-time as a secretary. At the time of the bankruptcy, she was married, and her husband had a stable income. She and her husband owned a home, and they lived above the poverty level. Under those circumstances, the court found no undue hardship existed, and it denied the debtor's request to discharge her educational loans.

The five cases described in *Correll* are not unlike other cases in which bankruptcy courts refused to discharge educational loans. Taken together, these cases constitute a litany of common woes—illnesses, divorce, lost jobs, worthless training programs, and changed career goals. Few cases are remotely similar to the kinds of abuses that Congress intended to halt when it passed the undue hardship provision of 11 U.S.C. § 523(a)(8)(B). Nevertheless, in most of these cases, courts have demonstrated far less compassion than the *Correll* court.

CONCLUSION

The Bankruptcy Code's harsh measures against individuals who default on their educational loans is not good public policy. Congress passed the undue hardship provision to stop college graduates from discharging their student loans just as they began reaping the economic benefits of their education. There was little evidence of this kind of abuse at the time Congress acted, and there has been little evidence of it since that time.

Instead, the data clearly show that most GSL defaulters are low-income students who attended vocational schools. Some of these debtors had inadequate information before assuming their indebtedness. Many defaulters are minority students and students from low-income families. Single parents also figure prominently among defaulters. Among the student loan borrowers who have actually tried to discharge their loans in bankruptcy courts, few appear to have filed in bad faith. And though they have not often found sympathetic courts, many defaulters who sought the aid of the bankruptcy courts demonstrated genuine hardship—sufficient hardship to have received a discharge had their debts not been educational loans.

Of course the danger of bad faith efforts to discharge student loans in bankruptcy is a real one. The undue hardship provision in the bankruptcy code is a sensible way to guard against such abuse. But most courts' interpretation of undue hardship has been unduly harsh. *In re Correll*'s interpretation of undue hardship, in which a bankruptcy court applied the undue hardship rule compassionately, provides adequate safeguards against bad faith efforts to discharge student loans without foreclosing bankruptcy protection for good faith debtors who are experiencing pressing financial difficulties.

REFERENCES

Brown, W. H., & Evans, K. L. A comparison of classification and treatment of family support obligations and student loans: a case analysis. *Memphis State University Law Review 24*, 623–650.

Brunner v. New York State Higher Education Services Corp., 831 F.2d 395 (2nd Cir. 1987).

Bryant v. Pennsylvania Higher Education Assistance Agency, 72 B.R. 913 (Bankr. E. D. Pa. 1987).

Cohn, J. (1994, April). Making college possible; new student aid program proposed by Bill Clinton. *Washington Monthly*, p. 24.

Collins, T. (1990). Forging middle ground: Revision of student loan debts in bankruptcy as an impetus to amend 11 U.S.C. § 523(a)(8)(B). *Iowa Law Review*, 733–766.

Dunham, D., & Buch, R. (1992). Educational debts under the bankruptcy code. *Memphis State University Law Review, 22*, 679–718.

Edelson, J. L. (1992). Higher education to a higher default: A re-examination of the Guaranteed Loan Program. *Annual Review of Banking Law, 11*, 475–508.

Eglin, J. J. (1993). Untangling student loans. *Society 30*, 52–59.

Greene, L. L. (1989). An economic analysis of student loan default. *Educational Evaluation and Policy Analysis 11*, 61–68.

Grubb, W. N. (1993). The long-run effects of proprietary schools on wages and earnings: Implications for federal policy. *Educational Evaluation and Policy Analysis 15*, 17–33.

Hallinan, C. G. (1986). The "fresh start" policy in consumer bankruptcy: A historical inventory and an interpretive theory. *University of Richmond Law Review,
21*, 49–153.

In re Brunner, 46 B.R. 752 (S.D. N.Y. 1985), *aff'd,* Brunner v. New York State
Higher Education Services Corp., 831 F.2d 395 (2nd Cir. 1987).

In re Bryant, 72 B.R. 913 (Bankr. E. D. Pa. 1987)

In re Correll, 105 B.R. 302 (W.D. Pa. 1989).

In re Coveney, 192 B.R. 140 (W.D. Tex. 1996).

In re Evans, 131 B.R. 372 (Bankr. S.D. Ohio 1991).

In re Faish, 72 F.3d 298 (3rd Cir. 1995).

In re Johnson, 5 Bankr. Ct. Dec. 532 (E.D. Pa. 1979).

In re Johnson, 121 B.R. 91 (N.D. Okla. 1990).

In re Kline, 155 B.R. 762 (Bankr. W.D. Mo. 1993).

In re Kraft, 161 B.R. 82 (Bankr. W.D. N.Y. 1993).

In re Law, 159 B.R. 287 (Bankr. D. S.D. 1993).

In re Mathews, 166 B.R. 940 (Bankr. D. Kan. 1994).

In re Malloy, 144 B.R. 38 (Bankr. E.D. Va. 1992), *rev'd,* 155 B.R. 940 (E.D. Va.),
aff'd without op., 23 F.3d 402 (4th Cir. 1993).

In re Pelkowski, 990 F.2d 737 (3rd Cir. 1993).

In re Phillips, 161 B.R. 945 (Bankr. N.D. Ohio 1993).

In re Richardson, 27 B.R. 560 (E.D. Pa. 1982).

In re Roberson, 999 F.2d 1132 (7th Cir. 1993).

In re Wardlow, 167 B.R. 148 (Bankr. W.D. Mo. 1993).

In re Woodcock, 149 B.R. 957 (1993), *aff'd and rev'd in part,* 45 F.3d 363 (10th
Cir.), *cert. denied,* 116 S. Ct. 97 (1995).

Johnson, J. (1989, June 2). U.S. sets tough penalties for student loan defaults. *New
York Times,* p. A10.

Knapp, L. G., & Seaks, T. G. (1992). An analysis of the probability of default on
federally guaranteed student loans. *Review of Economics and Statistics, 74,*
404–411.

Kosol, J. (1981). Running the gauntlet of "undue hardship"—The discharge of student loans in bankruptcy. *Golden Gate Law Review, 11,* 457–484.

Local Loan Company v. Hunt, 292 U.S. 234 (1934).

Myers v. Pennsylvania Higher Education Assistance Agency, 150 B. R. 139 (Bankr.
W.D. Pa. 1993).

National Center for Educational Statistics (1993). *Financing undergraduate education: 1990* (NCES 93–201). Washington DC: U.S. Department of Education.

Rieder, R. W. (1989). Student loans and bankruptcies: What can a university-
creditor do? *West's Education Law Reporter, 56,* 691–704.

Ryman, A. (1993). Contract obligation: a discussion of morality, bankruptcy, and
student debt. *Drake Law Review, 42,* 205–224.

U.S. General Accounting Office (1988, June). Defaulted student loans: Preliminary analysis of student loan borrowers and defaulters (GAO HRD-88-112BR). Washington DC: Author.

U.S. General Accounting Office (1993, August). *Student loan default rates at historically Black colleges and universities* (GAO/HRD-93-117FS). Washington DC: Author.

U.S. General Accounting Office (1997a, February 1). *High risk series: Student financial aid* (GAO/HR-97-11). Washington, DC: Author.

U.S. General Accounting Office (1997b, June 10). *Proprietary schools: Millions spent to train students for oversupplied occupations* (GAO/HEHS-97-104). Washington, DC: Author.

U.S. v. Smith, 862 F. Supp. 257 (D. Hawaii, 1994).

Winerip, M. (1994a, February 2). Billions for school are lost in fraud, waste and abuse. *New York Times,* p. A1.

Winerip, M. (1994b, June 19). House panel is facing vote on school aid. *New York Times,* Section 1, p. 16.

Winerip, M. (1994c, February 4). Overhauling school grants: Much debate but little gain. *New York Times,* p. A1.

CHAPTER 10

Condemning Students to Debt:

SOME CONCLUSIONS AND REFLECTIONS

Richard Fossey

As the previous nine chapters attest, the federal student loan program is the source of several significant public policy problems. First, one of its primary goals, to make higher education more accessible to low-income families, has not been achieved. In fact, as college costs rapidly accelerate, higher education may be less obtainable for these individuals than it was 20 years ago. Second, the program is plagued by problems of fraud, abuse, and misman-agement—especially in the trade school sector. The Department of Education has made some progress in this area, removing some of the most abusive trade schools from the loan program. Nevertheless, fraud and mismanage-ment have cost taxpayers billions of dollars. Third, a great many student borrowers have not benefited from the program. Countless thousands have accumulated debt for worthless training programs; and several million stu-dent debtors have gone into default, ruining their credit ratings and foreclos-ing them from further participation in the program.

Many factors have contributed to the program's shortcomings; but in the final analysis, its deficiencies can be traced to one primary cause: The federal student loan program is not, and never has been, the product of a coherent public policy. Rather, as Campaigne and Hossler observe in Chap-ter 8, it might be better described as a "pastiche of goals, programs, strate-gies, incentives, and disincentives" that has no overall philosophy or pur-pose. Over the years, the student loan program has been crafted in response to the desires of higher education's various stakeholders—colleges, universi-ties, trade schools, banks, and lending agencies. As a result, the program has become a thicket of statutes, regulations, agency guidelines, and confusing and contradictory policy objectives—often initiated at the behest of a partic-ular interest group.

Does this mean that the federal student loan program has been a disas-ter? No, it does not. Millions of individuals have paid for rewarding educational experiences with federally guaranteed student loans. And in the 30 years since these loans were first introduced, access to postsecondary education has greatly expanded.

Nor is it clear whether there is any realistic alternative to student loans as a major means of financing postsecondary education. In the past, state governments heavily subsidized higher education, making it available far below its true cost. In recent years, however, state education budgets are under pressure from a variety of sources—declining tax revenues, reduced political commitment to education in general, and competing demands for social services, particularly health care and prisons. Realistically speaking, state governments may not be able to underwrite higher education to the extent that they did in the early 1970s, even if they have the political will do so.

Nevertheless, everyone involved in student loan policy—legislators, researchers, and education officials—should be exploring ways to improve the student loan program and to identify and limit its harmful effects. And, in fact, this has been occurring. Various scholars and higher education professional groups have made a number of reasonable proposals to improve the way the student loan program operates.

In particular, the American Council on Education (ACE), in a 1997 report that was endorsed by more than 20 higher education associations, made 16 recommendations for reauthorizing the Higher Education Act, the primary student loan legislation. Each of these recommendations is reasonable, and if adopted, would make the federal student loan program more efficient and economical.

For example, the ACE report pointed out that the purchasing power of Pell grants, which are reserved for low-income students, has declined over the years. ACE urged Congress to increase funding for this program and to restore grants "as the central focus of student aid for low-income students" (p. 3).

ACE also made a number of proposals for making the student loan program less expensive for students. Specifically, it recommended the elimination of "up-front" fees—origination fees and insurance premiums—which cost students about 4% of the amount borrowed (p. 6). ACE also pointed out that student loan burdens were making it difficult for many graduating students to take low-paying jobs in the public service sector. It recommended that the program develop a more attractive loan forgiveness provision that would allow graduates with high loan obligations to pursue public service careers at relatively low salaries.

Echoing the General Accounting Office's concerns about the Department of Education's poor system for processing student loans, discussed in Chapter 1, ACE recommended that the loan delivery process be redesigned to be an "efficient, cost-effective, consumer-oriented system" on the model of Visa and Mastercard (p. 16). If such a system were in place, ACE pointed out, the department would have critical and timely information on loan volume, delinquencies, and defaults—something it does not have now.

ACE made other sensible proposals for improving the federal student aid program. For example, it suggested that Congress hold hearings on the promise of distance education and the appropriateness of directing more federal aid to students enrolled in distance learning programs. ACE also recommended streamlining the regulations for determining institutional participation and for monitoring institutional compliance. In addition, it recommended that historically Black colleges and universities and institutions serving Native Americans not be unduly penalized for having relatively high default rates, in recognition of their critical role in minority education.

Without a doubt, the ACE report contains many valuable suggestions for improving the student loan program. Nevertheless, when all is said and done, the ACE report takes the status quo pretty much for granted. In other words, its recommendations assume that the student loan program is a permanent fixture of higher education finance. In fact, ACE described the Higher Education Act as "the indispensable tool" for providing low-income groups greater access to higher education (p. 2).

ACE may be right in its conclusion. Like it or not, government, institutions, and students may have to reconcile themselves to the student loan program as a critical component of postsecondary education finance. We may never again return to a time when low-income and moderate-income students can expect to graduate from a public or private university without accumulating a significant amount of debt. If so, the task of higher education policy makers is to improve the student loan program without attempting to abolish or drastically alter it.

TOWARD A SENSIBLE STUDENT LOAN POLICY

On the other hand, perhaps it is time to stop tinkering with the status quo and to ask whether the federal student loan program needs to be fundamentally reconsidered. Such an undertaking would involve more than technical improvements to the student loan program. Rather, it would require a sober assessment of higher education's basic obligations to its students.

If such an assessment were to be made, surely it would be necessary to affirm these three elemental principles:

1. Postsecondary institutions have a moral obligation to control costs. In the past, as Howard Bowen observed in his classic book on higher education costs (1980), colleges and universities had little incentive to control their costs. Unrestrained by competition and supported by government and philanthropy, higher education institutions were relatively free to raise tuition, perhaps justifying these increases with "the comfortable belief that increased expenditures . . . automatically produce commensurably greater outcomes."

Today, it is evident that a college or university's cost decisions have serious implications for the institution's relationship with its students. As tuition costs have risen in recent years, more and more students and their families are forced to pay education expenses with borrowed money. Thus, every institution's decision that increases its costs—raises for administrators, reductions in faculty teaching loads, minority scholarship commitments—also increases the long-term economic burden for many of its students.

As student loan volume grows with each passing year, all the constituencies that benefit from the federal loan program should recognize a moral obligation to control their costs. This may seem obvious, but not every institution that has benefited from the federal loan program abides by this philosophy.

In particular, a significant number of the for-profit trade schools were organized for the sole purpose of collecting student-loan dollars from their students, charging high tuition without providing any worthwhile training. For example, the *New York Times* reported on one trade school that employed more student-loan processors and recruiters than instructors (Winerip, 1994).

In addition, some of the lenders and guaranty agencies that actually disburse and collect student-loan dollars have made unseemly profits from the growing student-loan market. USA Group, the nation's largest student-loan guaranty agency and a nonprofit organization, paid its chief executive a salary of $1 million in 1995 (Folkenflik, 1997), more than four times what the president of the United States was paid. The organization also hires lobbyists and contributes to political campaigns to make sure that the student loan program does not change in ways that would threaten its interests. In 1996, Senator Paul Simon challenged USA Group's nonprofit status with the IRS, based on its lobbying activities and campaign contributions (Ambrose, 1996).

Of course, it is easy to criticize the proprietary schools and guaranty agencies for exploiting student borrowers. Fraudulent trade schools and obscene executive salaries make good headlines. But even some of our most elite colleges and universities may have benefited from the federal student loan program at the expense of their students. In recent years, college costs have risen twice as fast as inflation. Although some higher education officials would deny it, it seems likely that the easy availability of student loans reduces the incentive for colleges and universities to contain their costs. Instead of controlling faculty salaries, increasing teaching loads, or taking other economy measures, many institutions simply raise their tuition, knowing their students will borrow the money to pay the bill.

This trend seems especially clear at private institutions, which have maintained enrollment levels in spite of steep price increases over the past several years. As one analyst remarked, "It seems inconceivable that private colleges could have stabilized their enrollments over the past decade without a healthy growth in student loans" (Arthur M. Hautman, quoted in Burd, 1997, p. A18).

Harvard, where I received my doctorate in 1993, illustrates this phenomenon. In 1989, when I entered the Harvard Graduate School of Education, annual tuition was about $12,000. At that time, faculty were required to teach three courses during an academic year—two courses during one semester and only one course in the other. Eight years later, annual tuition is $17,000; and faculty members still teach only three courses per year.

How much of Harvard's tuition increase could have been avoided if faculty teaching loads had been increased by a modest amount? For example, professors might be required to teach two courses each semester throughout the academic year—only 8 hours a week of classroom time. Instead, Harvard raised its tuition, something that might not have been possible if Harvard students had not had easy access to borrowed money.

This is not to say that mainline institutions have been indifferent to costs or that they have utterly failed to take economy measures. As ACE President Stanley O. Ikenberry (1997) explained in a recent report on tuition increases, institutions all over the country have engaged in a number of sincere and creative efforts to control their costs. Nevertheless, it seems fair to say that the higher education community—from the lowliest proprietary school to our most prestigious research universities—have acquiesced and encouraged the unchecked growth of a federal program that has placed long-term and burdensome debt obligations on tens of millions of Americans.

2. We should dismantle some of the harsh provisions we have in place to discourage student loan defaults. Currently, student loan defaulters are restricted in their access to bankruptcy protection. The IRS can seize defaulters' income tax refunds, and students who default on an education loan are prohibited from participating in the student loan program thereafter. In addition, by congressional action, lawsuits to collect on student loans have no time limitations. Unlike most private lawsuits to collect a debt, which must be brought within 6 years after the debt arose, student loan defaulters can be sued at any time—20 years or more after the loan became due.

Many of these harsh provisions were initiated to discourage "freedloaders," individuals who financed their postsecondary education with borrowed money and who had no intention of paying it back. However, as I argued in the previous chapter, there is little evidence to suggest that such fraudulent practices are common. Instead, most college loan defaulters are individuals who got little value from their educational experience or who encountered difficult life circumstances after leaving their studies—unemployment, divorce, or serious illness.

We should ask ourselves whether the nation might be better served if it tolerated a higher student loan default rate than it does now. We need to develop a more compassionate bankruptcy procedure for debtors who received no value for their student loan dollars or whose life circumstances make it unduly burdensome to repay their student loans. If we do not do this, we will condemn hundreds of thousands of individuals to many years of burdensome indebtedness, exactly the opposite of what the student loan program was intended to achieve.

In the same vein, Congress should restore the statute of limitations for suing student loan defaulters. If private creditors are required to sue debtors within 6 years, it seems reasonable to place the same obligation on the federal government, which has vastly greater resources for tracking down delinquent borrowers and collecting on its bad loans.

3. We must acknowledge a special obligation to provide inexpensive and worthwhile educational opportunities for low-income and minority individuals. Although there is controversy about many aspects of the student loan program, we know one thing for certain: A great many low-income and minority students have been excessively burdened by their decision to take out student loans. We know that these individuals disproportionately choose proprietary schools for their postsecondary training, that the training is often worthless, and that students who attend proprietary schools have high default rates. We also know that low-income and minority students are most likely to be enrolled in remedial courses at the postsecondary level, and that a high percentage of these individuals are student borrowers.

Regarding remedial education, higher education seems to be moving in the right direction. Several states have taken the responsibility for remedial education from research institutions and placed it exclusively in the control of less expensive community colleges. If secondary school reform efforts—ongoing for 15 years or more—are ultimately successful, we should see the number of postsecondary students who need remedial education begin to decline.

Limiting the damage done by renegade proprietary schools is proving to be more difficult. Thanks to legislative reforms contained in the 1992 reauthorization of the Higher Education Act, some proprietary schools with high loan default rates have been eliminated from the student loan program. However, the trade school sector has been remarkably adept at protecting their interests through lobbying and litigation. Thus far, historically Black institutions with high default rates have managed to evade effective sanctions.

As one commentator noted (Kane, 1996), proprietary schools are extremely difficult to regulate. Many are small, operate for short periods of time, and provide specialized programs in fields where it is difficult to develop strong accrediting bodies or standardized expectations (cosmetology, trucking, tourism, etc.). Many of the students who attend these schools are the targets of high-pressure recruiting tactics, and students often have inadequate information when they select a proprietary school. For example, students may be unaware that the training provided by proprietary trade schools can often be obtained at community colleges and state-supported trade schools at a far lower cost.

Perhaps it is time to remove proprietary schools from the federal student loan program altogether. Financial resources could then be shifted to community colleges and state-run vocational schools, which can provide relatively inexpensive training in settings that are easier to monitor and regulate than the nation's welter of private trade schools.

At the very least, we need to make sure that prospective students are adequately warned about the danger of borrowing money to attend a proprietary trade school. The extraordinarily high default rate of proprietary school students—four times higher than the rate for 4-year college students (Kane, 1996)—makes trade school enrollment the educational equivalent of "unsafe sex." The chances are extremely good that a trade school student's decision to borrow tuition money will ultimately destroy the student's credit rating, prohibit further participation in the student loan program, and leave the borrower in worse financial position than if the student had never entered the trade school.

CONCLUSION

Now in its 4th decade, the federal student loan program is a permanent part of the higher education landscape. Both students and institutions depend on the program, and it would be virtually impossible to eliminate or drastically reduce it, at least in the short term future. Nevertheless, year by year, the program grows ever larger, and we must face the fact that it has harmed rather than helped hundreds of thousands of student debtors.

We cannot address this problem with minor technical changes. Instead, we must reexamine the student loan program from a fresh perspective, with three basic principles in mind. First, higher education institutions must view cost containment not just as a marketing and fiscal issue, but as a moral imperative. Second, some provision needs to be made for relieving worthy debtors of their overbearing loan obligations. Third, the nation must take special care to make sure minority and low-income students have access to relatively inexpensive and worthwhile postsecondary education opportunities.

None of these basic principles is revolutionary. Nevertheless, if Congress, the Department of Education, and the higher education community were to adopt them as public policy, two beneficial goals would be achieved. First, such a policy would slow and perhaps reverse the nation's increasing reliance on student loans to finance higher education. Second, the loan program's harmful effects on some students—particularly low-income and minority students—would be diminished.

In sum, we must never forget that every dollar a student borrows to finance postsecondary education has the potential for jeopardizing rather than enhancing that student's future. Therefore, the federal student loan program must do more than satisfy various stakeholders and interest groups that have heretofore shaped student loan policy. It must continually be shaped to fit the larger national interest, which is to secure the blessings of economic security for everyone in our society.

REFERENCES

Ambrose, E. (1996, August 1). Sen. Simon levels charges at USA Group; Lawmaker criticizes tax-exempt status, top salaries and lobbying at student-loan guarantor. *Indianapolis Star.* p. c1.

American Council on Education (1997). Recommendations for reauthorization of the Higher Education Act. Washington, DC: Author.

Bowen, H. R. (1980). *The cost of higher education: How much do colleges and universities spend per semester and how much should they spend?* Carnegie Foundation for the Advancement of Teaching and Jossey-Bass.

Burd, S. (1997, May 30). Do federal loans encourage tuition increases? *Chronicle of Higher Education,* p. A18.

Folkenflik, D. (1997, March 2). Student loans generate profits: Middlemen provide guarantees, chase after defaulters. *The Sun* (Baltimore), p. 1A.

Ikenberry, S. O. (1997, April 23). Testimony to the Committee on Education and the Workforce, United States House of Representatives.

Kane, T. J. (1996). Lessons from the largest school voucher program: Two decades of experience with Pell grants. In B. Fuller & R. F. Elmore (Eds.), *Who chooses? Who loses? Culture, institutions, and the unequal effects of school choice.* New York: Teachers College Press.

Winerip, M. (1994, June 19). House panel is facing vote on school aid. *New York Times,* Sec. 1, p. 16.

About the Contributors

Mark Bateman is an associate professor in the College of Education at Baylor University, where he teaches in the area of higher education administration. Previously, he was an assistant professor of education at Louisiana State University. Professor Bateman received his EdD degree from the University of Indiana. His research interests include college choice, higher education finance, and college student services.

Alberto F. Cabrera is an associate professor of educational administration at the Center for the Study of Higher Education, Penn State University. He received his PhD degree in educational administration from the University of Wisconsin at Madison. Professor Cabrera specializes in research methodologies, college students, minorities in higher education, economics of education, and financial aid. In 1993, the Association for the Study of Higher Education granted him the Early Career Scholar Award in recognition for his contributions to the study of determinants of college persistence. He serves on the editorial boards of *Research in Higher Education, Review of Higher Education,* and the *Journal of Higher Education,* and he has published in such journals as *Research in Higher Education,* the *Journal of Higher Education, Economics of Education,* and the *Journal of Financial Aid.*

David A. Campaigne is a coordinator of campus outreach programs in the Division of Student Affairs at Georgia Southern University. He received a bachelor's degree from Indiana University and an MBA degree from UCLA 25 years before earning his PhD in Higher Education Administration from Indiana University. His research interests include strategic planning in higher education, the history of student life, and the intersection of intercollegiate life and educational policy.

Elchanan Cohn is a professor of economics and Fellow of the Business Partnership Foundation at the University of South Carolina, and editor-in-chief of the *Economics of Education Review.* He is author, coauthor, or editor of

10 books, including *The Economics of Education* (with Terry G. Geske), now in its third edition. He has contributed numerous articles to professional journals in economics, education, and business, including the *Review of Economics and Statistics, Journal of Political Economy, American Economic Review,* and *Journal of Education Finance.* He serves on the editorial board of the *Journal of Economic Education* and has been a consultant to the World Bank. He has conducted extensive studies on the economic returns to school efficiency of school operations, factors that determine learning in principles of economics courses at the college level, and equity of the school finance system in South Carolina.

Michael D. Coomes is an associate professor of higher education and student affairs at Bowling Green State University. He received his EdD degree from Indiana University. Previously, he held the position of director of financial aid at both Saint Martin's College and Seattle University. Professor Coomes's research interests include federal higher education policy, the application of student development theory to institutional policy, and the history of student affairs. He is active in the American College Personnel Association, the Association for the Study of Higher Education, and the National Association of Student Personnel Administrators.

Richard Fossey is an associate dean and associate professor in the College of Education at Louisiana State University in Baton Rouge, where he teaches education law and education policy. He received his doctorate in administration, planning and social policy from Harvard University and his law degree from the University of Texas School of Law. Prior to beginning an academic career, he practiced education law in Alaska, where he represented school boards in Aleut, Athabaskan, and Inuit communities. He is coauthor, with Michael Clay Smith, of *Crime on Campus: Liability Issues and Campus Administration,* published by Oryx Press and the American Council on Education. With Todd A. DeMitchell, he is coauthor of *The Limits of Law-Based School Reform: Vain Hopes and False Promises,* published by Technomic Publishing Company.

Terry G. Geske has been a professor of educational administration since 1984 at Louisiana State University. After receiving his PhD from the University of Wisconsin–Madison, Professor Geske served as a faculty member for 7 years at the University of Illinois at Urbana-Champaign. Professor Geske has published extensively in the areas of the economics of education and education finance policy. His major publications include *Financing Education: Overcoming Inefficiency and Inequity* (with Walter McMahon) and *The Economics of Education* (with Elchanan Cohn). Over the years, he has served as a consultant to various federal, state, and local governmental agencies, and he has also served two terms as a member of the Board of Directors of the American Education Finance Association. In 1992, Professor Geske was guest professor at the University of Salzburg in Austria.

James C. Hearn is a professor of higher education at the University of Georgia. He received his PhD degree from Stanford University and an MBA degree from the University of Pennsylvania (Wharton). Prior to entering his academic career, he worked in policy research on student aid issues for the American College Testing program and for a consulting firm in Washington, D.C. His teaching and research interests include higher education policy, organization, and finance. His studies of college enrollment, educational attainment, and student aid policy have appeared in sociology, economics, and education journals as well as in several edited volumes.

Don Hossler is a professor of educational leadership and policy studies in the School of Education at Indiana University, Bloomington. He has served as a department chair, executive associate dean of the School of Education and is currently serving as the Acting Vice-Chancellor for Enrollment Services on the Bloomington campus. His areas of specialization include: college choice, student financial aid policy, enrollment management, the desegregation of historically black colleges, and higher education finance. He earned a PhD in Higher Education from the Claremont Graduate School in 1979, where he worked with the noted economist of higher education, Dr. Howard Bowen. He joined the faculty at Indiana University in 1985. Recently, he conducted research and served as an expert witness in the *Knight v. Alabama* desegregation case; and he recently completed a national study of state funding policies for state systems of higher education. He has conducted research on change and reform in higher education in Russia. He is the author or co-author of 7 books and monographs and more than 20 articles and book chapters.

Jamie P. Merisotis is the founding president of the Institute for Higher Education Policy in Washington, D.C. The Institute for Higher Education Policy is a nonprofit, nonpartisan organization whose mission is to foster access to and quality in postsecondary education through the development and promotion of innovative solutions to important issues facing higher education. Recent studies produced by the institute include: *Life After 40: A New Portrait of Today's—and Tomorrow's—Postsecondary Students* and *College Debt and the American Family*. Mr. Merisotis previously served as executive director of the bipartisan National Commission on Responsibilities for Financing Postsecondary Education.

Thomas G. Mortenson is a higher education analyst based in Oskaloos, Iowa. His policy research focuses on opportunity for postsecondary education and training and the ways in which public policy fosters or impedes access to that opportunity. His studies have addressed academic and financial preparation for college, access, choice, persistence, attainment, and labor force entry of college graduates. He has been employed in policy research and budget analysis roles for the University of Minnesota, the Illinois Board of Education, Illinois State Scholarship Commission, and the American College Testing Program.

Currently, Mr. Mortenson is editor and publisher of *Postsecondary Education OPPORTUNITY*, a monthly research letter devoted to analysis and reporting on the demographics, sociology, history, politics, and economics of educational opportunity after high school. He is also half-time senior scholar at the Center for the Study of Opportunity in Higher Education located in Washington, D.C.

James Fredericks Volkwein is the director of institutional research and an associate professor of educational administration and policy studies at the University at Albany, State University of New York. He received his PhD degree from Cornell University and has held a variety of administrative posts within the State University of New York. Professor Volkwein serves on the editorial boards of several higher education journals and as editor-in-chief of the Jossey-Bass series, *New Directions for Institutional Research;* and he is currently writing a book on assessing student outcomes. His research interests include the assessment of student learning and growth, faculty governance and administrative structure, government regulation and university autonomy, academic program evaluation, faculty scholarly productivity, and the study of colleges and universities as complex organizations.

Index